Commander José Cas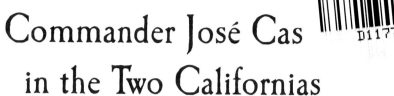 in the Two Californias

Including His Final Correspondence, 1856-1860

Julianne Burton-Carvajal

©2008

Noticias de Monterey Volume LVI: 1-4

A publication of the Monterey History and Art Association

– Special 50th Anniversary Edition –

&

Antepasados XIV

A publication of Los Californianos

ISBN 0-9651592-1-3

Set in Adobe Caslon Pro and Caslon Antique by JTC Graphics, Monterey, California
Printed by Vanard Lithographers, San Diego, California

For additional copies, contact:

Los Californianos
P.O. Box 600522
San Diego, CA 92160-0522
www.loscalifornianos.org

Monterey History & Art Association
5 Custom House Plaza
Monterey, CA 93940
(831-372-2608)
www.montereyhistory.org

Anthony's Gate Publications
925 Monterey Circle
Monterey, CA 93940
(831 645-9925)

Contents

Illustrations

Cooperating institutions, gratefully acknowledged, are abbreviated as follows:

ANC: Braun Research Library, Autry National Center, Los Angeles
BCC: Book Club of California, San Francisco
BL: The Bancroft Library, University of California, Berkeley
CSL: California History Room, California State Library, Sacramento
CHM: Colton Hall Museum, City of Monterey
GFC: Graves Family Collection
HL: Henry E. Huntington Library, San Marino
MPL: California History Room, Monterey Public Library
PHCVC: Pat Hathaway's California Views Collection, Monterey
PMH: Fenyes-Curtin-Paloheimo Papers, Pasadena Museum of History
SDHS: San Diego Historical Society Photo Collection
SPHS: San Pablo Historical Society
SCWHR Seaver Center for Western History Research, Los Angeles County Museum of Natural History

Cover: Drawing by H. Rimbault engraved by W.R. Ryan depicting Monterey after the American takeover of 1846; CSL.

Inside front cover: *Dramatis personae* in the final stage of Colonel José Castro's career:

Row 1, left to right: L'Abbé Henry J.A. Alric, 1990s drawing based on Parisian engraving, late 1860s.

Juan Bautista Alvarado, first native son to assume the governorship of Mexican California; SPHS.

Delfina Alvarado, his daughter, referred to by Castro as "*mi comadre*;" SPHS.

Prominent San Diegan Juan Bandini; BL.

Row 2: Baja California-born novelist María Amparo Ruiz de Burton; GFC.

Captain Henry Burton of the United States Army, husband of the novelist; SCWHR.

Esteban Castro, eldest son of José and Modesta Castro; CHM.

Colonel José Castro; this frequently reproduced engraving is also identified with two other Castros.

Row 3: Modesta Castro de Castro, wife of José Castro; CHM.

Modesta Castro de Dana, daughter of José and Modesta Castro; MPL.

Captain Manuel de Jesús Castro, younger cousin of José Castro; MPL.

Jessie Benton Frémont, wife of Captain John Charles Frémont, in 1861.

Row 4: Captain John Charles Frémont, 1856; see page 171 for full cartoon.

Baja California-born José Matías Moreno, Colonel Castro's successor; SDHS.

Prominent San Diegan Abel Stearns; CSL.

General Mariano Guadalupe Vallejo of Monterey and Sonoma; CSL.

Frontispiece: Unidentified Californio; PHCVC.

Introduction, Page 8: Unsigned, undated portrait of José Castro, possibly painted after his death; CSL.

Page 10, top: The Castro-Breen Adobe, San Juan Bautista, 2007; photograph by the author.

insert: Casa Castro on the Monterey Mesa in 1902, unidentified photographer; MPL.

bottom: Casa Castro, 2007; since 1985 the La Mirada venue of the Montery Museum of Art; photo by the author.

Page 13: Modesta Castro de Castro, wife of Colonel José Castro, and their eldest son Esteban; both CHM.

Bottom: Casa Castro on the Monterey Mesa, 1904 watercolor by Eva Scott Fenyes; ANC FEN.268.

Page 14: The Plaza at San Juan Bautista, drawn September 20, 1847 by William Rich Hutton; HL.

*Dedicated to the enduring legacy of Californios north and south,
who settled the last frontier of the Spanish empire, and to
Edna Emerson Cleave Kimbro (1948-2005) who cherished,
conserved, and illuminated their history and ours.*

CASTRO

Widely but inaccurately referred to in print as "General Castro," José Castro (1807-1860) was the out-standing military leader of California's Mexican era. He served as Interim Governor in 1835 and was appointed Commander General of Alta California a decade later. Without benefit of formal military train-ing, he attained the rank of Colonel in the Mexican Army. After the American takeover of 1846 and ratification of the Treaty of Guadalupe-Hidalgo two years later, Mexican officials recognized his qualifi-cations by appointing him Military and Political Chief (de facto Governor) of Baja California on three separate occasions: 1854, 1855 and 1859/60. Through a combination of previously unpublished personal correspondence and original research, this volume pieces together the untold story of Castro's final years as Vice-Governor (Sub-Jefe) of the harsh and isolated border region known as La Frontera, where one final betrayal led to an ignominious death and 150 years of misrepresentation.

Introduction

The Return of José Castro

Born in Monterey in 1807, Josef Antonio María de Jesús Castro would be known to his associates and to history as José Castro. As a native son or *hijo del país*, he would grow up to embrace the liberal democratic ideals behind the 19th century anti-colonial struggles for independence being waged throughout the Spanish-speaking Americas. From childhood, he was closely associated with two other Monterey youths, Mariano Guadalupe Vallejo and Vallejo's only slightly younger nephew Juan Bautista Alvarado. This trio would emerge as the most influential leaders of their day–only to see themselves unceremoniously swept aside after the United States Navy annexed California at Monterey on July 7, 1846.

José Castro was only twenty-one years old when first appointed *Secretario del Ayuntamiento* or Secretary to the Town Council of Monterey, an office he held from 1828 to 1831. He went on to assume a notable number of civic and military positions in both Upper and Lower California during his relatively short lifetime: Commissioner of Mission San Miguel in 1831 and later Administrator of Mission San Antonio; interim Governor from August of 1835 to January 1, 1836; President of the *Diputación* (Territorial Assembly) in 1836; Chief Executive of the Congress, Prefect and Political Chief of the Northern District in 1839; Chief of the Presidial Company at Monterey in 1842. Despite the fact that he had received no formal military training, his official appointments included serving the Mexican government as Commander General of Alta California in 1845-46 and as Vice-Governor of Northern Baja California from 1856 to 1860.

Castro was a key player in the most significant events of the fifteen years prior to the American takeover, including uprisings against Mexican-appointed California Governors Gutiérrez and Micheltorena, the "Isaac Graham Affair" in which several Americans were deported to Mexico, and the standoff with Captain John Charles Frémont and his band of "topographical engineers," who illegally occupied Gavilán Peak near Salinas, defiantly raising the American flag there.

As Commander General of the northern district of Alta California, Castro engaged in a protracted political struggle with Governor Pío Pico, a *sureño* (southerner) from Los Angeles, during their notoriously uncongenial "joint command." Castro led the resistance during both the renegade American takeover of June 1846, known as the Bear Flag Revolt, and the officially-sanctioned "annexation" a month later. Faced with leading his dwindling, demoralized troops against Commodore Stockton's patently superior forces, Castro and sixteen of his men retreated to Sonora and Sinaloa to seek reenforcements. Castro resided in Mexico for the duration of the US-Mexican War.

Returning to Monterey in 1848 after the Treaty of Guadalupe-Hidalgo, he endeavored to adjust to American-imposed political and fiscal regimes by finding new means of supporting his family and retaining ownership of their two homes and various land holdings. The following year, he and fellow Californios witnessed a veritable tidal wave of gold-seekers that rendered the Spanish-speakers strangers in their native land. Motivated by both personal need and a commitment to finding a viable alternative for other displaced Californios, Castro departed San Francisco by ship in early 1856 to assume the governorship of Baja California Territory at the invitation of the Supreme Government of Mexico. After four years in a position of lesser authority than the one he was promised, he was assassinated there in 1860–one more casualty of the tumult and strife rampant at that place and time.

José Castro and his wife, Modesta Castro de Castro, produced at least fourteen offspring. Tragically, half did not survive infancy. (See Genealogy, Part V.) Assassinated in his fifty-third year, Castro barely lived long enough to see his eldest son atttain adulthood. Modesta found herself widowed at forty-three with seven of her eight surviving children still living at home and the family homestead on the Monterey Mesa besieged by creditors.

Ernest J. García of Los Californianos has documented that José Castro and his family were the beneficiaries of several land grants, beginning with Rancho Vega del Río Pájaro in 1820, under the Spanish regime, and including a portion of Rancho San Justo at Hollister in 1839, part of Rancho

Above: Castro-Breen Adobe, San Juan Bautista, 2007; built by Colonel Castro's father José Tiburcio Castro in 1841.

Left: Casa Castro, stone with tile roof, in 1902; courtesy of California History Room, Monterey Public Library.

Below: Casa Castro-Work, known as La Mirada, second venue of the Monterey Museum of Art, 2007; built of stone by [Josef?] Antonio Maria Castro in the early 1800s.

Lomerías del Espíritu Santo near San Juan Bautista in 1842, some 48,000 acres of Rachería del Río Estanislao in 1843 (with fellow grantee Francisco "Pancho" Rico), Santa Rosa Island near Santa Barbara also in 1843 (with fellow grantee Carlos Carrillo), part of Rancho Sausal in Monterey Country (by paternal inheritance), and ex-mission lands at San Juan Bautista granted in 1846.

From the early 1840s, José and Modesta enjoyed a town home diagonally across the plaza from Mission San Juan Bautista and, from the mid-1840s, another on the Monterey Mesa overlooking the presidio and port of Monterey. In recent decades, both these former residences have become museums. The Castro-Breen Adobe in San Juan Bautista is a National Historic Landmark managed by California State Parks. Casa Castro-Work, also known as La Mirada, serves as the second venue of the Monterey Museum of Art.

Despite his pivotal role in Alta California history, José Castro has remained a side note in biographies of his contemporaries. While benefiting from abundant references sprinkled through a variety of historical texts, his biographers will have to reconcile highly contradictory depictions of their subject. The most scathing of these was written by a notoriously meddlesome American firebrand. In April of 1840, Thomas Jefferson Farnham described José Castro as *"a villain with a lean body, dark face, black mustachios, pointed nose, flabby cheeks, uneasy eyes, and hands and heart so foul as instinctively to require a Spanish cloak in all sorts of weather to cover them…"* (quoted in Joanne Levy, *Unsettling the West*). Nine years later, New York journalist Bayard Taylor registered a different impression in his best-selling account of gold rush-era California, *El Dorado, Adventures in the Path of Empire:*

> *General Castro—the redoubtable leader of the Californian troops in Upper and Lower California—is a man of medium height, but stoutly and strongly made. He has a very handsome face. His eyes are large and dark, and his mouth is shaded by moustaches with the gloss and color of a raven's wing, meeting on each side with his whiskers. He wore the sombrero, jacket and* calzoneros *[side-buttoned trousers] of the country. His temperament, I thought, seemed gloomy and saturnine, and I was gravely informed by a Californian who sat opposite me that he meditated the reconquest of the country!*

Bayard Taylor's concluding reference to Castro's threatened return evokes an expression that circulated widely among the beleaguered Californios following the American takeover. *"Cuando vuelva José Castro…"* ("When José Castro returns…") they would say expectantly to one another. Rumors of Castro poised to reclaim Alta California were circulating as early as October 1846 and, as Taylor's vignette testifies, persisted through 1849. Initially at least, such rumors would have inspired hope in the discouraged Californios, so abruptly relegated to minority status by the American takeover. The same rumors would have perhaps given the latter pause had not the almost immediate cry of "gold in them thar hills" opened the gates to a flood of Easterners and other hopefuls from countries around the world. Over time, as the Californios perceived the irreversibility of their displacement, the tone and meaning of this popular expression shifted until "when José Castro returns…" became a skeptical register of improbability—equivalent to the English expression "when pigs fly."

Hubert Howe Bancroft, undisputed dean of Western historians, summarized his view of José Castro in 1886 by declaring categorically: *"No Californian has been so thoroughly abused in what has passed for history. It should be stated at the outset that nine tenths of all that has been said against him by American writers has no foundation in truth."* Bancroft added that Castro's *"record as a public man in Upper California was, on the whole, not a bad one"* and concluded even-handedly, *"He had much energy, was popular with most classes, true to his friends, and as a public officer fairly honest."* (Reproduced in full in Part V.)

Part I of the present volume, "José Castro in Alta California," synthesizes what has been written about Colonel Castro's life and career to date. The cache of correspondence written by and to him that comprises Part II–transcribed, translated, and published here for the first time–spans the last four years of his life. Personal, official, and business-related letters offer unique insight into an often maligned figure who richly deserves another look. They also contain signposts leading to a number of ground-breaking discoveries.

The letters that comprise Part II came to light in the summer of 2004 when historians Edna Kimbro and Susan Doniger of California State Parks visited the San Francisco headquarters of the Society of California Pioneers in search of material related to the Castro-Breen Adobe at San Juan Bautista. Library Diretor Patricia Keats recalled a collection of letters relating to José Castro. Kimbro requested photocopies and passed them on to this compiler for translation and analysis. Edna Kimbro "slipped away" in her sleep a year later, on the night of her 57th birthday. Although she did not live to see this publication take form, she held her illness at bay long enough to learn from the transcriber-translator that what initially seemed to be a random assortment in fact traced the outlines of an unexpectedly cohesive, moving, and dramatic story.

Five of the letters were purchased by the Society of California Pioneers in 1959 from descendant Mrs. Modesta Castro Smith for the sum of $10. The other thirteen presumably arrived at a different juncture from the same or another family source. Reproduced here in three versions (facsimile, transcription into modern Spanish, and English translation) these letters register the all too infrequently documented point of view of the Californios, revealing the struggles and dislocations prompted by the abrupt transition from Novohispano life-ways to American rule.

The process of reconstructing the context of Castro's final years in Baja California and tracking the identity of the various people named produced an essay that contradicts what has until now been reproduced as historical fact. Taking into account pertinent material in Mexican archives as well as the University of California's Bancroft Library, Part III, "José Castro in Baja California," explores José Castro's service to rapidly changing Mexican regimes and the daunting challenges he faced during his four years as political and military leader of La Frontera, that newly vanquished nation's northwestern frontier. In addition to outlining the untold story of another Montereyan, his cousin Captain Manuel de Jesús Castro, his predecessor at the military colony inLa Frontera, Part III untangles the intricate web of enmity, conspiracy and betrayal behind Colonel José Castro's untimely death. Part IV brings together eight additional letters from key participants across a broader time span. Discovered subsequently at The Huntington Library, these substantiate conclusions drawn in Part III.

Historical investigations like these rely on the words of others–both primary (in letters from the principles) and secondary (from other historians). As a graphic means of acknowledging this composite quality, in Parts I and III quotations of more than a dozen words are italicized; longer quotations are also indented. Both essays are thoroughly referenced; credits in parentheses within the text refer to the List of Sources appended to each essay.

A timeline for José Castro, biographical sketches of key figures, and a complete ownership history of Monterey's Casa Castro/La Mirada. published here for the first time, have been prepared by the author-compiler, who has also supplied translations and transcriptions of Spanish texts throughout. Supplementary materials provided in Part V also include Bancroft's summary assessment of José Castro, US and Mexican press coverage of the conquest of the Californias, and a genealogy prepared by Los Californianos genealogist Judith Marie Rodriguez.

The joint sponsorship of Los Californianos and the Monterey History and Art Association has made possible this very first monograph dedicated to José Castro. The author-compiler also wishes to acknowledge the generous waiver of reproduction fees granted by the Society of California Pioneers, as well as grants from the University of California Consortium on Mexico (UC-MEXUS) and the Humanities Research Institute of the University of California at Santa Cruz (HRI-UCSC) providing assistance with illustration fees.

Distinguished Mexican historian Dr. Angela Moyano Pahissa secured copies of archival documents, contracted the services of paleographer Lourdes Alvarez, and made a visit to Monterey for consultation. Rebecca Lynn Kirk, who graduated with Honors from UC Santa Cruz in June of 2007, took responsibility for the initial research and drafting of Part I. She also secured permissions for illustrations and coordinated reimbursements in collaboration with David Symonik and the capable staff of the Humanities Budget Office at UC Santa Cruz. John Greenwald amiably assisted in securing outstanding reproduction rights. Historian Alan Rosenus provided helpful comments on Part I, while Rose Marie Beebe and Robert Senkewicz offered timely encouragement during the final stages.

Modesta Castro de Castro and her son Esteban Castro; courtesy of Colton Hall Museum, City of Monterey.

Modesta Castro de Castro and her son Esteban Castro successively owned Casa Castro on the Monterey Mesa–painted in 1904 by Pasadena artist Eva Scott Fenyes, who noted Esteban's ownership on the back.

The author-compiler would also like to thank Executive Director Dr. Peter Flagg, Library Director Patricia Keats, and board member William N. Swasey of the Society of California Pioneers for cooperation and support from the outset. Mary Triplett Ayers, Michael J. Ford, Boyd de Larios, Edna de Larios, Lance Beeson, and President Jane Cowgill of Los Californianos took an active interest in the project. Judith Marie Rodriguez and Ernest J. Garcia of the same organization generously shared their respective expertise in genealogy and land holdings. Leonard Espinosa insisted on the Index and will find his name listed there. Kudos to *Noticias de Monterey* collaborators John Castagna and Mary Aline for their stalwart assistance during the layout and copy-editing stages. Finally, a very special thank you to Peter Cole (Pedro Cole Soberanes) and the Diego Felipe y Tomas Soberanes Memorial Foundation. Errors and oversights, perhaps inevitable in a project as complex as this one, are the sole responsibility of the undersigned.

The correspondence reproduced here was undertaken 150 years ago, at a time and place where communications were notoriously slow and uncertain. Inevitably, much was lost or destroyed–either at the time, as some of these letters acknowledge, or during subsequent decades. These fragments, fortuitous survivors of an irretrievable whole, have been saved to history through the efforts of both heirs and historical organizations. Together, letters and the essays that accompany them constitute a long-awaited homecoming. Unjustifiably neglected over the past century and a half, José Castro returns in these pages to claim another hearing from posterity.

Julianne Burton-Carvajal, Ph.D.
Compiler, coauthor, transcriber, and translator
Monterey, September 2007

The plaza at San Juan Bautista on September 20, 1847, drawn and annotated by surveyor William Rich Hutton. Along with travel-ing companions Lieutenant William Tecumseh Sherman and Colonel Richard B. Mason, he lodged at the Castro Adobe, second from left. The notation above reads in part: "...after trying bed, slept in stack of pea straw." Courtesy of the Huntington Library.

Part I
José Castro in Alta California

Southeastern portion of Commander Castro's Monterey Headquarters

Woodcut of a Californio wedding party by Ernest Freed

José Castro in Alta California, 1807-1855

Rebecca Lynn Kirk and Julianne Burton-Carvajal

The Castro surname, derived from the Latin *castrum* (field), corresponded to more than one Northern California lineage. In fact, the Castros were the most abundant family line in northern Alta California. Place names like Castroville, Castro Valley, and the Castro District in San Francisco suggest the extent of their importance. José Antonio María de Jesus Castro, known as José Castro, is generally regarded as "the most prominent of the California Castros." (Greenwood 4)

Among Californio families, given names were multiple and often piously prefaced by José or María–and sometimes both. The similarity of names between José Antonio Castro and his father José Tiburcio Castro makes for confusion. The fact that José Tiburcio usually signed documents José T. Castro helps historians distinguish between the two men.

José and his wife Modesta shared a surname prior to their marriage. Adding to the coincidences, José Castro's father-in-law was also named José Antonio Castro. Multiplying the challenge to future historians and genealogists, José and Modesta followed the common practice of each giving their name to one of their offspring. (See Genealogy, Part V.)

The California branch of José Castro's lineage began with Macario Castro, a native of Sinaloa in northwestern Mexico, who came to Alta California in 1784 as a soldier (Greenwood 11). Macario's eldest son, José Tiburcio Castro, future father of José Castro, was born in Sinaloa but came to Alta California prior to 1800 with his mother, María Potenciana Ramírez de Castro (Greenwood 11). Stationed at Monterey in 1809 with the rank of corporal, José Tiburcio became *alcalde* (mayor and magistrate) of Monterey in 1827 and later served as Commissioner of Mission Soledad in 1831 and Mission San Juan Bautista in 1835-36 (Kimbro 2).

Early Years

Born at Monterey in 1807, José Castro was baptized Josef Antonio María de Jesús Castro at Mission Soledad on August 7, 1808. Between 1815 and 1820, he was educated at the Presidio of Monterey, where he studied with other *hijos del país* (Kimbro 2). The trio of José

Castro, Juan Bautista Alvarado and Mariano Guadalupe Vallejo received special attention from Governor Pablo Vicente de Solá, a strong advocate for education, who "*gave them government reports and newspapers from New Spain to read, as well as copies of the classics, like Don Quixote.*" Among his friends, Castro stood out as "hawk-eyed" and "volatile" (Rosenus 7, 8).

In 1828, Castro assumed his first government office, Secretary to the Monterey *Ayuntamiento* (town council), a post he held until 1831 (Kimbro 2). It was during this period that the three friends experienced their first uprising. Mariano Vallejo was acting commandant of the Monterey Presidio at the time. What became known as the Joaquín Solís revolt began on the night of November 12, 1829, when disgruntled soldiers in the service of Mexico imprisoned Vallejo, Alvarado and Castro in the Presidio cavalry barracks and held them for three weeks (Miller 24-5; Rosenus 142; 256, n.38).

In January of 1831, while still serving as Secretary to the Town Council, Castro was sent to Mission San Antonio as Administrator after Governor José María Echeandía issued a secularization decree that reduced the missions to parish churches and put their lands and accumulated wealth quite literally "up for grabs." Echeandia's successor as Governor of Alta California, Manuel Victoria, quickly countermanded that decree and abolished the position of mission administrator, a move that only temporarily delayed the inevitable pillaging of the missions' wealth. At this point, Castro and Alvarado both returned to Monterey, where they learned that Governor Victoria had ordered criminal proceedings against them for allegedly attempting to arouse the neophytes, as the Indian converts attached to the missions were called (Miller 29, 30).

Faced with these charges, the men secretly fled on horseback to Mission Santa Clara (Miller 30). Unemployed and out of favor in the capital, Castro and Alvarado successfully petitioned Governor Victoria for a permit to hunt sea otters, which they intended to send to market in China. Their hunting season was limited to April and May of 1831. While their company of hunters was based at Yerba Buena Cove, the two friends resided at the Presidio of the future San Francisco as guests of

Lieutenant Mariano Guadalupe Vallejo, adjunct at that post (Miller 30).

It was during this period that the trio fell into disfavor with the Catholic Church. Vallejo, who had traded cattle hides and tallow with the captain of the ship *Leonor* in return for several boxes of prohibited books, shared his prize with his two friends under a pledge of secrecy. After Castro let a pious lady friend in on their secret, all three young men were excommunicated. Promulgated in the churches, the writ of excommunication decreed that all of the sacraments, including marriage, were to be denied the offenders and any person who had dealings with them (Miller 31).

Just three weeks later, Alvarado was entrusted with several thousand pesos to be given to Fray Narciso Durán, Father President of the missions (Miller 31-2). When Alvarado reminded the priest that the writ of excommunication prohibited all believers from interactions with him, Father Durán promptly reinstated all three young men, writing to the trio: "*I give you permission to read the prohibited books—even Voltaire, Telemachus, Rousseau, etc., and even the Protestant Bible—with the sole condition that they shall not be placed in the hands of irresponsible or unintelligent people*" (Nunis 311).

Setting aside the hero of Greek mythology, the mention of two exponents of the French Enlightenment indicates that Liberal political ideology was filtering into even the provincial backwater of Alta California. Ideals of independence and representative democracy would soon inspire the trio to rise up against the rulers assigned to them by a succession of distant, embattled, short-lived regimes in Mexico City.

Once the writ of excommunication had been revoked, the young free-thinkers were free to marry, as Castro did later that year, wedding María Modesta Victoriana Castro at Carmel Mission on August 12, 1831. (Kimbro 2). Nine years her husband's junior, Modesta had also been born in Monterey. On July 2, 1832, the couple welcomed a daughter, María Isabela de la Visitación, and in 1834 Modesta gave birth to a son, José Gabriel Esteban. (Two letters to José Castro from his son Esteban and two from his wife Modesta are included in Part II.)

Castro's intellectual curiosity was not curbed by the short-lived writ of excommunication. The learned English-born merchant William E.P. Hartnell opened his *seminario* (college) in Monterey in 1833, the first Alta California institution of higher learning. According to eminent historian Doyce B. Nunis, Jr., "Hartnell and Nathan Spear had already begun tutoring select pupils privately… As a result of these efforts, a group of Californios became relatively well educated" (Nunis 310). This group included José Castro, Juan Bautista Alvarado, Mariano Guadalupe Vallejo, José Antonio Carrillo, Manuel Jimeno, and Pablo de la Guerra. Castro and Alvarado maintained a life-long interest in reading, and their libraries rivaled those of their friend Vallejo and their former teacher W.E.P. Hartnell (Miller 134-5). A portion of latter's library is on permanent display at the Carmel Mission Museum; travels and tragedies presumably scattered José Castro's book collection.

Prior to his untimely death in September of 1835, Governor José Figueroa—the only one in the string of governors sent from Mexico City to win broad support from the Californios—named Castro, then senior member of the *Diputación* (Assembly), as political head of the territory, and Lieutenant-Colonel Nicolás Gutiérrez military commandant (Miller 40). From August 1835 until January 1836, Castro served as *Jefe Político ad interin* (temporary Governor) at the capitol in Monterey (Kimbro 2). In January, when an order from Mexico City consolidated the offices, Castro was required to turn over political authority to Gutiérrez (Miller 40; *Testimonios* 240). Alvarado suspected that Mexico City officials preferred Gutiérrez over Castro because the former had been born in Spain (Miller 40). Indeed, this persistent bias in favor of *peninsulares* (Spaniards born on the Iberian Peninsula) over *criollos* (people of Spanish descent born in the New World) was a principal motive for the independence movements that swept the Spanish colonies from 1812 onwards, culminating in fledgling republics from Mexico south to Argentina.

Rebellion Against Governor Gutiérrez

Just four months later, on May 1, 1836, Gutiérrez turned over his office to Colonel Mariano Chico, gubernatorial appointee of the newly reconstituted Mexican government. Alvarado and Vallejo later wrote that they, along with José Castro and others, began planning a revolution against Governor Chico from his first month in office. Such action proved unnecessary, however, because authorities in Mexico City replaced Chico after only three months (Miller 41-2). The subsequent reappointment of Nicolás Gutiérrez as Governor left Castro and his compatriots dissatisfied.

In October of 1836, Alvarado instigated a revolt against Gutiérrez, calling upon Castro to lead the citizens in arms (Miller 47). Alvarado and Castro made San Juan Bautista their headquarters for this "revolution," which Castro commanded from November 5th to 29th as head of the rebel forces (Kimbro 2). Castro's army, called the Vanguard of the Division of Operations, was supplemented by Isaac Graham's *rifleros americanos*, a group of well-armed American mountain men (Miller 47; Rosenus 18; Kimbro 2-3).

On November 3rd, the rebel forces approached Monterey "under the cover of darkness and heavy fog" and surrounded the weakly fortified El Castillo (current site of the Monterey Presidio), demanding that Gutiérrez surrender. On the third day, increasingly frustrated by the Governor's hesitation, Castro ordered a shot fired from the battery. The cannon ball went through the roof of the governor's residence, scattering his supporters and hastening his surrender (Miller 47, Spencer-Hancock 237, Rosenus 18).

A few days before Castro took command of the rebel forces, Governor Gutiérrez had been on the verge of executing Don Miguel Avila, husband of Doña María Inocenta Pico. The death sentence was averted, and Doña Inocenta credited José Castro with saving her husband's life. Consequently, when Castro and his forces were preparing to attack the quarters of Governor Gutiérrez, which were near Doña María Inocenta's house, she was anxious to provide all possible assistance. Many years later, when interviewed by one of Hubert Howe Bancroft's oral historians, she would recall:

> *I was naturally furious because of Gutiérrez's despicable behavior against my husband, so I sent word to José Castro and offered him gunpowder, saddles, and other supplies for the campaign. In fact, I offered him everything I had…Whenever Don José Castro, my daughter Josefa's godfather, would remember the things I did to help make that revolt a success, he would laugh so hard…That revolt did free us from people who wanted to treat us more despotically than what we had ever experienced during the absolute rule of the Spanish governors.*
> (*Testimonios* 306-8)

Immediately following the surrender of Gutiérrez, Alvarado wrote a decree proclaiming California "a free and sovereign state" and converting the *Diputatión* into a Congress (Miller 49). Castro served as Chief Executive (Acting Governor) until December 7, 1836, when Alvarado himself became Interim Governor (Miller 49; Kimbro 3). That same month, the pair of revolutionaries triumphantly, if only temporarily, renamed two northern California towns after themselves: "San José de Alvarado" and "San Juan de Castro" (formerly San Juan Bautista; Miller 49; Kimbro 3).

Political successes notwithstanding, this period proved to be a time of great personal loss for José and Modesta. Their eldest daughter María Isabela died in September of 1836 at the age of four, following the death of her infant sister, María de los Dolores, six months earlier. On October 10, 1837, the couple produced another daughter, María Visitación Francisca, who did not live to see her third birthday. A fifth daughter, Rufina Felicidad, baptised on March 3, 1840, was the first of their girls who would survive to adulthood.

Alvarado Assumes the Governorship

During 1837 and 1838, Castro was kept busy putting down potential uprisings by countrymen and hostile Indians from the Central Valley (Kimbro 3). On February 25, 1839, members of the old *Diputación* met to compile a *terna* (slate of candidates) for permanent governor, from which the central government in Mexico would make their selection. In order of preference, the list consisted of Juan Bautista Alvarado and José Castro of Monterey, followed by Pío Pico of Los Angeles (Miller 64). Alvarado was named to the post.

On February 28th, Castro was made Prefect of the First, or Northern District, a position that conferred a yearly salary of $2000, included a secretary (José María Covarrubias, a French Basque from Santa Barbara), and gave Castro the authority to issue land grants.

On April 4, 1840, the legislature at Monterey discussed a rumored plot against the government by the Kentucky-born distiller Isaac Graham and his followers, a rough-and-ready bunch of hunters and trappers. The following day, former English sailor William Garner confirmed the alleged plot to take over the government, denouncing Graham as head of a conspiracy that involved capturing Castro and Alvarado, who were to be killed if they could not be taken prisoner (Miller 80). Alvarado interpreted this news as an indication that the Americans wanted California for themselves and would go to any lengths to take it. Retrospectively, he suspected that this goal had motivated Graham's assistance in the 1836 revolt against Governor Gutiérrez.

On April 6, 1840, under orders from Alvarado, Castro and his secretary Covarrubias began rounding up the foreigners and locking them in the Monterey jail until the total number of prisoners came to about 100 (Kimbro 4; Miller 80). According to Angustias de la Guerra, those apprehended were "*either foreigners whose residence in the country was not legally documented, or foreigners accused of being involved in planning the revolution to take over the country*" (*Testimonios* 256).

On April 25, 1840, Castro and Covarrubias sailed from Monterey to the supply depot of San Blas, Mexico, with "*forty-five prisoners, about half of whom were American and the others English-born*" (Kimbro 4; Miller 81). The prisoners were released within a year through the intervention of American and British officials in Mexico (Nunis 312). Many of the exiles returned to California on July 15, 1841 (Kimbro 5). Graham, who reentered Alta California with $36,000 from the Mexican government for his inconvenience, was not the only prisoner to walk away with monetary gain because "*the [Mexican] government was required to pay a considerable amount of money to compensate the prisoners for the damages and suffering they endured*" (*Testimonios* 256).

Castro was apparently not as well-served as the prisoners whom he escorted. After accompanying them from the port of San Blas to Tepic, where they were to stand trial, the escorting officer was sent to Mexico City, where British and American ministers filed charges against him, alleging mistreatment of the prisoners (Miller 81-2). Defended by Brigadier General Manuel Micheltorena, Castro was eventually exonerated and returned to Monterey in September of 1841, two months after his former wards (Miller 83; Kimbro 5). No evidence suggests that he received any monetary reparations for *his* inconvenience.

Based on findings by Amelie Elkinton and Randy Milliken, Edna Kimbro reported that, during his son's unexpectedly prolonged absence, José Tiburcio Castro requested a leave from his post at Monterey in order to supervise construction of the Prefecture at San Juan Bautista. Kimbro believed that both the Prefecture and the Castro family residence may have been constructed upon the remains of former Mission buildings, and that the latter was built as a father's gift.

Castro could not have occupied the new family home at San Juan Bautista until he returned in September from his detention in Mexico. In early July of that same year, 1841, his father José Tiburcio died at age 64. According to an interpretive panel installed by California Parks and Recreation at the renovated Castro-Breen Adobe, José Tiburcio's will divided the 200 pesos he had received for constructing that residence into two equal parts: 100 pesos to be shared equally by his surviving son and daughter, and the remaining 100 for the Indians who had assisted in the construction. The conjunction of Castro's prolonged absence and his father's untimely death may have freighted the San Juan residence with unhappy associations from the outset.

The Castros resided in San Juan from about 1839 until at least 1843 (Kimbro 4). José's and Modesta's participation in church affairs, including serving as *padrinos* (godparents) for several family members as well as for a number of Indians, is one means of confirming their residence (Kimbro 4). On July 23, 1842, a sixth daughter, María Modesta Castro, called Modestita, was born to the couple. This was apparently a time of prosperity for the family, although some preferred to portray it as profligate. Angustias de la Guerra, consistently hostile to Castro in her late-life oral testimony, claimed that Castro "finished off all of [Mission San Juan Bautista's] assets" (*Testimonios* 255).

In 1842, Castro was made was chief of the Presidial Company at Monterey. For a good portion of the 1840s, he was headquartered at the capital, where he was involved in Californio politics as well as in settling disputes between local Indians and Californio residents, exacerbated by secularization of the missions.

After what would come to be known as "the Isaac Graham Affair," Lieutenant Colonel Castro conferred with General Vallejo in San Jose regarding the mounting danger posed by the resident foreigners. Together with Governor Alvarado, they appealed to the Mexican government for arms and aid (Miller 91). Understandable resentment about the accusations leveled against him by Graham and his cohort notwithstanding, Castro's overall attitude toward Americans remained surprisingly positive.

The Revolt Against Governor Micheltorena

On January 22, 1842 another recently installed Mexican regime appointed Manuel Micheltorena Governor and General Commander of California. The new governor was accompanied by 100 Mexican soldiers whose unruliness and thievery earned them the racializing epithet *"cholos"* (ruffians of mixed blood) among the wary, offended Californios. In the first year of his governorship, Micheltorena officially promoted Castro to Lieutenant Colonel, a rank previously conferred by Californio comrade-in-arms Juan Bautista Alvarado.

By August of 1842, Alvarado was no longer willing to recognize Micheltorena's authority as Governor (Rosenus 49). Indebted to Micheltorena for assistance during the Isaac Graham Affair, and to Alvarado for a lifetime of friendship, Castro may have tried to mitigate the growing tension between the two, but Alvarado eventually decided to revolt against Micheltorena, taking Castro with him. Several resentments prompted the uprising, including the fact that Micheltorena was not a native Californian, that *"his army of hardened criminals and Mexican convicts insulted and threatened residents,"* and that he had failed to react decisively in 1842 when US Naval Commodore Thomas ap Catesby Jones mistakenly "captured" Monterey without the sanction of his own government (Miller 102; Kimbro 5).

The revolution against Micheltorena commenced on November 14, 1844 when:

A party of about fifty young Californios, led by Lieutenant Manuel Castro [José Castro's cousin], *Jesús Pico, and Antonio Chávez drove off all the government horses from Monterey to the Salinas Valley, seized government munitions in San Juan Bautista, and appealed for popular support of their movement.* (Miller 102)

Four days later, Micheltorena issued a proclamation to dissuade others, particularly foreigners, from supporting the revolt (Miller 103).

Some thought it suspicious that Castro took control of the rebel army so quickly because it was unlike him to oppose his *patrón* (boss or superior), particularly when Micheltorena had so recently promoted him (Rosenus 62-3). According to the ever-skeptical Angustias de la Guerra, *"Micheltorena [had even] brought the communi-qué [of his promotion] to Castro himself and placed the insignias on him with his own hands"* (*Testimonios* 261).

Vallejo's view was that Castro and Micheltorena had agreed to stage a revolt as a means of providing the Governor with an honorable excuse for leaving California, and correspondence to this effect was rumored to exist (Rosenus 63). At the end of November, Micheltorena's armed force and the rebel army confronted each other twelve miles south of the pueblo of San Jose (Miller 103). When the revolt began, Castro had been on an expedition with twenty-five men in the interior valley; he now commanded a rebel army of about 220 recruits (Miller 103).

On December 1, 1844, a formal peace agreement was signed. Under its terms, Micheltorena pledged that, within three months, he would discharge his *cholo* soldiers and the officers of his infantry battalion (Miller 104). To ensure that the terms were fulfilled, Alvarado and Castro were to be permitted to maintain a contingent of fewer than 100 armed men, the "Division of the North," at San José (Miller 104).

Promptly violating the terms of the agreement, Governor Micheltorena returned to Monterey to solicit help from foreign residents, notably the American mountaineer Isaac Graham and the enterprising Swiss John Sutter (Miller 104-5). In return for his assistance, Sutter was promised a large land grant and the approval of provisional grants that he had made to American settlers in the Sacramento Valley. Emboldened by this promise, Sutter announced his intent to capture Castro and Alvarado, dead or alive (Miller 104-5).

On January 1, 1845, Captain Sutter and his men left New Helvetia. One week later, they joined forces with Micheltorena at the Salinas River. (Miller 105) Meanwhile, having gotten word of Sutter's scheme against them, Castro and Alvarado left San Jose on January 2nd, proceeding to southern California in the expectation that it would be more difficult for Micheltorena to command his foreign troops further from home (Rosenus 67). They also reasoned that the rival *sureños* would be similarly opposed to the *cholos*, and would likewise disapprove of Micheltorena's duplicity and be angered by his recruitment of foreigners and Indians (Miller 105).

On January 21st, Alvarado's and Castro's Division of the North arrived at the plaza of Los Angeles (Miller 106).

Shortly thereafter, Castro's men captured some of John Sutter's American sharpshooters (Rosenus 68). Toward the end of January, Pío Pico, then President of the Departmental Assembly, called an extraordinary meeting. On February 7th, Micheltorena refused to cooperate with the list of demands put forward by the Assembly (Miller 106-7). The following week the same body passed a decree deposing Micheltorena and declaring Pío Pico temporary Governor (Miller 107). Finally, on February 22nd, the Commissioners, along with Micheltorena and Castro, signed the Treaty of San Fernando.* Alvarado, who thought the terms overly favorable to Micheltorena, ascribed this to Castro's indebtedness to the Governor (Miller 109).

One of the terms of the agreement made Castro *Comandante General* (General Commander) of California (Miller 109; Kimbro 5). With the Treaty of San Fernando:

> *Enemies jettisoned their fears, and friendships temporarily disrupted by the dispute traveled again along old channels. For instance, when Sutter was seized, his captors said they were glad to see him, and… [Castro] clasped Sutter in the customary California* abrazo *[embrace].* (Rosenus 69)

When Micheltorena departed California on March 31, 1845, Mexican rule seemed to have come to an end. Californios were in command of their native land at last, but their hard-won autonomy was to be short-lived.

In 1844, Castro had been *"occupied with selling real estate and fighting the Indians in the Tulares (San Joaquin Valley) who had been stealing horses and harassing settlers"* (Kimbro 6). On February 2nd of that year, another daughter, María Candelaria Griselda, came into the world, followed on December 18, 1845 by José Tiburcio Castro, namesake of his recently deceased grandfather. Paternal namesake José María Castro, Jr. was born in 1846 or 1847. Castro returned from his two-year Mexican sojourn by March 6, 1848, and probably earlier, given the birth of his son José Job Castro on November 20, 1848, followed by the baptismal ceremony at Carmel Mission.

Contending with the Americans

Ostensibly built by its Swiss owner for protection from Indian attacks, Sutter's Fort at New Helvetia on the Sacramento River promptly became an arrival station for Americans venturing to California by wagon train. In 1843, Castro declared that John Sutter's ex-soldiers would be permitted to settle permanently in California under the government's protection. The guarantee offered by Castro also applied to Americans in San Jose and elsewhere in the territory (Rosenus 72). Castro appointed Charles Weber, Alvarado's Prussian-born ally, as captain of the militia in the interior, writing to him that:

> *You may freely offer to all [foreigners] whom you find useful and industrious all the guarantees they may desire for establishing themselves in this department…You will also inform them that the friendly feeling of this office toward them is already secured to them by the treaty of San Fernando…*

In 1845, a total of 173 Americans immigrated to California between the spring thaw and the onset of autumn (Rosenus 74). Castro briefed this disconcertingly large number of newcomers at Sonoma, explaining the Mexican laws to them, and then penned a decree extending "the sentiment of hospitality," adding that, *"Considering that most of the said expedition is composed of families and industrious people, I have deemed it best to permit them provisionally to remain in the Department…"* (Rosenus 75).

The unexpectedly amicable resolution to the revolt against Micheltorena notwithstanding, future interactions between Californios and Americans were not destined to end on such friendly terms. Later in 1845, tensions between the US, Mexico, and the Californios mounted. It was *"a time when the air was full of rumors of war, of foreign aggression, of an English protectorate, of American hopes and designs…"* (Jones 65).

On July 10, 1845, longtime local merchant Thomas Oliver Larkin, recently appointed US Consul to Mexico in Monterey, sent a letter to the US Secretary of State James Buchanan stating that the new central govern-

---

* The 1845 confrontation with Governor Micheltorena, known as the *Battle* of Cahuenga, concluded with the Treaty of San Fernando and is not to be confused with the *Treaty* of Cahuenga, which was signed in January 1847, following the Battle of San Gabriel between the Californios and the Americans.

ment in Mexico City was assembling a military force in Acapulco with the objective of removing Pío Pico and José Castro from office (Hague and Langum 112). Larkin was especially alarmed by a rumor that Great Britain was directly involved in Mexico's action. The Californios were aware of the plans against them, and Castro was preparing defensive action (Hague and Langum 113).

Larkin wrote Buchanan that California leaders had repeatedly told him that they *"will fight all troops Mexico may send here, to the* last *drop of their blood…They wish to govern themselves."* However, he added enticingly, failing self-governance the Californios would *"prefer to see the United States troops, to those from Mexico, …govern the country"* (Hague and Langum 113). Larkin maintained that *"British interest in California was evident in the recent appointment of a salaried vice consul [and that] the French, too, were showing considerable interest in California affairs"* (Hague and Langum 113).

Concerned about the increasing number of American immigrants, Castro and Andrés Castillero traveled to Sutter's Fort in late October of 1845 to negotiate its purchase (St. Clair 285; Haas 337). They hoped that government ownership of the Fort would prevent its further use as an American gathering place, thereby stemming the influx of immigrants from the states and territories, but Sutter rejected their offer. That December, tensions increased after the United States Congress voted to annex Mexican Texas (Haas 337).

Meanwhile, by being *"disorganized and unable to defend the locals against Indian depredations, yet meddling in local affairs and trying to collect taxes and tariffs,"* the Mexican government had lost the allegiance of many Californios, who began to consider *"forming some other allegiance that promised protection and stability…Though some supported the American causes, Californio elites probably would have preferred some sort of independence under British or French protection"* (Monroy 176). By some reports, Castro himself was planning for separation from Mexico in 1847 or 1848, once he judged that a sufficient number of foreigners had arrived to steer allegiance away from Mexico and to adequately garrison California (Monroy 176).

Internal tensions within Alta California were also on the rise. In their split commands, Castro and Pico became promptly and predictably estranged from one another, never managing to agree on how to govern the territory jointly. Castro believed that Alta California needed to strengthen its military defenses against potential US hostility, while Pico insisted that the most effective defense would be to have Californio residents commit more deeply to the territory by making them landowners (*Lands of Promise* 465). Pico sought to move the Customs House, principal collector of territorial revenue in the form of duties, from Monterey to San Pedro, the port of Los Angeles while Castro reportedly wanted it moved north to San Francisco (*Testimonios* 40). According to Dorotea Valdez, *"Don Pío Pico was conspiring with [James Alexander] Forbes to turn the territory into an English protectorate. Meanwhile, Castro, with the assistance of General Vallejo, was doing his best to have the country annexed to the United States"* (*Testimonios* 40). The entrenched animosity between Castro and Pico would eventually have great bearing on the fate of California.

Beginning in the summer of 1845, Captain John Charles Frémont of the U.S. Topographical Corps led a group of men *"through Mexican territory, including parts of the present states of New Mexico, Colorado, Utah, and California, allegedly to determine, among other things, a route for a railroad to the Pacific, terminating either in California or in the Oregon Country"* (Haas 337). Frémont's party, consisting of "about sixty heavily-armed mountain men" (Hague 357) arrived in California in early January of 1846 without seeking permission from the authorities (Hague and Langum 11). Manuel Castro, Prefect at Monterey, asked American Consul Thomas Larkin to explain the "unauthorized presence of American troops in California." Shortly thereafter, Commander General José Castro asked Captain Frémont himself to do the same (Hague and Langum 120).

Larkin assured both Castros that most of Frémont's hired men were "not army troops," and explained that the party was in Monterey *"only to purchase supplies for the expedition [and afterwards] would reassemble and depart for Oregon."* Frémont insisted that "the objectives of the expedition were… scientific and commercial." According to this account, when Castro *"did not reply to the explanation provided, Frémont and Larkin assumed that he was satisfied"* (Hague and Langum 120). An earlier account stresses that Castro's approval was more explicitly conditional, granting Frémont permission to *"winter in the San Joaquin Valley, away from the [coastal] settlements, where the men would not be likely to annoy the people…[and to] extend his explorations in the spring as far south as the Colorado River"* (Bidwell 2).

Overall, Californio officials in Monterey treated Frémont quite courteously (Jones 62), despite a couple of incidents that may have fueled their suspicions about his true intent and character. In the spring of 1846, a dispute occurred in the San Jose Valley concerning horses belonging to a ranchero named Sebastián Peralta (Rosenus 83). Frémont's men had allegedly stolen the horses and refused to surrender them when confronted by their rightful owner (Jones 64). Frémont's response to this matter was overtly aggressive and hostile, referring to Peralta as a "straggling vagabond" who *"should have been well satisfied to escape [the American camp] without a severe horsewhipping"* (Rosenus 83). In addition, while still at Monterey, Frémont had made the intimidating announcement that *"ten thousand Americans were about to start from the Mississippi Valley to California"* (Jones 64).

Early in the spring of 1846, Frémont and his party resumed their expedition. It is logical to assume, as Bidwell did early on, that

> *When Castro gave him permission to explore towards the Colorado River he no doubt supposed [that Frémont] would go south or southeast from where he was camped in the San Joaquin Valley, and on through the Tejon Pass and the Mojave Desert; but, instead, [Frémont's group] started to go west and southwest through the most thickly settled parts of California, namely, the Santa Clara, Pajaro, and Salinas Valleys.* (Bidwell 3)

Frémont's party arrived in the Salinas Valley on March 3rd (Miller 112) and went to William Hartnell's residence at Rancho Alisal. Three of his men were sent to purchase supplies at the ranch of José Castro's uncle, Don Angel Castro and, *"Under the influence of liquor, one of Frémont's men insisted that the ranchero's daughter become his companion"* (Rosenus 84; Jones 64). In the brief scuffle that ensued after this inappropriate advance, "the American drew his pistol," an even more overtly offensive act (Rosenus 84). Frémont's men were immediately asked to leave the premises, and the encounter apparently ended without further incident.

On March 5th, Castro had an official order delivered to Frémont stating that his unauthorized presence in the area was in violation of Mexican law, and demanding his immediate departure (Miller 112). Castro presumably "based his peremptory order on positive instruc-

tions which he had received from Mexico by the *Hannah*" (Jones 65). Frémont refused to issue a written reply, telling the messenger, Lieutenant José Chávez, that he had no intention of complying with the order (Rosenus 85). He then left Rancho Alisal with his men and ascended a nearby mountain–*Pico Gavilán* or Hawk's Peak, subsequently called Frémont Peak (Hague and Langum 11). From this strategic position overlooking the Salinas Valley, Frémont raised the American flag in blatant defiance of international protocol (Kimbro 6; Rosenus 85).

Castro began assembling forces at San Juan Bautista and brought his troops into line at the base of the mountain, challenging Frémont to descend and fight on the plain below (Rosenus 85; Hague and Langum 11; Kimbro 6). On March 8th, Castro issued a public proclamation stating that a "band of robbers" commanded by Frémont, had *"…without respect to the laws and authorities of the Department daringly introduced themselves into the country"* and were "committing depredations, and making scandalous skirmishes" (Cleland 196).

On March 9th, Alvarado's militiamen joined forces with Castro's troops, and Consul Larkin sent Frémont a note advising him to retreat (Miller 114). Late that night, Frémont finally abandoned his position, "departing the peak from the rear" (Kimbro 6) and moving rapidly northward, through the San Joaquin and Sacramento Valleys toward the Oregon Territory (Bidwell 3).

The testimony of one of Castro's men explains that their commander was against pursuing Frémont: *"He said that it was not necessary to shed blood, and that he did not want the responsibility of spilling Californian blood. Everyone was ready to fight and felt very mad at Señor Castro for not letting them go"* (Escobar 3). Angustias de la Guerra accused Castro of putting his personal safety first: *"It did not matter how much Alvarado and the others who were with him urged him to [pursue Frémont]. Castro was not keen on placing his valuable self in the line of fire. He preferred to come to a friendly agreement, either by scheming or some other means, as long as he protected his own hide"* (*Testimonios* 262).

Instead of giving chase, Castro sent the civilian soldiers home and duly reported the incident to Governor Pico and to the Minister of War in Mexico City (Miller 114). At the end of March, when Frémont arrived at the Marysville buttes just north of Sutter's Fort:

He found the settlers in that vicinity were greatly excited over the report that General Castro intended to drive all of the Americans from the country. A second rumor said that he had instigated the Indians to massacre all of the families and burn all of the crops. This was indeed alarming news, but it was not true. (Tinkham 2)

In mid-March of 1846, soon after the confrontation with Frémont, Castro sent an agent to Mexico to appeal for aid and called a *junta mixta* (a meeting including both military officials and civilian residents) of the Northern District (Miller 115). Vallejo and others suspected that Castro had called the meeting "to solidify his own plans to overthrow Pico" rather than to discuss the American threat (Miller 115). This was apparently not the case, however, since Governor Pico had himself been invited, although in the end "…no one from the south attended" (Hague and Langum 117). The *junta*, which convened on March 27th, began at Castro's home in Monterey and then moved to US Consul Thomas Larkin's residence (Miller 115; Hague and Langum 117). Castro had prepared a dramatic opening statement:

> *How greatly to be pitied is the condition to which Mexico has reduced us! …The mother country…refuses us arms, money and materials of war which we are so lacking for our defense. She does not do this because she has forgotten us long since, for she very well recalls us to mind in order to send us her minions, who, dressed in the garb of soldiers and civil officials, penetrate into our society [to corrupt our morals and rifle our strongboxes].* (Miller 115, partially retranslated by the Editor)

He went on to warn of the rapidly increasing number of American immigrants, predicting–quite correctly, as it turned out–that within just two years they would outnumber the Spanish-speaking residents who had been in Alta California for generations (Miller 115-6). Commenting on the enterprising character of the Americans, Castro drew laughter with an even more far-sighted prediction: *"The Americans are so clever that some day they will build ladders reaching to the sky, and once there, they will change the face of the whole universe and even the color of the stars"* (Miller 116). He also spoke of possible defensive measures, such as going to the Sacramento region in July to prevent the entry of more immigrants (Rosenus 89).

Before an audience who assumed that he "favored full independence with no foreign ties," Castro spoke out unexpectedly in favor of annexing California to Catholic France (Hague and Langum 117; Miller 116). Other participants spoke variously in favor of a British protectorate, unfettered independence, and association with the United States (Hague and Langum 117). Alan Rosenus states that, contrary to Larkin's fears–and to the hopes of some Californios: *"The governments of England and France had no desire to seize California… England's main objective was to block American ownership of the province; she did not want the territory herself… Because of the huge Mexican debt, papers signed in Mexico City or London could give the province to Britain without any need for war"* (72). It was clear that the uncertain fate of California would have to be decided soon.

Some historians claim that, contrary to his statements at the *junta*, Castro secretly favored the Americans. Harlan Hague writes that Castro *"showed Larkin a plan for declaring California independent from Mexico as soon as a sufficient number of immigrants had entered the province to ensure success, probably by 1847 or 1848"* (357). William Carey Jones, brother-in-law to John Charles Frémont and officially delegated to report on conditions in California, wrote that *"Larkin had obtained from Castro a general assent to a scheme for revolutionizing the country in favor of the United States, and Castro was merely going to wait until the Americans had become sufficiently numerous to ensure success"* (64).

The accuracy of these statements can be neither verified nor disproved due to the dearth of supporting documentation, while Larkin's brief on behalf of a peaceful transition to American rule in California is clear from the historical record. In late April or early May, he reportedly told Castro and Vallejo that he expected the American flag to be flying over Monterey within thirty days. Castro, exasperated by the uncertainty of recent months, reportedly replied that war was preferable to peace since affairs would finally be settled. Larkin then suggested that Castro *could*, without the necessity of war, *"secure to himself, and his friends, fame, honor, permanent employ, and pay,"* but Castro reportedly did not respond to this overture (Hague and Langum 127; Rosenus 98). Regardless of the potential for tangible reward, it would seem that José Castro was unwilling to relinquish California without a fight.

On April 2, 1846, six members of the *junta* and the military secretary signed a declaration recognizing General

José María Paredes as President of Mexico, and disavowing acts of the previous administration, including the appointment of Pío Pico as Governor (Miller 117). According to the same source, on April 11th members of the Northern group signed a statement with the following resolutions: 1) Commander General Castro's presence was necessary in the northern towns, which must be fortified and defended against possible foreign invasion; 2) Governor Pico should come to Monterey to take part in the defense of the Department; 3) if he did not comply with the invitation, Castro was authorized to establish his headquarters at Santa Clara as he deemed best; 4) these arrangements would prevail until Andrés Castillero arrived with orders and resources solicited from Mexico.

Pío Pico did not react favorably to these demands. He and Castro each charged the other with dictatorial ambitions. Pico reportedly hoped that *a conference in the south would offset the effect of the junta that [had] met in Monterey.* On June 3, 1846, he called a secret session of the Los Angeles Departmental Assembly, which proceeded to denounce and suspend José Castro for his "illegal assumption of powers" (Hague and Langum 132-3; Rosenus 99-100). The Assembly authorized Pico to take the necessary steps to "save the country," by which they meant remove Castro from command (Hussey 122). Pico decided to feign compliance with Castro's demands for assistance against the foreigners by raising a military force, but with the actual goal of unseating Castro (Miller 118).

Since May, Castro and José Antonio Carrillo had been in the Santa Clara Valley, recruiting an army for use against either Pico or the Americans, as necessity dictated (Rosenus 100; Miller 118). On June 5, 1846, with Lieutenant Francisco Arce, Castro paid a visit to General Vallejo at his gracious home and headquarters at Sonoma (Rosenus 101). Primarily concerned with impending war against Pico, Castro successfully petitioned his old friend to provide him with 170 horses plus weapons and ammunition for his men. (Rosenus 102).

Castro then proceeded to Santa Clara, leaving Lieutenant Arce to bring the horses "round the bay by way of the Sacramento and San Joaquin Rivers" (Hansen 226). Rumors that Castro was intent on driving the Americans from the province now abounded. Armed Mexican horsemen were reputed to be riding toward the Sacramento Valley, burning and ravaging the countryside (Rosenus 102; Hague and Langum 136).

What would come to be known as the "Bear Flag Revolt" will forever remain an enigma; whether the Americans involved truly believed the rumors and thought they were taking defensive action can never be determined. On June 10th, Frémont, recently returned with his men from the buttes above the Yuba River, instigated the capture of Lieutenant Arce and the band of horses by a group of a dozen Americans and Englishmen (Hansen 226; Hague and Langum 136). He took this action independently, prior to the receipt of any official orders or word of a declaration of war between the United States and Mexico (Bidwell 3). It is likely that much of his motivation was personal resentment based on his earlier encounter with Castro. According to Hussey's account, *"Arce was told that if Castro wanted the remaining horses he could get them at Frémont's camp"* (122). As Hague and Langum note:

> Castro had issued no proclamation against the settlers; he had taken no action to drive them away; he had gathered no troops to march against them. It was true that he was plotting, collecting a force, and preparing to march, but almost certainly against Governor Pico, not against the Americans. (138).

The Americans Take Action and Take California

Frémont played a surprisingly small role in the events that followed. It is said that he *"promised aid to the Bear Flaggers, but never actually gave it."* (Hansen 226) William B. Ide, one of the group's members, reportedly urged the men to further action, arguing that *"to desist now…was to condemn themselves [and] stultify all their previous acts; but one course lay open to them…they must be conquerors or they were horse-thieves"* (Jones 80).

Thus inspired, the group captured Mariano Guadalupe Vallejo's home and headquarters at Sonoma on June 14th, seizing more horses and taking as their prisoners General Vallejo himself, his brother Salvador, and eventually the American merchant Jacob P. Leese, who had volunteered to act as translator (Hague and Langum 137). On June 17th, Castro *"called upon all Californians to resist, en masse, the adventurers who, inspired by the contemptible policy of the United States agents, had seized Sonoma"* (Hussey 123). Northern Californios under Castro's command immediately engaged in skirmishes against the Bear Flaggers, as did some of the ranchers in the Sonoma region.

On June 23rd, Governor Pico, who was heading northward to fight Castro, learned of the events in Sonoma and called upon his countrymen *"to fly in all haste in pursuit of the treacherous foe"* (Hussey 123). Angustias de la Guerra believed that Pico did not feel particularly threatened by the news from Sonoma, and that it was not until he learned of the capture of Monterey by the US Navy that he abandoned his original plan to attack Castro in order to focus instead on the foreign threat (*Testimonios* 261-2). By June 29th, "All organized resistance to the Bear Flag movement north of the bay was now ended, and Castro retreated southward to strengthen his forces" (Hussey 124).

After the capture of Sonoma by the Bear-Flaggers, Castro from his headquarters in Santa Clara began *"issuing proclamations that guaranteed protection to all foreigners not in arms. The Sonoma rebels would have to take their chances with the fortunes of war, but Castro vowed that he would never 'lightly proceed' against any residents until their crimes had been proved"* (Rosenus 139-40). Hearing that the Americans planned to engage them, Castro and his troops left for San Juan Bautista to obtain arms and ammunition (Kimbro 6).

After long days of indecision and self-confinement, US Naval Commodore John Sloat finally raised the American flag over Monterey's Custom House on July 7, 1846, sending word to Castro and Pico to surrender (Kimbro 6; Haas 341). Upon learning of the capture of Monterey, Castro reportedly exclaimed, *"What can I do with a handful of men against the United States? All who wish to follow me, right about face; I am going to Mexico"* (Tinkham 3).

Whether or not this was Castro's original intention, he quickly decided to fortify southern California instead. On July 9th, he refused Sloat's order and announced his determination to defend California as long as he could count on a single man to accompany him "in this cause which is as just as it is national" (quoted in Hussey 126). As Angustias de la Guerra concludes:

> *In light of the critical circumstances in which California found itself, and with the assistance of some friends, Castro and Pico made peace with one another because it was necessary to gather all the troops and individuals who were available to de-*

> *fend California, and there were not many of them.*
> (*Testimonios* 262)

Castro's 160 men united with 100 of Pico's at Rancho Santa Margarita on July 12th (Kimbro 6; Haas 341-2). Four days later, on July 16th, Governor Pico issued orders in Santa Barbara that *"all citizens of the territory, whether native-born or naturalized, take up arms"* (Haas 341-2). Later that month, Castro and Pico held a meeting at Rancho Santa Margarita at which they decided on a joint retreat toward Los Angeles (Cameron 11).

Castro posted his soldiers at present-day Compton (Rosenus 170) while Frémont and his men arrived in San Diego on July 29th, and Commodore Robert Field Stockton, who had taken over Sloat's command, sailed from Monterey on August 1st (Monroy 177). Five days later, Stockton arrived at San Pedro, where he began preparing his 360 troops for the fifteen-mile march to Los Angeles (Rosenus 170).

Castro offered to negotiate for peace, under the condition that Stockton suspend "all hostile movements" toward Los Angeles (Rosenus 170-1). Stockton responded provocatively that hostilities would not end until Castro himself raised the American flag over California (Rosenus 171; Haas 342). Castro replied in cavalier fashion that if Stockton *"marched upon the town he would find it the graves of his men,"* to which Stockton retorted, *"Tell the General to have the bells ready to toll, as I shall be there tomorrow"* (Tinkham 3).

During negotiations, General Castro's forces had diminished as his undersupplied troops grew increasingly war-weary. At this point, he found himself with barely 100 men (Rosenus 171). On August 9th, at his Campo de la Mesa near Los Angeles, Castro decided that, under the circumstances, he could do no more to defend Alta California and determined instead to retreat to Sonora (Hussey 128), leaving his command in the capable hands of his younger cousin Manuel de Jesús Castro (Miller, 124). That same day, he sent a dispatch to Pico that was both an apology and a letter of resignation:

> *After having done all in my power to prepare for the defense of the department and to oppose the invasion of the United States forces…, I am obliged today to make known to you with regret that it is not possible to accomplish either objective, because, notwithstanding your efforts to afford me all the aid in your power, I can count on only 100 men, badly*

armed, worse supplied, and discontented…so that I have reason to fear that not even these few men will fight when the necessity arises. (Rosenus 171)

On August 10, 1846, accompanied by his secretary Ensign Francisco Arce, Castro left Alta California for Sonora, Mexico, *"where he would ceaselessly petition the Mexican government for arms and soldiers to retake California"* (Haas 342). Meanwhile, the Los Angeles Departmental Assembly decided to dissolve itself rather than be taken over by the American forces (Hussey 128). Pico, forced to choose between "ignominy and emigration," signed over the mission lands in his possession to his associates and decided to head for Mexico as well (Hussey 128; Monroy 177). Some accounts report that Pico departed for Mexico on August 10th, the same day as Castro, while Edna Kimbro and others maintain that he did not depart until early September (Monroy 177; Kimbro 7). By the time Stockton arrived in Los Angeles, his men met "only insignificant resistance from the fractious and demoralized forces" (Monroy 177).

On the eve of his departure, in addition to his letter of resignation to Pico, Castro composed a farewell to his fellow Californios:

With my heart full of the most cruel grief, I take leave of you. I depart the country of my birth, but with the hope of returning to destroy the slavery in which I leave you; for the day will come when our unfortunate fatherland can punish this usurpation, as rapacious as it is unjust, and under the gaze of the world exact satisfaction for its grievances. Friends, I confide in your loyalty and patriotism… (Rosenus 172, from Bancroft 5:269, n.16)

The official Mexican newspaper, *El Diario del Gobierno*, published Castro's account of the conquest of the Californias in October (Phillips 108). By the first week of December, 1846, Jessie Benton Frémont, wife of the explorer, and her sister Eliza Benton Jones had translated it into English for the *Daily Union* newspaper of Washington DC.* (Reproduced in Part V.) Phillips summarized Castro's account:

[It] reported both provinces lost [and] all civil and military authorities fled, including Governor-General Don Pio Pico. It further stated that Fré-

mont and his men with Commodore Stockton and the Marines were in the City of the Angels, that Colonel Alvarado and other officers were hid in the woods, and that General Castro himself was thirty days on the road to Sonora. (108)

That same month, Jessie Frémont provided the *Union* editor with a translation of Castro's proclamations to the people of California and to the Consuls of France, Spain, and Great Britain, originally published in Mexico City.

Meanwhile, *The Californian*–California's first newspaper, published at Monterey–was fanning the fears of Castro's return by advising its readers on October 26th:

Every American who can get a rifle and a horse ought to turn out, or expect to be driven to the mountains, or massacred, for the Californians has [sic] determined to fight, almost every man has turned out, they say they will be killed if taken, and they are determined to conquer or die. Castro is hourly expected from Sonora, with four hundred men, which added to their present force will make about fifteen hundred men, and all well-mounted.

Intriguingly, the same issue contained a contradictory article a few lines below:

Many of the citizens remain at their ranches, from a fear of some warlike movements on the part of the few Californians who have taken the field, but our force at this place is sufficiently large to protect the town from any trouble from them, and we should be much pleased to see the good citizens return to their [town] houses. From the best information we can get, there are only a few persons who have nothing to lose, and are unwilling to go to work, who are engaged in the present out-break, [and] all of the good and substantial citizens of this place, are not only quiet, but much opposed to this movement.

This edition of the paper also echoes José Castro's prediction of a growing influx of Americans: *"We may reasonably expect a very large emigration next fall…"* Although the U.S. and Mexico were still at war, *The Californian* writes encouragingly that *"[American] emigrants will be agreeably disappointed; instead of finding the Californians*

*The daughters of Senator Thomas Hart Benton of the Missouri Territory had been taught both Spanish and French as children because both languages were spoken among their father's constituency.

a cold, morose and uncivil race, they are affable, generous, and obliging, and the females invariably kind, attentive, and hospitable" (October 26, 1846).

Despite fears and hopes of Castro's reconquest, the war in California ended on January 13, 1847 with the capitulation of the Californio forces to Frémont (in preference to Stockton) and the Treaty of Cahuenga. (See note on page 22.) There were many reasons for the Californios' inability to effectively resist the American forces. As one historian observes, *"California was a remote outpost of Mexico and had been neglected to the point where there was little in the way of a fighting force [and] little funds to purchase essential equipment…[Some Californios] also were disenchanted with Mexican dominion to the point that they were indifferent to the outcome or even favored American victory"* (Beck 3). Another writes, *"For decades, [Californios] had not been able to stem the tide of American immigration, control the California Indian frontier, or secure monetary aid, arms, and soldiers from Mexico, despite the constant appeals of General Castro and former Governor Pío Pico"* (Haas 344). In addition, the infamous friction between Castro and Pico made unity against the invaders difficult and, as a result, they were unable to defend their territory effectively (Beck 3, Monroy 176). Dorotea Valdez even went as far as to declare many years later, in her "dictation" for Hubert Howe Bancroft: *"If the Americans had not taken the country in 1846, by 1847 every Californio would have been killed in a civil war due to the bitter hatred that existed [between north and south]"* (*Testimonios* 40).

Lizbeth Haas emphasizes widespread resistance to the American takeover when she writes that in fall of 1846, *"Los Angeles, Santa Barbara, San Diego, Santa Inés, San Luis Obispo, and surrounding lands were retaken by a Californio army composed of both soldiers and civilians… [Californio citizens] engaged in small, but daily, acts of resistance, and criticized…José Castro and Pío Pico for leaving the country rather than defending it"* (Haas 343). Writing more than a century earlier, Hubert Howe Bancroft concluded with mixed condescension and realism: *"[Castro] was not a very able man, [but even] with ten times his ability and resources, no resistance could have been offered to the US; he was not a very brave man, but he showed no cowardice in the operations of 1846"* (Bancroft 19:752, reproduced in full in Part V.)

Transition to American California

Based in Mexico until the cessation of hostilities between that country and the United States, Castro made occasional visits to Alta California, presumably to pursue business ventures and to visit family and compatriots. He was *"back in California by March 6, 1848 when he received permission from [Territorial] Governor [Richard B.] Mason to keep the San Juan Bautista Mission orchard"* (Kimbro 7).

That spring, the nine-member Breen family, Irish-American immigrants who had spent a starving, snowbound winter in the Sierra Nevada with other members of the infamous Donner Party, arrived in the San Juan Valley. Patrick, his wife Margaret, and their seven children had all survived the unspeakable ordeal, but were traumatized and destitute as a result. The José Castro family, "the most politically connected in the region" and also holders of "prime ranch lands and real estate," allowed the Breens to occupy their property on former San Juan Bautista Mission land (Kimbro 5, 7).

Sources conflict as to whether this two-story, 8-room balconied residence–adjacent to the Plaza Hotel and diagonal to Mission San Juan Bautista–was in use by Castro's own family when he opened its doors to the the destitute Irish-American family who shared the same Roman Catholic faith as his own. Some historians maintain that Castro "vacated his own house" or "turned his house over to the newcomers," while others state that it "was not then being actively used" or was "under-utilized" ("General" 71; Enright 351; Kimbro 5, 7). Whichever the case, Castro was remembered favorably for this gesture, as exemplified by an 1881 article entitled "General Castro's Hospitable Nature" that describes him as having a "heart full of generous impulses and kind feelings" ("General" 71). A source from the 1950s echoes this assumption of generosity, maintaining that *The Breens were a large family in want and Castro had a native charity"* (Enright 351).

When one of the Breens' sons returned from the gold fields with $12,000 in cash, the windfall gave his struggling family a fresh start, catalyzing their rapid rise to prominence in Central California ranching, real estate, and politics. On December 18, 1848, Patrick Breen Sr. purchased the two-story San Juan Bautista adobe from José Castro and promptly turned the building into the

United States Inn. The hotel venture was short-lived, but the Breen family continued to live there until 1874. The building is still known as the Castro-Breen Adobe, with the latter family's heirlooms providing the basis for ongoing displays and interpretation (Kimbro 8).

Jessie Benton Frémont–wife of John Charles Frémont and daughter one of the nation's most influential senators, Thomas Hart Benton of Missouri–arrived in Monterey in mid-1849 after sailing both coasts of the continent with her young daughter Lily–not to mention having traversed the intervening jungles of Panama by canoe and mule. Her keen eye immediately read the effects of the gold rush on the little town of Monterey:

> *There was a small garrison of married officers [in residence] with their families, but no man of any degree voluntarily kept away from the mines or San Francisco; it was their great opportunity for sudden money-making. Domestic manners were even more upset than in San Francisco, where the Chinese could be had [for household labor]. Here it was like after a shipwreck on a desert shore; the strongest and the most capable was king, and, to produce anything like comfort, all capacities had to be put to use…*

> *It was barely a year since the gold had been discovered, but in that time every eatable thing had been eaten off the face of the country, and nothing [had been] raised. I suppose there was not a fowl left in the northern part of the state, consequently not an egg; …Since there were no longer vaqueros or herdsmen, flocks and herds had dispersed. There were no cows, consequently no milk. Housekeeping [under circumstances such as these]…becomes a puzzle.* (Frémont 68-9)

Jessie also took note of the toll that American rule had taken on the native Californios, as manifest for example in her reference to *"the shameful injustice of our government in disregarding its treaty stipulations, and despoiling them."*

José Castro was not the only member of the family to offer hospitality to incoming Americans. In June of 1849–while he was tending to business in San Juan Bautista and elsewhere, and while and the restless John C. Frémont was shuttling between San Francisco and the Mariposa property that had once belonged to Juan Bautista Alvarado, which Thomas Oliver Larkin had astutely purchased on Frémont's behalf–Modesta Castro allocated two rooms of their Monterey home to Jessie and Lily Frémont (Kimbro 8, Freeman 2).

Jessie Benton Frémont begins the Monterey section of her memoir, *A Year of American Travel*: *"The winds of San Francisco had renewed the trouble with my lungs, [so] we went down by steamer to Monterey, where there was a very different climate."* According to her first biographer, one-time neighbor Catherine Coffin Phillips, husband and wife discussed possible housing arrangements upon her arrival. Admiring the location, Jessie proposed gamely to her consummate outdoorsman that they *"make permanent camp anywhere within sight and sound of this beauty."* Her husband reportedly answered, pointing to a low house on a hill:

> *Our home for the present is to be here. Madame Castro, wife of the Mexican General, holds no enmity toward me, although her husband is still exiled in Mexico [sic]. She lives here with her little daughter Modesta [and] will give us two large rooms for our own home.* (Phillips 153)

The Castro home may indeed have been the only option available, as reported by Freeman (2). Certainly, hotel accommodations were few, and the 48 delegates to the California Constitutional Convention were poised to arrive for an indefinite period of deliberations. Fortunately, the accomodations pleased the young wife, who had grown up enjoying the best that the nation's capital had to offer. According to Jesse's description:

> *The largest and best building in town was the Governor's residence [sic]; it occupied double the usual space, and was really a good building, with very thick walls and a charming great garden, surrounded by hedges of roses. I was fortunate to have one wing of this, where I made my first housekeeping. The large window of one room looked into the bay, with its great crescent-shaped sweep towards Santa Cruz; the boom of its long rollers was with me all the time…"* (Frémont 73).

No suggestion of difficulties between the Castro and the Frémont families has emerged. On the contrary, the women and their offspring got along very well. Jessie recalled: *"The other wing of the house was occupied by Madame Castro herself, and her very nice little girls made charming playmates for mine"* (Frémont 101). Indeed,

Elizabeth (Lily) Frémont was the same age as little Modestita Castro. Conversant in Spanish from childhood, Jessie was introduced to Modesta's friends and ended up borrowing books from one of them (Phillips 155-6). The historical record shows that even John Charles Frémont put a high degree of trust in Modesta Castro. After a rich vein of gold was discovered on his Mariposa property, he "*sent the buckskin bags of the precious metal down to be stored in an adobe building behind the Castro house*" (Phillips 156).

While it may seem curious that Modesta would have offered hospitality to the family of her husband's former adversary, many Californio families had become so impoverished by that time that their inbred hospitality and generosity were reinforced by need. According to Edna Kimbro, "*If that were the case, it could provide a great incentive to sell their San Juan Bautista real estate holdings to the Breens. It also explains why José would be in San Juan at the time*" (8). The letters published in this volume confirm the family's dire financial straits, which would have also been a motivating factor in José's decision to accept the military position offered to him by the Mexican government a few years later.

After the Constitutional Convention convened on September 3, 1849, John Sutter, future California Senator William M. Gwin, and other delegates enjoyed dinners at the Castro home hosted by Jessie on improvised plank tables modestly covered with unbleached muslin strips "briar-stitched together with red thread" (Phillips 158). Jessie received help in providing hospitality from Mrs. M'Evoy, a cook from Australia, and two local Indians, Gregorio and Juan, who provided game for the table and assisted her in myriad ways (Frémont 74, 94, 101).

Referring to the growing breach between pro-slavery and free states and territories, Jessie recalled lobbying the constitutional delegates to make California a slavery-free state:

> *… Our rooms in the Castro house were very pretty, with their French and Chinese fittings. My army and navy allies helped me to keep them orderly, and although I had then only the two Indian men [as servants] we managed to be very comfortable. We had the grand wood fires; everyone sent me birds and squirrels of their shooting, and these are never so good as when broiled on the coals. …, In short, my pretty rooms were the headquarters of the anti-slavery party, and myself the example of happiness*

and hospitality without servants [slaves]." (Frémont, 94)

While the Frémonts were poised to come into considerable wealth from their California land acquisitions, the Castros were faced with the expensive and cumbersome process of reconfirming their titles before the Land Commission soon to be set up for the purpose in San Francisco. It was imperative for them to find the wherewithal to pay the necessary attorneys' fees as well as the newly imposed property taxes. José Castro was involved in a number of property transactions during these years. In specifying several of them, Edna Kimbro noted that some "appear to have been somewhat irregular in nature" (Kimbro 9). Given the predictable confusion during a period of transition between two very different sets of legal and economic regimes, it would be unrealistic to expect transparency.

On July 22, 1852, Rosalia Vallejo de Leese purchased a tract of land known as Rancho Sausal from joint owners Castro, his wife Modesta, his sister María Francisca, and her husband Santiago Moreno. The owners were to be paid $1750 when the sale was confirmed (Kimbro 8), but Castro signed over his and Modesta's interest to James McKinley "*for payment of a debt contracted back in 1845 at 2.5% interest per month.*" (Kimbro 8) It is pertinent to note that this loan was made before the American takeover, and that annual the rate of interest was 30%, the going rate during those years.

On March 4, 1853, a contract was signed in San Francisco by Castro, his cousin and fellow military officer Manuel de Jesús Castro, Juan Bautista Alvarado, and Jacques Antoine Morenhout, French consul to Mexican California between 1846 and 1848. This had do with a property at Cabo San Quentín on the Pacific coast of northern Baja California, the title to which had been awarded to Castro in 1841 (Miller 146). The land contained salt deposits, but Castro had not developed the extraction facilities, and the buyers intended to begin exploiting the deposits (Miller 146). "*Subsequent correspondence between Alvarado and the partners indicates that the salt business was unsuccessful in producing income, at least for Don Juan*" (Miller 146). Indeed, Letter 5, written on December 24, 1856 by Alvarado to Castro, refers to the failure of one of their salt quarrying enterprises and the misfortunes that have befallen the Californios:

> *The same official who delivers this to you will inform you how disastrous the expedition to Sal was,*

and that this is the reason your order is not being sent to you, and will likewise let you know just what my own daily lot is like, and how every day things get more difficult for us, as they do for all the Californios in general. Do your best to put together some kind of capital for your family [in Baja California], because here there is no hope for us…

Even after peace between Mexico and the U.S. was ratified in mid-1848, Castro was unwavering in his political allegiance. Despite American assurances such as the one published in *The Californian* on August 15, 1846 –*"We shall advocate an oblivion of all past political offences and allow every man the privilege of entering this new era of events unembarrassed by any part he may have taken in previous revolutions"*–Castro refused to swear allegiance to the United States (*Californian* 8/15/46; Kimbro 8). In this refusal, *"He–and another man of his name–were the sole exceptions among all Mexican subjects in California who by positive act and declaration declined the proffer of American citizenship"* ("General" 71).

Perhaps the Americans would have slept more soundly had they succeeded in convincing Castro to accept US citizenship. Instead, accounts of him as a *"rather mysterious individual, still greatly feared by the Americans"* persisted. During the Constitutional Convention of 1849, when he let himself be seen in a few public places, *"Word went around that he was planning to retake California."* Alan Rosenus adds knowingly that at this juncture, *"No doubt some of the long-term residents reported this with a wink and a smile"* (203).

José and Modesta Castro produced at least three more children, in addition to one of unknown name and gender who was born and died in 1850. The three were Cesario Castro, born February 25, 1851; Moisés Castro, born in 1853; and Eleanora Elizabeta Castro, born in April of 1854. When José Castro departed on the ship *Oregon* in February of 1856 to assume the governorship of Baja California, Modesta was pregnant with their fourteenth child, who was delivered and buried within weeks of the father's departure.

Castro was eventually appointed Military Commander and Political Sub-Chief of Lower California–a position that he held until, as Edna Kimbro notes wryly, *"He died loyal to the Mexican government that he had defied throughout his youth"* (9). Several of Dr. Angela Pahissa Moyano's many books and articles give a sobering sense of the wrenching reversals that dominated the political landscape in post-independence Mexico–a period in which the only constant was frequent and often violent change. Parts III and IV explore the complexities of Castro's Baja California years.

Baja California historian Pedro L. Martínez notes summarily that, during the last four years of his life, *"Castro surrounded himself with [former] soldiers and officers of his [command], many of whom were fugitives from justice in the neighboring terrain. He liked to drink a lot and in one of his drunken sprees he was murdered by one of his own men, Manuel Márquez, on April 14, 1860"* (Martínez 387). Kimbro's account, which gives Castro's date of death as April 5, 1860, refers to the incident as "foul play, perhaps assassination by Manuel Márquez…" (Kimbro 9). Upon Castro's death, his political command was assumed by his delegated second, Feliciano Ruiz de Esparza, who reportedly, *"in reprisal for the assassination of his chief, shot twelve men without any form of trial, which caused stormy agitation along the border"* (Martínez 387). This blood-soaked, byzantine saga is summarized in Part III.

As the pair of letters from Modesta to her husband reproduced in Part II suggest, the Castros never managed to regain the material security they had apparently enjoyed prior to the American takeover. E.S. Harrison paints a cloying picture of Modesta's waning years:

In a gloriously fertile nook adjacent to the old adobe, Castro's widow,…in the sad days of poverty and want which followed the footsteps of retreating wealth and high position, cultivated a garden and made tomales [sic], which she sold to support herself and family… (Kimbro, 10)

Because there were at least four "Casas Castro" in Monterey, it is difficult to determine which is the one invoked by Harrison without more concrete information. The stone house on the Mesa once belonged to Modesta's paternal grandmother, Victoria Beltrán de Castro, who inherited it from her husband, soldier Antonio María Castro. Edna Kimbro's research indicated that Modesta Castro de Castro purchased the property from attorney Miguel Avila in 1836 and later deeded it to her eldest son. In 1904, Esteban Castro in turn deeded it to his longtime companion, the widow Adelaida Limas, "for love and affection." In 1917 the property belonged to Francisca Dana de Díaz, daughter of Modesta Castro de Dana, who became Francisca Díaz-Tucker upon her second marriage. (See Part IV.)

Castro Ranch House. Built & occupied by Genl Castro. The ranch was called Agua fria (or Spring) Ranch because of a fine spring of it. It is now called "Workman's bay Ranch". It's back of the Del Monte Links, about 2 miles from Monterey. Old Mrs Castro says "Mr Jacques (said to have owned 100.000 or more, acres hereabouts) bought the ranch — or 400 square Vares of it, from Genl Castro. The house is unoccupied & fast going to ruin. 3rd May '09 4 p.m.

Preceding page, top: Castro Headquarters by Will Sparks, courtesy of Hauk Fine Arts.

Bottom: Castro ranch house in the Agua-jito tract, on Castro Road bordering the Del Monte Golf links; subsequently home to philanthropist Margaret Jacks.

Above: watercolor sketch of Casa Castro on the Monterey Mesa, subsequent home Mrs. Dana de Diaz, Gouverneur and Ruth Morris, Maude and T.A. Work, Zizi and Frank Work; renamed La Mirada by the Monterey Museum of Art in 1985.

Right: rear patio of Castro Headquarters in Monterey, site of bull and bear fights.

Eva Scott Fenyes of Pasadena painted these three watercolors between 1904 and 1911.

Local tradition maintains that the Castro Adobe on Castro Road in the Rancho Aguajito tract was originally built to shelter herdsmen and shepherds. That modest dwelling was in the hands of another branch of the Castro family when Pasadena watercolorist Eva Scott Fenyes painted it in 1909. In the mid-20th century, much expanded, it became the gracious home of Monterey benefactor Margaret Jacks, a daughter of local land baron David Jacks.

Another adobe, known as Castro Headquarters, occupied a sizeable piece of land located on today's Tyler Street between Alvarado and Pearl, convenient to Governor Alvarado's "palace." Artist Tulita Westfall, born and raised in her family's ancestral Boronda Adobe on the Monterey Mesa opposite Casa Castro, left drawings of yet another Castro Adobe which probably was located on today's Frémont Street. According to the artist's note, it belonged to Modesta at the time the sketch was made circa 1910.

Edna Kimbro's research, completed in 2004, indicated that Modesta remained in Monterey, living "in the Casa de Castro on the Mesa" (Kimbro 9), but Modesta's obituary from the *Monterey New Era* indicates that she was residing with one of her sons, probably José Jr., in Alameda at the time of her death in June 1899. Thomas Savage's 1888 memoir, recently published as an appendix to Rose Marie Beebe's and Robert Senkewicz's much-applauded collection *Testimonios*, places Modesta with another offspring in San Luis Obispo during the mid-1880s (376). During the decades of her widowhood, she would presumably have spent extended periods of time with her children and grandchildren at their various locations.

Modesta Castro de Castro was widowed in her forty-fourth year; she outlived her husband for almost four decades. Letters 6 and 7 from her to her husband, as well as Letter 2 from Castro to his son, and Letters 4 and 8 from Esteban to his father, give some sense of the family's close bonds of affection and mutual regard. Two passages of William Heath Davis's 1889 memoir, *Seventy-Five Years in California*, provide a rare glimpse of the Castros' marriage from outside the family circle. Having described *"Mrs. General Castro of Monterey"* as *"beautiful and queenly in her bearing"* (112), he recalled a visit to the Castro home in Monterey with American Consul Thomas O. Larkin:

I was introduced to Mrs. General Castro and we chatted for some time very pleasantly. I saw by the General's expression, when she went into the next room for a few minutes, that he was proud of her"

Modesta's body was returned by train to Monterey on July 5, 1899. After a funeral service held at the railway depot, she was buried in the Catholic Cemetery, opposite and below the stone house where she had lived with her extended family for almost two decades.

Reversals and Betrayals

Considering José Castro's life as summarized here, reconstructed in Part III, and more intimately revealed through the correspondence reproduced in Parts II and IV, reversals and betrayals emerge as the most salient motif. The incident of the anti-intellectual *señorita* who tattled to the priest about forbidden books is amusing in the retelling, although perhaps not at the time, but the other instances are hardly a laughing matter.

Castro might have felt some qualms when arresting Isaac Graham and his riflemen in 1840, after the assistance they had provided in the 1836 rebellion against Governor Gutiérrez. However, the tables were turned once more when what began for Castro as a voyage to escort prisoners ended with his own imprisonment –and a year of legal manoeuvering to secure his freedom. Just three years later, he was involved in a revolt that brought about the overthrow of the Mexican official who had won his release. Micheltorena in his turn signed a treaty and then immediately violated it by enlisting gringo adversaries against Castro and his troops.

Castro's good faith efforts to accommodate the material needs of the group of "topographical engineers" who accompanied John Charles Frémont were rebuffed by the visitors, who blatantly defied local regulations. Yet less than four years later, Frémont was able to rent a wing of the Castros' Monterey home for his wife and daughter. Ongoing animosity and mistrust between Castro and his southern counterpart Pío Pico kept Californio forces divided, distracting them from the growing American threat.

When the Americans failed to make good on their promises of just and democratic treatment for the Californios, Castro turned to the government of Mexico and the people of Baja California, hoping to create a refuge where his compatriots from Alta California could restart their lives. However, he was to learn the hard way that neither governmental nor local support would be forthcoming. On the contrary, Castro and the people whom he sought to help were made to feel unwelcome on both sides of the border. The suspicious circumstances of Castro's ignominious death, allegedly "in a drunken brawl, at the hands of one of his own men" conforms to this stubborn, tragic pattern of reversals and betrayals. In the concluding four years of Colonel Castro's career, this terrible pattern is only magnified.

One attempt to obtain a sympathetic account of Castro's life was unsuccessful. *Testimonios: Early California through the Eyes of Women, 1815-1848* includes a reference to an effort by Bancroft's principal oral historian, Thomas Savage, to obtain a "dictation" (interview) from Castro's widow: *"It would have been perhaps but fair to obtain from the widow something in Castro's favor, as so much has been said against him,"* wrote Savage in his personal memoir, included in the collection. *"But those who should have done the needful towards it didn't seem to manifest any interest"* (376). Possibly Modesta felt that her trust and her husband's had already been betrayed one time too many.

The abundance of brief, scattered references to José Castro, unaccompanied by any sustained examination, has contributed to his contradictory reputation. Considered in the context of this biographical summary, the eighteen letters in Part II not only provide the basis for a more accurate and multidimensional view of the man himself, but also offer a window onto the shared experiences of two generations of Californios who endured their homeland's transition to American rule. As expressed so hauntingly in this cache of letters, the forced reordering of gracious and venerated lifeways by "an enterprising people" with a markedly different code of values occasioned untold upheaval and grief for the Californios.

During the first decades of American statehood, there was little interest or impetus to give "equal time" to the California side of the story. The generation of the 1880s —which included Herbert Howe Bancroft, Charles Lummis, Helen Hunt Jackson, and Josiah Royce—was more disposed to focus on the experience of the Californios and Native Americans. Historians of the present generation–Douglas Monroy, Rosaura Sánchez, Ramón Gutiérrez, Lisbeth Haas among others–provide an overdue counterweight. The heroic recuperation of writings from the Spanish, Mexican, and early American eras undertaken by Rose Marie Beebe and Robert Senkewicz has solidified the very foundations of California history. The return of–and to–José Castro presented in these pages is a modest contribution to the broader quest for a more nuanced and empathetic understanding of our shared California heritage.

Entry display at the Castro-Breen Adobe Museum, San Juan Bautista

Sources for Jose Castro in Alta California

Anonymous. "Prospectus." *The Californian*. Monterey: Colton & Semple, 15 Aug. 1846.

-- "News from the War." *The Californian*. Monterey: Colton & Semple, 21 Oct. 1846.

-- "Precipitency." *The Californian*. Monterey: Colton & Semple, 23 Jan. 1847.

-- "From the Seat of War." *The Californian*. Monterey: Colton & Semple, 23 Jan. 1847.

-- "General Castro's Hospitable Nature." *History of Monterey County*. San Francisco: Elliott & Moore, 1881. 137.

-- "Señora Modesta Castro – (Death of)." *The Monterey New Era* 5, July 1899: 3.

-- "Histories of Pair of Handsome Residences Have Been Confused." *Monterey Peninsula Herald*. 1 June 1970: 20B.

-- *Santa Cruz County Historical Journal*. Issue 3: Branciforte Bicentennial Edition. Santa Cruz: Art and History Museum, 1997.

Atkinson, Fred W. *100 Years in the Pajaro Valley: From 1769 to 1868*. Watsonville: Register and Pajaronian Press, 1934.

Bancroft, Hubert Howe. *History of California, 1542-1890*. San Francisco: History Co, . Vol. 19 (1886): 752.

Barrows and Ingersoll. "Stephen Castro." *Memorial & Biographic History of the Coast Counties of Central California*. Chicago: Lewis, 1893: 237.

Beck, Warren A. and Ynez D. Hasse. "The Mexican War and California: The Bear Flag Revolt and the Anglo-American Conquest of California." Online. http://www.militarymuseum.org/BFR.html. 28 Sep. 2005.

Beebe, Rose Marie and Robert M. Senkewicz, eds and translators. *Lands of Promise and Despair: Chronicles of Early California, 1535-1846*. Santa Clara and Berkeley: Santa Clara University and Heyday Books, 2001.

-- *Testimonios: Early California through the Eyes of Women, 1815-1848*. Berkeley: Heyday Books, 2006.

Bidwell, John. "Frémont in the Conquest of California." *The Century Illustrated Monthly Magazine*. Feb. 1891, vol. XLI, no. 4. Online. http://sfmuseum.org/hist6/Frémont.html. 14 Sep. 2005.

Burton-Carvajal, Julianne, ed. *The Monterey Mesa: Oldest Neighborhood in California*. City of Monterey: 2002.

Cameron, William R. "Rancho Santa Margarita of San Luis Obispo." *California Historical Society Quarterly*. San Francisco: March 1957. XXXVI: 1: 11.

Davis, William Heath. *Seventy-Five Years in California*. San Francisco: John Howell Books, 1962. Original edition 1889.

Denton, Sally. *Passion and Principle: John and Jessie Frémont, the Couple Whose Power, Politics and Love Shaped Nineteenth Century America*. New York: Bloomsbury USA, 2007.

Enright, John Shea. "The Breens of San Juan Bautista." *California Historical Society Quarterly*. San Francisco: Dec. 1954. XXXIII: 4: 351.

Escobar, Agustin. "Reminiscence of Agustin Escobar." Monterey, 1877. Online. Accessed Nov. 7, 2007. http://sunsite.berkeley.edu/MaderaMethod/zescobar.html.

Freeman, Cathleen A. "Monterey's La Mirada Adobe." 1996. Online posting; rife with inaccuracies. http://www.mchsmuseum.com/lamirada.html.

Frémont, Jessie Benton. *A Year of American Travel: Narrative of Personal Experience. 1848-49*. San Francisco: Book Club of California, 1960.

Greenwood, Roberta S., Maryellen Ryan, Edna E. Kimbro, Trudy Harvest, and Gary S. Breschini. *Historical Investigation of Rancho El Sausal, Salinas, Monterey County, California*. Salinas: Archaeological Consulting, 1984.

Haas, Lisbeth. "War in California, 1846-1848." *California Historical Society Quarterly*. San Francisco: summer & fall 1997. LXXVI: 2, 3: 337-44.

Hague, Harlan. "The Jumping off Place of the World: California and the Transformation of Thomas O. Larkin." *California Historical Society Quarterly*. San Francisco: Winter 1991/92. LXX: 4: 357.

Hague, Harlan and David J. Langum. *Thomas O. Larkin: A Life of Patriotism and Profit in Old California.* Norman: University of Oklahoma Press, 1990.

Hansen, Woodrow J. "Robert Semple: Pioneer, Promoter, Politician." *California Historical Society Quarterly.* San Francisco: Sept. 1962. XLI: 3: 226.

Harlow, Neal. *California Conquered: The Annexation of a Mexican Province, 1846-1850.* Berkeley: University of California Press, 1982.

Hawgood, John A., ed. *First and Last Consul: Thomas Oliver Larkin and the Americanization of California, a Selection of Letters.* Palo Alto: Pacific Books, 1970.

Hussey, John A. "California's Day Book." *California Historical Society Quarterly.* San Francisco: June 1946. XXV: 2: 122-28.

Jones, William Carey. "The First Phase of the Conquest of California." *Papers of the California Historical Society.* San Francisco: California Historical Society, Vol.1. Part 1, 1887.

Kimbro, Edna E. "Castro-Breen Adobe Historical Overview." Report Prepared for California Department of Parks and Recreation. 9 June 2003: 1-7.
-- "Spanish-era Settlement of the Mesa, 1795-1822," in Burton Carvajal, ed., *The Monterey Mesa: Oldest Neighborhood in California.* City of Monterey: 2002, pages 11-26.

Pablo L. Martínez. *A History of Lower California.* Mexico: Editorial Baja California, 1960. Republished as *Historia de Baja California,* 2003.

Miller, Robert Ryal. *Juan Alvarado: Governor of California, 1836-1842.* Norman: University of Oklahoma Press, 1998.

Monroy, Douglas. *Thrown Among Strangers: The Making of Mexican Culture in Frontier California.* Berkeley: University of California Press, 1990.

Nunis, Jr., Doyce B. "Alta California's Trojan Horse: Foreign Immigration." *California Historical Society Quarterly.* San Francisco: Summer & Fall 1997. LXXVI: 2, 3: 310-12.

Osio, Antonio María. *The History of Alta California: A Memoir of Mexican California.* Translated by Rose Marie Beebe and Robert M. Senkewicz. Madison: University of Wisconsin Press, 1996. (Originally written in 1851; not published to date in Spanish.)

Phillips, Catherine Coffin. *Jessie Benton Frémont: A Woman Who Made History.* San Francisco: John Henry Nash, 1935.

Robinson, Alfred. Footnote to "Business Letters of Alfred Robinson." *California Historical Society Quarterly.* San Francisco: Dec. 1944. XXIII: 4: 374.

Rosenus, Alan. *General M.G. Vallejo and the Advent of the Americans: A Biography.* Albuquerque: University of New Mexico Press, 1995.

Spencer-Hancock, Diane and William E. Pritchard. "El Castillo de Monterey: Frontline of Defense Uncovering the Spanish Presence in Alta California." *California Historical Society Quarterly.* San Francisco: Summer 1984. LXIII: 3: 237.

St. Clair, David J. "New Almaden and California Quicksilver in the Pacific Rim Economy." *California Historical Society Quarterly.* San Francisco: Winter 1994/95. LXIII: 4: 285.

Tinkham, George H. "The California Conquest." California Men and Events, Time 1769-1890. Accessed Aug. 15, 2007
http://www.usgennet.org/usa/ca/state1/tinkhamch4.html

Weber, David J. *The Mexican Frontier, 1821-1846: The American Southwest Under Mexico.* Albuquerque: University of New Mexico Press, 1982.

Montereyano *in typical dress*

Part II
Letters from the Society of California Pioneers

Detail of 1868 map by J. Ross Browne, with X added to mark pertinent locations, courtesy of The Huntington Library

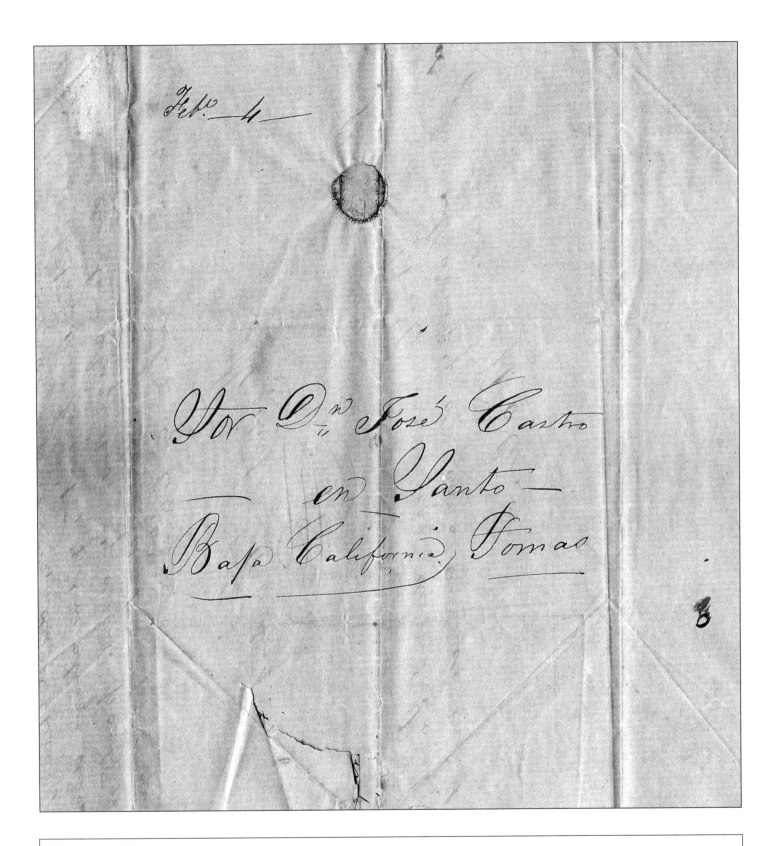

Feb.º 4

Sor D.ⁿ José Castro
en Santo —
Baja California, Tomas

Correspondents made their own "envelopes" by addressing the back of their folded letters or by adding an extra sheet for protection. This sheet, with its red wax seal, was prepared by Ambrosio Gómez, scribe for Modesta Castro de Castro, to transmit Letter 7, hand-delivered by Señor Sosa.

Eighteen Letters Written by and to Jose Castro, 1856-1860

The following eighteen letters pertaining to José Castro–courtesy of the Alice Phelan Sullivan Library, Society of California Pioneers, San Francisco–are reproduced in three formats: facsimile, Spanish transcription, and English translation. In the trasncriptions, the non-standardized mid-19th century Spanish of eleven different correspondants has been rendered into correct modern-day Spanish.

The fourteen letters *to* José Castro are the actual documents that he received and retained, while the four letters *by* him are period drafts or copies made in order to preserve a record of his correspondence. No mail service existed between the two Californias or within Baja California itself. Because transport was notoriously slow and unreliable, many a letter never reached its addressee. Express service was scarce and costly; an alternative was to entrust the mail to travelers, as Señora Modesta Castro de Castro did with Letters 6 and 7.

When I received the set of 46 photocopied pages in summer 2004, I began by arranging them in sequence in order to assess their contents and significance. It was both intriguing and gratifying to see a storyline gradually emerge from documents that initially seemed a disconnected miscellany. Two bills of lading turned out to be unrelated, leaving five family letters (3, 4, 6, 7, 8), six pieces of official correspondence (2, 10, 13, 14, 16, 18), five letters to and from business associates (1, 5, 9, 11, 12) and two personal communications from La Frontera residents relocated to the San Diego side of the border because of rampant disturbances on the other side (15 and 17).

The intensive transcription process and extensive research process turned out to be mutually illuminating. Based on a growing familiarity with the historical record, I was gradually able to identify most of the proper names mentioned in the letters and to compile biographical sketches for fifteen individuals. Reciprocally, the content of the letters began to illuminate and–to a significant degree–challenge the recorded history.

Until summer 2007, when the various parts of this volume were at last ready for layout, I continued to ponder where the three undated letters might fit. The following sequence begins and ends with two overviews by José Castro–the first to the President of Mexico, the last probably to an incoming Governor of Baja California. (This latter post changed occupants all too frequently, contributing to the Territory's chronic instability.)

In Letter 1 of April 7, 1856, Colonel Castro appeals his personal dilemma and the future of his displaced countrymen to President of Mexico Ignacio Comonfort. This letter holds particular interest as Castro's own carefully worded summary of the preceding decade, articulating both his "critical situation" and his strategy for the future.

I have opted to conclude the sequence with Castro's de facto balance sheet for his Baja California years. Letter 18 (undated copy to an unspecified recipient) summarizes his failures and frustrations, registers his pride in maintaining order thanks to to a band of loyal countrymen, and addresses the pending threats that will, in the end, not only take his life but also suppress his achievements.

Letter 2 (undated) is addressed to a "Friend and Compadre"–probably former Governor of Alta California Juan Bautista Alvarado, who is the author of Letters 5 and 10. In Letter 3, dated April 10, 1856, Castro's eldest son Esteban addresses his absent father from his new position as head of household, his youth and inexperience manifest in every line. Foremost among the updates he must convey are expected glad tidings turned to sad ones. Learning that the daughter born just weeks after he departed for Mexico had already been buried would account for the unguarded anguish of Castro's undated Letter 4. This latter sequencing is only plausible, however, if Esteban's letter of April 10th reached his father at Mazatlán by the end of that month–a timely delivery indeed.

Transcription, Translation and Editorial Interventions

More than a dozen different handwriting styles made the transcription process unusually challenging. Uneven levels of education and the lack of standardized spelling conventions further complicated the task. Challenges to intelligibility include abbreviations and unusual proper names, "orphaned" syllables that should be joined, composite words that should be separated, extra letters (particularly *h*, which can appear as *b*), *s* written as a forward slash, and the often indistinguishable consonants *r, rr, n,* and *m*. Rather than reproducing the irregularities of mid-19th century provincial Spanish, the transcription incorporates present-day conventions of spelling and accentuation.

Names that appear in **bold type** in this and subsequent sections can be identified in "Biographical Sketches" (page 188). Material inserted in the process of transcription or translation appears between [square brackets]. Uncertain renderings and indecipherable words are marked by [?]. For greater clarity, separations have been introduced to form new sentences and new paragraphs. Punctuation generally conforms to English-language usage.

It is useful to note that *pesos* and dollars were used interchangeably during the period spanned here. Castro's official title–*Subjefe Político y Militar del Partido Norte del Territorio de Baja California*–has been shortened in translation to Vice-Governor of La Frontera. Introductory notes, and titles echoing a line in each letter, orient the reader.

E. S. Presidente D. Ygnacio Comonfort.

Pto. de Mazatlan Abril 7. del 1856

Ecmo. Sr.

Al dirigirme á S. E. por segunda vez en particular, me permitirá que lo haga con la franqueza propia de mi caracter, manifestandole mis desgracias en estos terminos.

El año de 1846, siendo Comandante Gral. de la Alta Califa. la guerra con los Norte Americanos en aquella época, por la falta absoluta de recursos para resistirlos en aquel pais, me obligó á evacuarlo, sin capitulación, sin juramentarme, sin faltar á la dignidad de soldado y sin ningun otro compromiso al hacerlo prócsimo objeto unirme al ejercito y cooperar como soldado en tan justa lucha: permanecí fuera de aquel pais dos años, dejando en él una regular fortuna para vivir. Volvi despues de este tiempo y no encontré mas capital que mi trabajo personal: Conservé á pesar de mi desgracia, el unico de los Californios, los derechos de ciudadano Mejicano, con la esperanza de prestar alguna vez mis servicios, la ninguna fortuna; la necesidad de trabajar personalmente para asistir á mi numerosa familia; me impidió tal vez salir como debia. Con el tiempo que transcurrió, un constante trabajo, y sacrificios mil, me facilitaba ya un modo honesto de vivir, cuando recibí el nombramiento de Comande. prâl. y Géfe Politico de la Baja California. Supuse por esto, que el Spmo. Gobo. Consideraba mi critica posicion en aquel pais, lo mismo entendieron los antiguos Californios, los empleados de los

43

= diferentes naciones en aquellos pueblos, y aún los ame
ricanos como lo manifesto la prensa en aquellos dias.—
Resuelto pues á marchar para cumplir con las ordenes
supremas, permanecio en este puerto, cuando con sorpresa
vi variar las disposiciones del Gobierno, nombrandome 2.º Ca
bo á las ordenes del Gral Blancarte á quien debia rele
var como estaba entendido. ¿Que puedo hacer en este empleo?
Hacer lo que se me mande como soldado y nada mas. No
era esta mi mente como tengo manifestado, pues la princi
pal, y por la que me decidí á venir fué por que estando yo
al mando politico y militar podia proteger con la emigra
cion á multitud de familias de los antiguos Californios
que sufren vejaciones, y esperaban ser protegidos por un hombre
conocido por ellos. Tal esperanza para aquellos y para mi ha
cambiado completamente.

Por los compromisos en que se encuentra el Gral Blan
carte, por las escaceces que ha sufrido, dificil sería que aún
mis pagas se dieren con puntualidad, para atender con par
te de ellas á mi familia compuesta de mi muger y ocho
hijos, fiados solamente en mi para subsistir.

En la frontera de la Baja California por la inmedia
cion á la Alta, podria aun ser todavia util á mis paisa
nos Californios como les habia ofrecido, y alli tambien formar
pequeñas Colonias, siendo esto á mi individuo un bien por la
inmediata proteccion que pudiera impartir á mi familia;
de lo contrario Sr. mi posicion es demaciado critica, y obedez
co á las disposiciones Spmas, con la esperanza de que el Gob.º no
olvidará lo que á S.E. le digo particularmente.

Al verificarlo Sr.ª

Letter 1: "With the Candor that Corresponds to My Character…"

Colonel Castro composed this letter after his second voyage to Mazatlán to assume the governorship of Baja California, only to learn (again) that another was to occupy the promised position. In this unique autobiographical summary, he recapitulates his conduct and setbacks since 1846 and requests reassignment to Baja California's northern section (La Frontera), where he hopes to employ his considerable leadership experience and, in the process, encourage the resettlement of Californio families displaced by the American takeover—among them his own.

Su Suprema Excelencia Presidente Don Ignacio Comonfort.
Puerto de Mazatlán. Abril 7 de 1856.

Excelentísimo Señor:

Al dirigirme a Su Excelencia por segunda vez en particular, me permitirá que lo haga con la franqueza propia de mi carácter, manifestándole mis desgracias en estos términos.

El año 1846, siendo Comandante General de la Alta California, la guerra con los Norte Americanos en aquella época, por la falta absoluta de recursos para reprimirlos en aquel país, me obligó a evacuarlo–sin capitulación, sin juramentarme, sin faltar a la dignidad de soldado, y sin ningun otro compromiso. Al hacerlo fue mi objeto unirme al ejército [mexicano] y cooperar como soldado en tan justa lucha.

Permanecí fuera de aquel país dos años, dejando en él una regular fortuna para vivir. Volví después de este tiempo y no encontré más capital que mi trabajo personal. Conservé a pesar de mis desgracias, el único de los Californios, los derechos de Ciudadano Mexicano, con la esperanza de prestar alguna vez más [mis] servicios.

La ninguna fortuna, la necesidad de trabajar personalmente para asistir a mi numerosa familia, me impidió tal vez salir como debía. Con el tiempo que transcurrió, un constante trabajo y sacrificios mil, me facilitaba ya un modo honesto de vivir cuando recibí el nombramiento de Comandante General y Jefe Político de la Baja California.

Supuse por esto que el Supremo Gobierno consideraba mi crítica posición en aquel país. Lo mismo entendieron los antiguos californianos, los empleados de las diferentes naciones en aquellos pueblos, y aún los americanos, como lo manifestó la prensa en aquellos días.

Resuelto pues a marchar para cumplir con las órdenes supremas, permanecía en este puerto cuando con sorpresa vi variar las disposiciones del Gobierno, nombrándome Segundo Cabo a las órdenes del General Blancarte quien debía relevar como estaba entendido.

¿Qué puedo hacer en este empleo? Hacer lo que se me mande como soldado y nada más. No era ésta mi mente, como tengo manifestado, pues la [razón] principal, y por la que me decidí a venir, fue porque estando yo al mando político y militar podía proteger con la emigración a multitud de familias de los antiguos californios que sufren vejaciones y esperaban ser protegidos por un hombre conocido por ellos. Tal esperanza para aquellos y para mí ha cambiado completamente.

Por los compromisos en que se encuentra el General Blancarte, por las escaceces que ha sufrido, difícil sería que aún mis pagas se diesen con puntualidad, para atender con parte de ellas a mi familia, compuesta de mi mujer y ocho hijos, fiados solamente en mí para subsistir.

En la frontera de Baja California con inmediación a la Alta, podría aún ser todavía útil a mis paisanos californianos como les había ofrecido, y allí también formar pequeñas colonias, siendo esto a mí [como] individuo un bien por la inmediata protección que pudiera impartir a mi familia. De lo contrario, Señor, mi posición es demasiado crítica, y obedezco a las disposiciones Supremas, con la esperanza de que el Gobierno no olvidará lo que a Su Excelencia le digo particularmente.

Al verificarlo SS [Su Seguro Servidor]

His Supreme Excellency President Don Ignacio Comonfort
Port of Mazatlán
April 7, 1856

Most Excellent Sir,
Upon addressing Your Excellency personally for the second time, permit me to do so with the candor that corresponds to my character, revealing my misfortunes to you in these terms.

In the year 1846, being Commander General of Upper California during the war with the North Americans, the absolute lack of resources needed to suppress them in that country obliged me to evacuate it–without capitulating, without taking any oath, without imperiling the dignity of a soldier, and without making any other compromise.

It was my goal to unite with the [Mexican] army and collaborate as a soldier in that very just war. I remained outside that country for two years, leaving behind there a veritable fortune for living [expenses].

I returned after the time I've stated and did not find any capital other than my own personal labor. Despite my misfortunes, I retained, alone among the Californios, the rights of a Mexican Citizen, with the hope of lending my services some other time. The absence of income, the need to go to work myself in order to aid my sizeable family, perhaps prevented me from leaving as soon as I should have.

With the passage of time, constant labor and a thousand sacrifices, I had managed to arrange an honest mode of living when I received the appointment to be Commander General and Political Chief [Governor] of Lower California. I assumed in light of this that the Supreme Government was aware of the critical nature of my position in that country – just as the former Californios, along with the employees from various nations then living in those towns and even the Americans themselves understood it to be, as the press of those days made clear.

Determined to march in compliance with supreme orders, I was staying at this Port when, to my surprise, I saw the Government's disposition change and myself named Second Lieutenant under the orders of General Blancarte, whom I was to be relieving, as was understood.

What can I do in this position? Simply whatever I am ordered to do and nothing more. This was not what I had in mind, as I have made clear, since my principal [motive], the one that decided me to come to this country, was that being myself in military and political command, I could protect–through immigration–a multitude of former Californio families who suffer vexations and were hoping to be protected by a man already known to them. For them and for me, that hope has changed completely.

Because of commitments that General Blancarte has already made, it is unlikely that even my wages would be paid on time so that, with a portion of them, I might attend to my family, which is made up of my wife and eight children, who depend solely upon me for their subsistence.

On the border of Lower California close to the Upper California frontier, I could still be of use to my Californio countrymen, as I have offered to be in the past, and there too I could organize little colonies, something that would [also] be of individual benefit because of the immediate protection I could offer my family.

Otherwise, Sir, my position is too critical, and I will obey the Supreme orders with the hope that the Government will not forget what I say most particularly to Your Excellency.

Upon verification SS [Your Sure Servant]

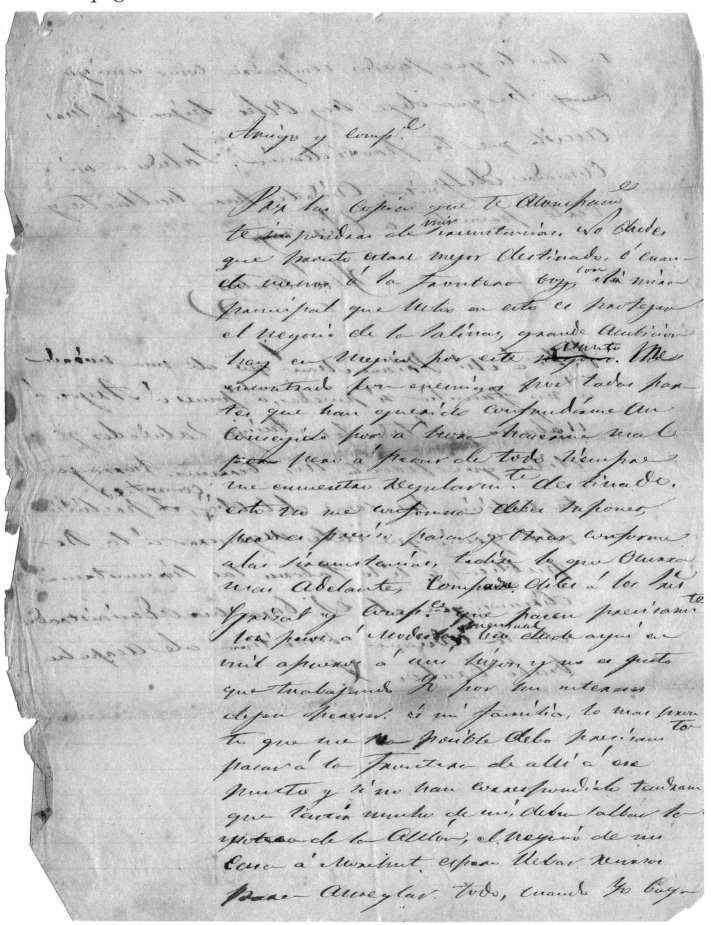

Amigo y comp.

Por las copias que te acompañan
te impondras de mis [...]. No dudes
que pronto estaré mejor destinado, ó cuanto menos á la Frontera, [...] con mira
principal que llevo en esto es proteger
el negocio de las Salinas, grande ambicion
hay en Mejico por este asunto. Me
encuentro por enemigos por todas partes, que han querido confundirme [...]
conseguido pues á [...] traerme mal
por [...] á pesar de todo siempre
me encuentro regularmte destinado.
esto no me conforma [...] imponer,
[...] preciso pasar, y obrar conforme
á las circunstancias, todo lo que verás
mas adelante, compañero dales á los
Yznaga y comp.es que paren precisamte
los [...] á Modesto [...] [...] aqui en
mil apuros á mi mujer y no es justo
que trabajando [...] por sus interesses
dejen [...] á mi familia, lo mas [...]
te que me [...] posible debo precisamte
pasar á la Frontera de allí á ese
punto y si no han correspondido tendran
que [...] mucho de mi, debe salbar la
[...] de la Aduana, el negocio de mi
casa á Modesto, espero llevar nuevos
[...] arreglar todo, cuando yo baya

tu haor lo que puedas compadre como amigo

[...] de que depe hay ocho hijos. Sin mas

[...] que te providencia, Saludes a mi

Comadre Delfinita. Cuidate para hablarte y

[...] pronto a Dios [...]

José [...]

P. D. a mi [...] Mau que de una [...]

a mi familia si puedes, a Gomes o Arjas, a

Habana y a todos los Amigos Saludados y

diles que pronto nos veremos. [...]

te noticia, las cosas del año, y preludio

del genio que debe [...] a la Re—

publica y si lo [...] las circunstancias

diremos que el S. [...] administrador

de la aduana maritima de Acapulco

brabo brabo. X.

Letter 2: "I Have Found Myself with Enemies on All Sides…"

This undated letter, copied on both sides of a transparent sheet, was probably addressed to Juan Bautista Alvarado, Castro's close friend from childhood, godfather (compadre) *to one of his offspring, and Governor of Alta California from 1836-1842. Castro, Alvarado, and Mariano Vallejo organized an abalone harvesting venture as early as 1821. In the 1850s, Alvarado was residing at Rancho San Pablo with frequent stays in nearby San Francisco, presumably the port alluded to in the letter. Grisar Byrnes & Co. acquired the salt extraction concession at San Quintín, Baja California in 1866; in 1853 it belonged to Alvarado, José Castro, his cousin Manuel Castro, and Jacques Moerenhout, French (Vice)Consul at Monterey–possibly already in partnership with the Grisar group. (The word* aulón, *like the English* abalone, *derives from the language of the Rumsien tribes who inhabited the Monterey region. Delfinita was one of Alvarado's daughters.)*

Amigo y Compadre,

Por las copias que te acompaño te impondrás de mis circunstancias. No dudes que pronto estaré mejor destinado o cuando menos a La Frontera voy, con la mira principal que lucho en esto es proteger el negocio de las Salinas. Grande ambición hay en México por este asunto.

Me he encontrado con enemigos por todas partes que han querido confundirme. Han conseguido por ahora hacerme mal, pero a pesar de todo siempre me encuentras regularmente destinado. [?] No me conformo, debes suponer, pero es preciso parar y obrar conforme a las circunstancias. Te diré lo que ocurre más adelante.

Compadre, diles a los de Grisar y Compañía que pasen precisamente 100 pesos mensuales a Modesta. Veo desde aquí en mil apuros a mis hijos, y no es justo que trabajando yo por sus intereses [de los socios] dejen fracasada[?] a mi familia.

Lo más pronto que me sea posible debo precisamente pasar a La Frontera, de allí a ese puerto, y si no han correspondido, tendrán que [?] mucho de mí. Deben salvar la exportación de la aulón, el negocio de mi[?] casa. A **Morenhout** espero llevar [remisas?] para arreglar todo cuando yo vaya.

Tú haz lo que puedas, Compadre, como amigo. Ve que dejé allí [a] ocho hijos sin más auxilio que la Providencia. Saludos a mi comadre Delfinita. Cuídate para hablarte y verte pronto. A Dios.

[firma de] José Castro

P.D.
A mi primo **Manuel [de Jesús Castro]** [díle] que dé una mirada a mi familia si puede. A **[Ambrosio] Gómez**, a [José] Abrego, y a todos los amigos, salúdalos y díles que pronto nos veremos. Preocupante noticia, las cosas del otro [comandante?]. La proclividad [?] del genio que debe asegurar[?] a la República, y si lo favorecen[?] las circunstancias, diremos que vaya un [ilegible] Administrador de la Aduana Marítima de Acapulco–"Bravo, bravo."

Friend and Compadre,

Via the copies that I enclose, you will [be informed] of my circumstances. Have no doubt that very soon I will have found a better path or [else] I will go to La Frontera with the principal goal that I fight to achieve in all this: to protect our enterprise of the Salinas [salt quarries]. There are great ambitions in México regarding this matter.

I have found myself with enemies on all sides who have wished to confound me. For the time being they have succeeded in damaging me [but] you will always find me on the right path. You should assume that I will not put up with this, but it is necessary to pause and to work as circumstances dictate. I will tell you later what is happening.

Compadre, tell the people from Grisar & Company to turn over exactly 100 pesos every month to Modesta. From here I can see that my children are in a thousand straits, and it is unjust that while I am working in the interest of our associates, they leave my family [in need].

As soon as I possibly can, it is my duty to go to La Frontera and from there to that port where you are [San Francisco], and if [our associates] have not done their share, they will have [to answer] to me. They should save the abalone business, the one at my house. Tell [Jacques] **Morenhout** that I hope to bring revenues in order to arrange everything when I come.

You do what you can, Compadre, as a friend. [You can] see that I left eight offspring in need there with no greater aid than Providence. [Give my] greetings to my Comadre Delfinita. Take good care of yourself so that I can talk to you and see you soon. A Dios.

[signature of] José Castro

P.S.
To my cousin **Manuel [de Jesús Castro]** [tell him] that he should look in on my family if he can. [Give] **[Ambrosio] Gómez**, [José] Abrego, and all our friends [my] greetings and tell them that we will be seeing each other soon. The news of the other [commander?] is worrisome. Such a proclivity [?] should be a disgrace to the [Mexican] Republic, and if circumstances favor [?] we will say [hail to the?] Administrator of Maritime Customs at Acapulco–"Bravo, bravo."

Sor. D. José Castro
Monterey Abril 10 de 1856

Querido Padre.

Hasta hoy no hemos tenido ninguna
novedad la familia esta buena y yo solo estoy en la casa, cuido de las vacas.
El 28 de Febrero tubo mi madre una niña
que se parecia á Rufinito y murio el
siete de Marzo, fueron sus padrinos Don
Pancho Rico y la Madre
Vivimos bien aunque tenemos necedad
de algun dinero, Nadie conoce mejor q.
V. Monterey y las personas que viven
á qui, por nada hacen ningun favor
á no ser, muy pequeños, de mis amigos,
La Casa tiene hoy el Gravamen de
(1600$) y esta puesta en venta, no
la han vendido, porq. la ley obliga á da
tres meses de avisos cuando el dueño
esta fuera del Estado. El Sor Moreno
consul de Monterey Dice que hará
lo posible por sacarla pero que es muy

dificil consegir dinero de finca fuera de la
ciudad de san Francisco, yo hare de mi parte todo lo posible, mañana salgo para San
Juan con este fin. Aunque Rematen, que
darán todavia siete meses y medio en que
se puede redimir.

Entre los comerciantes solamt.e D. Diego se
ha manejado bien con la Casa los demas
todos han serrado las puertas y dinero es
muy dificil consegir y si algo nos con-
siderán es porq.e esperan algo de cambio en
nuestra fortuna, digo esto de la genera
lilidad.

Yo hago lo mejor que puedo, en todo, soy
mucho mas arreglado y pongo mas aten-
cion en los negocios de la casa, al mismo
tiempo me ocupo poco del ingles.

Nosotros tenemos grandes deseos de recibir
cartas de usted, mi Madre le encarga q.
no deje de escribir siempre que tenga
oportunidad.

Reciba v. espresiones de mi Madre de
Modestita y el buen afecto de su hijo
que le ama y venera

Estevan Castro

Letter 3: "For My Part, I Will Do Everything I Can…"

Writing two months after his father's second departure for Mazatlán, Castro's eldest son, 21 years of age and probably at this point the only literate person in the household, has the painful task of transmitting two devastating pieces of news: first, the birth and death one week later of the last child that Modesta Castro de Castro would bring into the world, two weeks after Castro's ship departed; second, the lien to force the sale of the family home, Casa Castro on the edge of the Monterey Mesa, overlooking the original Spanish-era presidio and church. Modesta's mother, María Merced del Socorro Ortega de Castro, who lived nearby, was godmother to the infant. Rufinita, the eldest surviving daughter, would have been 14 years old. Esteban's comments regarding unsympathetic and opportunistic Montereyans expose the breeches exacerbated within the community once the traditional barter-and-credit system was abruptly replaced by a cash economy. Like other families of that place and time, the Castros kept livestock at their townhouse for their own subsistence if not also as a source of income.

Señor don José Castro.

Monterey. April 10, 1856.

Querido Padre,
Hasta hoy no hemos tenido ninguna novedad [de usted]. La familia está buena y yo solo estoy en la casa. Cuido de las vacas.

El 28 de febrero tuvo mi madre una niña que se parecía a [mi hermana] Rufinita y murió el 7 de marzo. Fueron sus padrinos don **Pancho Rico** y la Madre [Abuela].

Vivimos bien aunque tenemos necesidad de algun dinero. Nadie conoce mejor que usted Monterey y las personas que viven aquí. Por nada hacen ningun favor, a no ser muy pequeños, de mis amigos.

La casa tiene hoy el gravamen de $1600 y está puesta en venta. No la han vendido porque la ley obliga a dar tres meses de avisos cuando el dueño está fuera del Estado. El Señor **Morenhout**, Cónsul [de Francia] de Monterey, dice que hará lo posible por sacarla, pero que es muy difícil conseguir dinero de finca [raíz] fuera de la ciudad de San Francisco. Yo haré de mi parte todo lo posible. Mañana salgo para San Juan [Bautista] con este fin. Aunque rematen, [dicen] que darán todavía siete meses y medio en que se puede redimir.

Entre los comerciantes solamente don Diego se ha manejado bien con la casa. Los demás todos han cerrado las puertas y dinero es muy difícil de conseguir. Y si algo nos consideran es porque esperan algo de cambio en nuestra fortuna. Digo esto de la generalidad [de los comerciantes].

Yo hago lo mejor que puedo, en todo. Soy mucho más arreglado y pongo más atención en los negocios de la casa. Al mismo tiempo me ocupo [un] poco del inglés.

Nosotros tenemos grandes deseos de recibir cartas de usted. Mi madre le encarga que no deje de escribir siempre que tenga oportunidad. Reciba usted expresiones [de cariño] de mi madre, de Modestita, y el buen afecto de su hijo que le ama y ver desea.

[firmado] Estevan Castro

Casa Castro after 1879,
with cattle and poultry
in the foreground and
a train on the horizon at left.

Señor Don José Castro

Monterey, April 10, 1856

Dear Father,
Until today we have had no news [of you]. The family is fine and I am alone in the house. I am looking after the cows.

On February 28th my mother had a little girl who looked a lot like Rufinita and died on the 7th of March. Her godparents were Don **Pancho Rico** and Mother [Grandmother].

We are getting along fine although we have need of some money. Nobody knows Monterey better than you do, and the people who live here don't do any favors for any reason, except for a few little ones from my friends.

The house has a lien of $1600 as of today and is for sale. They have not sold it because the law requires giving three months' notice when the owner is out of the state. The [French] Consul at Monterey, Mr. **Morenhout**, says that he will do whatever possible to take it off [the market] but that it is very difficult to obtain real estate funds outside the city of San Francisco. For my part, I will do everything possible. Tomorrow I leave for San Juan [Bautista] with this goal. Even if they auction off the house, they will still give a term of seven and a half months in which it can be redeemed.

Among the merchants, only Don Diego has dealt fairly with our household. All the others have closed their doors, and money is very hard to obtain. And if they extend us a little credit, it is because they hope to get something in exchange if our fortune improves. I'm referring to the majority [of the shopkeepers] when I say this.

I do the best I can in everything. I am much more orderly and I pay more attention to the business of the house. At the same time, I'm studying a little English.

We have great desires of receiving letters from you. My mother requests that you not fail to write whenever you may have the opportunity. Please receive the [caring] expressions of my mother and Modestita and the solid affection of your son who loves you and wishes to see you.

[signed] Estevan Castro

Sr. Dn. Estevan Castro.

Querido Hijo.

Llegue á esta punto el 1.o del pasado de donde he tenido que dirijirme al gobierno pidiendole explicaciónes. y me encuentro con mil dificultades el mes que entra espero estar en la baja lifornia de allí pasar á la frontera y de llí á besarlos esto no pasara del mes de Sep.re ó mas antes si fuere posible, cociendo remediar mi pobon y la de U. pues que me veo en peor, dile á tu madre ese infra, que pronto estare ahi con N.s Yo estoy muy afligido, y desesperado pensando en tu estado que [tacha] que no haya que haser para remediar pronto las necesidades que beo desde aqui que pasan, ntfran pronto espero en Dios besarlos, al Sor Moreno le escribo para que consiga algun aucilio para U. á mi Primo Manuel, á mi Comp.e Alsonde se que nada pasan. pues escribeles, pidiendoles algun aucilio diciendoles q.e á te lo mandó desde aqui Hijo en este momento que me ocupo de escribir les se, despedasa el Alma, esta carta lleba el corazon de tu Padre, Abrasa á tu madre a mi nonbre á Mbestita á cada uno de los niños a Dios. a Dios hijo hata la bista

Letter 4: "Believing that I Might Remedy my Position and Yours, I Seem to Find Myself in Even Greater Difficulties…"

Castro's undated letter to his son struggles to find the right words to comfort the entire family as they face one devastating loss after another. His tenderness in the face of despair reveals a side of his character heretofore seen only by those closest to him. This is the only instance where he crosses out phrases and substitutes others in his struggle to master his emotions.

Señor Don Esteban Castro.
Querido hijo,

Llegué a este punto el 12 [¿18?] del [mes] pasado, de donde he tenido que dirigirme al Gobernador, pidiéndole explicaciones, y me encuentro con mil dificultades.

El mes que entra espero estar en la Baja California. De allí pasaré a La Frontera y de allí a verlos [a ustedes]. Esto no pasará del mes de septiembre, o más antes si es posible.

Creyendo remediar mi posición y la de ustedes, parece que me veo en peor. Dile a tu madre que sufre [no sufra] que pronto estaré ~~a su lado~~ con ustedes. Yo estoy muy afligido y desesperado pensando en su estado, ~~que sufren mucho~~ que no hallo qué hacer para remediar pronto las necesidades que veo desde aquí que pasan. Pronto espero en Dios verlos nuevamente.

Al Señor **Morenaut** [Morenhout] le escribo para que consiga alguna cuenta[?] para ustedes. A mi primo Gabriel y a mi compadre **Alvarado**, separado[?] [?], pero escríbeles pidiéndoles algun arribo, diciéndoles que te lo mando desde aquí.

Hijo, en este momento que me ocupo en escribirles, se [me] despedaza el alma. Esta carta lleva el corazón de tu Padre. Abraza a tu madre a mi nombre, a Modestita, a cada uno de los niños.

A Dios, a Dios, hijo, hasta la vista.

Señor Don Estevan Castro.

Dear Son,
I arrived at this point on the 18th [12th?] of the present [month], whence I have had to address myself to the government, requesting an explanation. I find myself in a thousand difficulties.

I hope to be in Baja California next month. From there I will cross the frontier, and from there [sail north] to see [all of] you. This will not be later than the month of September, or earlier if possible.

Believing that I might remedy my position and yours, I seem to find myself in even greater difficulties. Tell your mother, who is suffering, that I will soon be ~~at her side~~ with all of you.

I am very afflicted and desperate thinking of your state and ~~how you all suffer~~ because I cannot discover what to do in order to promptly remedy the neediness that I can see from here you must be enduring.

I am writing to Señor **Morenhaut** to ask him to find some funds for you. To your cousin Gabriel or my Compadre **Alvarado**, write them separately[?] requesting some quantity to rescue you from these financial difficulties, telling them that I have directed you to do so from here.

Son, as this moment as I occupy myself in writing this letter, my soul breaks into pieces. This letter carries with it your Father's heart. Embrace you Mother in my name. To Modestita, to each one of my children, a Dios. Go with God, my Son, until we meet again.

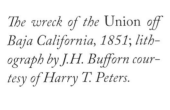

The wreck of the Union *off Baja California, 1851; lithograph by J.H. Bufforn courtesy of Harry T. Peters.*

68

Sn. Franco Dicre 24 de 1856.

Mi estimado Compadre.

Los mismos oficiales que re
gresan te informarán cuan desgraciada fué la expe
dicion de Sal y por cuyo motivo, no van tus encargos, y esto mismo te indicará cual será mi posicion
particular que cada dia se va poniendo mas dificul
tosa juntamente con la de todos los Californios en
general.

Procura por estos puntos ~~aqui~~ Arreglar algu
na fortuna para tu familia por que aqui no hay
esperanza para nosotros.

Estevan se halla aqui actualmente
ha sido nombrado miembro de la Lejislatura y le ha
ce competencia Smith el Yerno de Hartnell
por que alega no ser Ciudadano Americano en el
supuesto de que tu renunciastes la dicha nacionalidad Americana. Sin embargo para tu eleccion
en Monterey y para todo lo demas en la presente
cuestion no dejamos tus amigos de hacer cuantos
esfuerzos podamos para tu colocacion en la
Camara: el se ha sabido atraer el carino y la
simpatia de todos los que lo conocen y esto
deve ser para ti muy Satisfactorio.

Livenleur atu enla carcel consecuente a la
declaracion de Agustin Town y ala que ultima-
mente ha dado un tal Litaueur Framer tambien
que dijo haber el mismo escrito el titulo en
Mejico en 52 siendo Secret.º privado de Limen-
teur. Aqui hay un misterio y a todos nos ha
sorprendido este acontecimiento. el saldra con
fianza en estos dias y parece que no le da un
pepino cuidado de eso.

Espero que vendras en Febrero Rocit
no bien ahora mismo vamos a ver a Palmer
aber si conseguimos por mucho favor 200 pesos
para tu hijo que se va al Sacramento y lo
necesita mucho: el se ha resistido siempre á dar
un solo centavo pero veremos lo que sucede

Grandes cosas han ocurrido aqui
durante tu ausencia que seria muy largo referir

Asi que nos veamos te informaré
de todo

Soy tu amigo y comp.º

J.B. Alvarado

aqui
Se habla de una expedicion de 1000 hombres
para auxiliar a Gandara en Sonora
pero hasta ahora es muy baga la noticia

Letter 5: "Here There Is No Hope for Us…"

Former Governor of Alta California Juan Bautista Alvarado–lifelong friend, comrade-in-arms, business associate and godfather or "co-parent"–laments the lack of returns from their joint salt extraction venture and the widespread financial difficulties of the Californios. His mention of Esteban Castro's pending appointment to the State Legislature would have been a rare piece of good news. The jailed Frenchman, Jose Yves Limantour, infamous for fraudulent land deals, would have been the talk of San Francisco just then. Alvarado's postscript refers to the repeated incursions of filibusters into Mexican territory in search of lands and wealth under the pretext of "liberating" the population of the target area. As explained in Part III, many of these expeditions were launched from San Francisco. In this instance, the volunteers would be seeking to defend the Sonorans from the filibusters. The address portion of this letter appears on page 58.

Al Señor Coronel del Ejército Mexicano Don José Castro, Baja California

San Francisco. Diciembre 24 de 1856.

Mi Estimado compadre,

Los mismos oficiales que regresan te informarán cuán desgraciada fue la expedición de Sal, y por cuyo motivo no van tus encargos, y esto mismo te indicará cual será mi posición particular, que cada día se va poniendo más dificultosa justamente con la de todos los californianos en general. Procura por esos puntos arreglar alguna fortuna para tu familia porque aquí no hay esperanzas para nosotros.

Esteban se halla aquí actualmente. Ha sido nombrado miembro de la legislatura, y le hace competencia Smith, el yerno de [William E.P.] Hartnell, porque alega [que Esteban] no es Ciudadano Americano, en el supuesto de tú renunciastes la dicha nacionalidad Americana. Sin embargo para su elección en Monterey y para todo [lo vemos?] en la presente cuestión, no dejamos tus amigos de hacer cuantos esfuerzos [podamos] para su colocación en la Cámara. El se ha sabido atraer el cariño y la simpatía de todos los que lo conocen, y esto debe ser para tí muy satisfactorio.

[Jose Yves] **Limantour** está en la cárcel, consecuente a la declaración de Agustín Jouan y a la que últimamente ha dado un tal Litaneur, francés también, que dijo haber él mismo escrito el título [de propiedad] en México en [18]52, siendo secretario privado de Limantour. Aquí hay un misterio y a todos nos ha sorprendido este acontecimiento. El [Limantour] saldrá con fianza en estos días y parece que no le da ningún cuidado de eso.

Espero que vendrás en Febrero. Rocit[?] no viene. Ahora mismo vamos a ver a Palmer, a ver si conseguimos por mucho favor 200 pesos para tu hijo que se va a Sacramento y lo necesita mucho. El [Palmer] se ha resistido siempre a dar un solo centavo, pero veremos lo que sucede.

Grandes cosas han ocurrido aquí durante tu ausencia que serían muy largas de referir. Así que [cuando] nos veamos te informaré de todo.

Soy tu amigo y compadre.

J.B. Alvarado.

Aquí se habla de una expedición de 1000 hombres para auxiliar a [al Gobernador] Gandara en Sonora, pero hasta ahora es muy vaga la noticia.

To Señor Don José Castro, Colonel of the Mexican Army
Baja California

San Francisco, December 24, 1856

My Esteemed Compadre,

The same officials who return [with this letter] will inform you how disastrous the expedition for Salt was, and that this is the reason why your order is not being sent to you. This will likewise indicate to you just what my own daily lot is like, and how every day things get more difficult for us, as they do for all the Californios in general.

Do your best to put together some kind of capital for your family in those parts, because here there is no hope for us.

Esteban is here [in San Francisco] at present. He has been appointed to the [State] Legislature and Smith, [William E.P.] Hartnell's son-in-law, is giving him some competition, since he [Esteban] is not an American citizen according to the supposition that you renounced said nationality. Notwithstanding all this, in the Monterey elections and everything [we perceive necessary] in the current situation, your friends will not cease to make whatever efforts we can lend to his placement in the Chamber. He has known how to win the sympathy and affection of everyone who makes his acquaintance, something that should be a great satisfaction to you.

[Jose Yves] **Limantour** is in jail as a consequence of the testimony given by Agustín Jouan as well as the more recent deposition of someone known as Litaneur, another Frenchman, who claims to have written the same [property] title in México in 1852 [when serving] as Limantour's private secretary. There's a mystery here, and we have all been surprised by these events. He [Limantour] should be released any day now and seems quite unconcerned about the whole thing.

I hope you will come in February. Recit [?] will not come. Right now we are going to pay a call on Palmer to see if we can obtain the huge favor of 200 pesos for your son, who is on his way to Sacramento and in great need of them. He [Palmer] has always resisted giving even a single cent, but we'll see what happens.

Great events have occurred here during your absence that would take a long time to recount. Until we meet again, be sure to keep me informed of everything.

Your friend and compadre,
[signed] J.B. Alvarado

There is talk here about an expedition of 1000 men to aid [Governor] Gandara in Sonora, but until now the news is very vague.

Monterey Febrero 4. de 1857

Sor Dn José Castro.

Mi muy querido, y amable esposo.

Tengo mucho gusto en dirigirte esta cartita, segura de que la recibiras, y no tendrá ningun estravio como las otras que te emos escrito; pues, segun me dice el Sor Sacramento, no as recibido ninguna durante el tiempo que estas en ese puerto, siendo asi, que te emos escrito varias.

Respecto al negocio de la casa, y el dinero que tu mandaste, te digo, que no habiendo recibido instrucciones tuyas nos habiamos resuelto á dejar perder la casa, pero, biendo que las leyes, le permitian á nuestro acredor, embargarnos el ranchito los Animales, y todo lo que pudieramos tener, á la precente, y en lo futuro, hasta no completar la suma $250 nos determinamos al fin despues de largas reflecciones á dar el dinero, quedando siempre indecisas sin saber si hicimos bien ó mal, puesto que tu no nos dices una palabra,

para dicho efecto Estevan entregó al Sor Zabala
$1500. Ahora, yo, ignoro conque obfeto Estevan á
separado los otros mil pesos que restan, pero lo
que si sé es, que consiguió con Zabala que le a-
guardara seis meses, mas, por los mil pesos sin pagar ningun interes. y si en este tiempo no se le
paga dá, seis meses mas, pagandole interes. pero
yo te aseguro y te confieso que quisiera definitivamente salir de todo este negocio con la urebe-
dad que sea posible, de consiguiente no mas espero que benga Estevan y pienso entregarle
á Zabala lo restante. esto es si tu no me escribes
pronto y me instruyes de lo que debo de hacer.
pero espero con confianza que me escribiras lo mas
pronto que sea posible.

Por otra parte, debo advertirte que yó tomé
$250. pesos. no para ayudarme ni auciliarme en las
necesidades diarias y precisas de la casa. sino para
pagar tanto piquito ó abonar pues no puedes cre
lo que me mortifico con esto, mas bien quiero su
frir y padecer nesecidades que berme atormentada
por tanta deudita que tu no ignoras, y que me
cobran muy á menudo.

Esposo mio, espero en Dios, y en primer lugar,
y por la espereencia que con razon debemos te
ner que si la suerte nos protefe ynos ayuda
en lo venidero, sabremos cultivarla y aprovechar
la. Enfin, toda la familia se encuentra buena
hay el Sor Sacramento te dirá mejor los deseos

que tenemos todos de verte, tanto que si no
puedes venir pronto, te ruego mandes por nosotros.

Recibe miles de espreciones, de Estevan,
de Modestita, de Toscaito, y un abrazo de cada uno de los chiquitos, y de mi parte recibe el mas cinsero afecto de tu esposa que
verte desea, con salud y felicidad.

Modesta Castro,

P. O.

Recibe memorias de mi Padre,
de mi Madre, y de cada una de mis
Hermanas.
Vale.

Letter 6: "If Luck Protects and Assists Us in the Future…"

Alluding to several letters lost in transit, Castro's wife takes comfort in the assurance that a family friend will personally deliver this one, which updates her husband on efforts to save the family home and the various decisions reluctantly made without benefit of his counsel. This letter reveals Modesta's admirable strength and composure in the face of threats to home and welfare. Tellingly, it expresses how the newly imposed indebtedness wounds her dignity while also reaffirming her commitment to her husband and her hopes for the future. Señor Zavala was a Monterey merchant involved in property transactions. Señor Sacramento, bearer and perhaps also scribe for this letter, is also mentioned in Letters 7 and 15.

Señor don José Castro en Santo Tomás, Baja California.
Monterey. Febrero 4 de 1857.

Mi muy querido y amable esposo,
Tengo mucho gusto en dirigirte esta cartita, segura de que la recibirás, y no tendrá ningún extravió como las otras que te hemos escrito; pues, según me dice el Señor Sacramento, no has recibido ninguna durante el tiempo que estás en ese punto, siendo así que te hemos escrito varias.

Respecto al negocio de la casa y el dinero que tú mandaste, te digo que no habiendo recibido instrucciones tuyas, nos habíamos resuelto a dejar perder la casa, pero viendo que las leyes le permitían a nuestro acreedor embargarnos el ranchito, los animales y todo lo que pudiéramos tener, a la presente y en lo futuro, hasta no completar la suma [de] $2.500, nos determinamos al fin después de largas reflexiones a dar el dinero, quedando siempre indecisas sin saber si hicimos bien o mal, puesto que tú no nos dices [ni] una palabra para dicho efecto. Esteban entregó al Señor Zavala $1500. Ahora yo ignoro con qué objeto Esteban [ha] separado los otros mil pesos que restan, pero lo que sí sé es que consiguió con Zavala que le aguardara seis meses más por los mil pesos sin pagar ningún interés, y si en ese tiempo no se le paga, dar seis meses más, pagándole intereses.

Pero yo te aseguro y te confieso que quisiera definitivamente salir de todo este negocio con la brevedad que sea posible. De consiguiente no más espero que venga Esteban y pienso entregarle a Zavala lo restante. Esto es si tú no me escribes pronto y me instruyes de lo que debo de hacer. Pero espero con confianza que me escribirás lo pronto que sea posible.

Por otra parte debo advertirte que yo tomé $250 pesos, no para ayudarme ni para auxiliarme en las necesidades diarias y precisas de la casa, sino para pagar tanto piquito o abonar, pues no puedes creer lo que me mortifico con esto. Más bien quiero sufrir y padecer necesidades que verme atormentada por tanta deudita que tú no ignoras, y que me cobran muy a menudo.

Esposo mío, espero en Dios en primer lugar, y por la experiencia que con razón debemos tener que si la suerte nos protege y nos ayuda en lo venidero, sabremos cultivarla y aprovecharla.

En fin, toda la familia se encuentra buena. Hoy el Señor Sacramento te dirá mejor los deseos que tenemos todos de verte, tanto que si no puedes venir pronto, te ruego mandes por nosotros. Recibe miles de expresiones de Esteban, de Modestita, de Joseaíto y un abrazo de parte de los chiquitos, y de mi parte recibe el más sincero afecto de tu esposa que verte desea, con salud y felicidad.

Modesta Castro [firmado por el escribano]
P.D.
Recibe memorias de mi padre, de mi madre, y de cada una de mis hermanas. Vale.

Señor Don José Castro in Santo Tomás, Baja California
Monterey, February 4, 1857

My very beloved and kind husband,

I take great pleasure in addressing this letter to you in full confidence that you will receive it and that it will not go astray like the others we have written to you, since, according to what Señor Sacramento tells me, you have not received a single one from us during the time you have been at your present location, despite the fact that we have written you several.

Regarding the business of the house, and the money that you sent, I must tell you that, not having received instructions from you, we had resolved to let the house be lost. But–seeing that the laws allowed our creditor to put a lien on our little ranch, our animals, and all that we might possess, both in the present and the future, until it totaled the equivalent of $2500–after prolonged reflection we finally decided to give over the money, always remaining unclear whether we were doing right or wrong, since you have not said a word to us on the matter. Estevan gave Señor Zavala $1500. I have no knowledge of Estevan's motive for withholding the remaining thousand pesos, but what I do know is that he got Zavala to agree to wait another six months for the thousand pesos without our paying any interest. And if within that time the remainder is still unpaid, he will give us an additional six months with payment of interest.

But I assure you and confess to you that I wish to be definitively finished with this business as soon as possible and therefore, as soon as Estevan returns, I intend to give Zavala the remaining amount–that is, as long as you don't write me promptly giving me instructions on what I should do. It is my confident hope that you will write to me as soon as possible.

In addition, I should let you know that I took 250 pesos, not for the benefit of my own daily needs or those of the household, but rather to pay down even a little bit of the debt, since you would not believe how much mortification this causes me. I would rather suffer and go without than see myself tormented by so many debts, of which you are not unaware, and which they approach me to collect with great frequency.

My husband, I put my hope in God above all, and in the experience that we have rightfully acquired together, that if luck protects and assists us in the future, we will know how to nurture and benefit from it.

In conclusion, the entire family is well at present. Señor Sacramento will tell you better than I can the wishes we all have for you. If you cannot come soon, I beg you to send for us to join you. Receive thousands of expressions [of affection] from Esteban, Modestita, Joseaíto, and a hug from each of the little ones. For my part, receive the most sincere affection from the wife who longs to see you in good health and happiness.

[signed by the scribe] Modesta Castro

P.S.
My father, my mother, and each of my sisters sends you their best regards. That's all for now.

Monterey Marzo 5 de 1857.

Sor. Dn. José Castro.

    Mi muy apreciado José.

El Sor. Sora estubo aquí y me dijo
tenia algun dinero para tí, combino con migo
en dejarme alguna cantidad en San Francisco
por el Sor. Abrego y como este Señor ha vuel
to y no me ha dado nada, hasta ahora
no sé el fin y actualmte. me encuentro muy
necesitada.

    Recibí la carta que le mandaste
á Estevan y se la remití por el Express
y me dice se ha estraviado, por lo que te
encargo que en la primera oportunidad que
se presente le escribas. Con respecto á la
situacion de la familia, el Sor. Sacramento
te dirá bastante, no dejes de contestarme
la carta que con el dicho Señor te escribí el
cual te recomiendo que siempre que puedas le hagas algun servicio por que aqui se
manejó muy bien, Leonor y todos los niños
se acuerdan mucho de él y lo saludan

    Modestita Josecito y todos los de la fami
lia te saludan cariñosamente

    Estevan está bueno y todavia en el ejercicio
de su empleo sigue manejandose bien
para con migo.

    Recibe el afecto de tu esposa que te apre
cia y B. T. M.

        Modesta Castro de Castro

Aumento
Sor. D. José

Yo Secretario de su Esposa y al mismo
tiempo amigo de U, no puedo menos de
dirijirle estas lineas para saludarlo
y reproducirle mi amistad que jamas en-
tibiara la distancia que nos separa, y en
recompensa quiero tener el gusto de merecerle un recuerdo en alguna de las suyas
que dirija á su familia, y será mayor mi
placer si usted me dá una noticia de
la tienda que se para en ese pais.

        Queda á su disposicion su af.mo
amigo que lo aprecia y B. S. M.

                        Ambrosio Gomez

Letter 7: "Reiterating My Friendship, Which the Distance that Separates Us Will Never Render Lukewarm…"

Dictating another letter to her husband just a month after the preceding one, Modesta alludes once more to lost correspondence, Esteban's absence (while the Legislature is in session in Sacramento), and the family's continuing need for funds. José Abrego was a Monterey merchant. Leonor was one of Modesta's sisters. Castro later granted property in La Frontera to family friend (and scribe) **Ambrosio Gómez**. *Letter 11 from Alvarado reports that allegations of robbery and murder drove* **Gómez** *across the border to La Frontera.*

Monterey. Marzo 5 de 1857.

Señor don José Castro.

Mi muy apreciado José,

El Señor **[Antonio L.] Sosa** estuvo aquí y me dijo [que] tenía algún dinero para ti. Convino conmigo en dejarme alguna cantidad en San Francisco por el Señor [José] Abrego, y como este señor ha vuelto y no me ha dado nada, hasta ahora no sé el fin, y actualmente me encuentro muy necesitada.

Recibí la carta que le mandaste a Esteban y se la remití por el Express, y me dice que se ha extraviado, por lo que te encargo que en la primera oportunidad que se presente le escribas.

Con respecto a la situaron de la familia, el Señor Sacramento te dirá bastante. No dejes de contestarme la carta que con dicho señor te escribí, al cual te recomiendo que siempre que puedas le hagas algún servicio porque aquí se manejó muy bien. Leonor y todos los niños se acuerdan mucho de él, y lo saludan.

Modestita, Josesito y todos los de la familia te saludan cariñosamente.

Esteban está bueno y todavía en el ejercicio de su empleo. Sigue manejándose bien para conmigo.

Recibe el afecto de tu esposa que te aprecia y BSM (besa su mano).

Modesta Castro de Castro [firmado por Ambrosio Gómez]

Aumento

Señor don José,
Yo secretario de su esposa y al mismo tiempo amigo de usted, no puedo menos de dirigirle estas líneas para saludarlo y reproducirle mi amistad que jamás entibiará la distancia que nos separa, y en recompensa quiero tener el gusto de merecerle un recuerdo en alguna de las suyas que dirija a su familia, y será mayor mi placer si usted me da una noticia de la vida que se pasa en ese país.

Queda a su disposición su afectuoso amigo que lo aprecia y BSM (besa su mano).

[firma de] Ambrosio Gómez

Monterey, March 5,1857
Señor Don José Castro

My very esteemed José,

Señor **[Antonio L.] Sosa** was here and told me that he had some money for you. We agreed that he would leave a certain quantity for me at San Francisco in care of Señor Abrego, but since that gentleman has returned without giving me anything, I am unaware at present how this will all turn out and for the time being find myself in great need.

I received the letter that you sent to Esteban and forwarded it to him by express, but he tells me that it has gone astray, which is why I request that you write him again upon the very first opportunity that presents itself.

Regarding the current situation of our family, Señor Sacramento will tell you a great deal. Don't fail to answer the letter that I sent to you in care of this aforementioned gentleman, for whom I urge you, whenever possible, to perform any service he might find himself in need of, because here he has handled himself very commendably. Leonor and all the children remember him frequently and send him their greetings.

Modestita, Little José, and the rest of the family send you affectionate greetings. Esteban is doing well in the exercise of his employment and, with regards to me, also conducts himself very well.

Receive the affection of your wife who holds you in high esteem and kisses your hand.

Modesta Castro de Castro [signed by Ambrosio Gómez]

Addendum

Señor Don José,
As your wife's secretary and at the same time your personal friend, I cannot but send you these lines in order to convey my greetings and reiterate my warm friendship, which the distance that separates us will never render lukewarm. And in return, I wish to have the pleasure of warranting a mention in one [of the letters] that you address to your family members, and my pleasure will be even greater if you give me news of how life is lived in that country.

Your affectionate friend who remains at your disposition and kisses your hand,

[signature of] Ambrosio Gómez

Sacramento Marzo 12/57

Sor. D.n Jose Castro
Santo Tomas

Querido Padre: Nuestras necesidades hoy
no son tan Graves, como desde que v.
se fue hasta dos meses pasados; Pero
aun no tenemos un pequeño capital
libre de acredores, las deudas de la casa
son cerca de dos mil pesos
Segun me informó él Sor. Sacramento
y él Sor. Sosa de la Frontera, he formado buena idea de ese País, tengo una
buena opportunidad de conocerlo ahora
que usted está en él. Usted conoce mejor lo q. me conviene, es muy provable
que yo obtenga el nombramiento de
Inspector de la Aduana para San
Luis Obispo, que vale dos mil p.s
anuales, he tocado ha este recurso y
encaso que sus negocios tengan mal
resultado, esto será muy benefico

Tengo muchos deceos de estar con V.
y en muy pocos dias estaria en
caso q. V. crea conveniente, tal vez
le seria util en algun negocio, lo que
no faltará en un Pais tan nuevo como
ese.

Dentro de tres meses sabré si tiene buen
resultado este empleo; pero antes quiero
estar con usted.

Su hijo que le ama

Estevan Castro

Letter 8: "You Know Better What Is Best for Me..."

This letter, written eleven months after Letter 3, demonstrates how quickly eldest son Esteban Castro has matured. He shows exquisite tact in offering the salary of his pending appointment as Customs Inspector at San Luis Obispo in case his father's business ventures do not work out, and conveys the depth of his filial bond by voicing preference for reunion with his father over his own career prospects in Alta California–while leaving the final decision up to his parent.

Sacramento. Marzo 12, 1857.
Señor don José Castro.
Santo Tomás.

Querido Padre,

Nuestras necesidades hoy no son tan graves como desde que usted se fue hasta dos meses pasados, pero aún no tenemos un pequeño capital libre de acreedores. Las deudas de la casa son cerca de dos mil pesos.

Según me informó [informaron] el Señor Sacramento y el Señor [Antonio L.] Sosa de La Frontera, he formado [una] buena idea de ese país. Tengo una buena oportunidad de conocerlo ahora que está usted en él. Usted conoce mejor lo que me conviene. Es muy probable que yo obtenga el nombramiento de Inspector de la Aduana para San Luis Obispo, que vale dos mil pesos anuales. He tocado a este recurso y en caso [de] que sus negocios tengan mal resultado, esto será muy benéfico.

Tengo muchos deseos de estar con usted, y en muy pocos días estaría en caso que usted crea conveniente. Tal vez le sería útil en alguna negocio, lo que no faltará en un país tan nuevo como ése.

Dentro de tres meses sabré si tiene buen resultado este empleo, pero antes quiero estar con usted.

Su hijo que le ama.

[firma de] Esteban Castro.

Sacramento, March 12, 1857
Señor Don José Castro
Santo Tomás

Dear Father,

Our needs right now are not as acute as they were from the time you went away until two months ago, but we still lack a little stock of capital free from creditors. The household debts come to nearly 2000 pesos.

According to what Señor Sacramento and Señor Sosa from La Frontera have told me, I have formed a good idea of that country, and I now have a good opportunity to get to know it in person, since you are there. You know better what is advisable for me. It is very likely that I will be named Customs Inspector at San Luis Obispo, which is worth 2000 pesos a year. I have mentioned this resource [because] in case your business ventures turn out badly, this salary will be very beneficial.

I greatly desire to be with you, and I could be in just a few days should you think it convenient. Perhaps I could be useful to you in some business opportunity, which must not be lacking in a country as new as that one.

Within three months, I will know if this job of mine will work out, but I'd like to be with you even sooner.

Your son who loves you,

[signature of] Estevan Castro

Sr. Coronel Don José Castro.

    Santo Tomás.

    San Diego á 15 de Marzo 1857

    Estimado amigo.

El Sr. Norrlin vino en el Vappor del 9— Se halla hoy
á unas 10 leguas de aquí en un rancho, de paseo, hoy
ó mañana lo espero— Me ha autorizado para decir
á vd. que no tenga cuidado por el asunto del Guano,
pues aun que es verdad que otras manos quicieron,
y aun quieren meter en el su cuchara, no hay cuidado, que el negocio está bien calculado y andando.

    Me dijo, que ya habia escrito á vd. sobre esto,
y para que desechara todo cuidado en el asunto.

    Sin mas por hoy me repito suyo y buen amigo.

              José Matías Moreno

Letter 9: "The Deal is Carefully Calculated and Moving Along…"

José Matías Moreno, a native Baja Californian who resided in San Diego for most of his adult life, emerges as a principal player in Parts III and IV. Well-connected to the Mexican authorities and tireless in pursuit of his personal agenda, Moreno initially cooperated with Colonel Castro but later resolved to have him removed from his Baja California post. Much of what is known to date about José Castro in Baja California derives from reports written by Moreno, who briefly assumed Castro's former post. In Letter 18, Castro refers to Moreno as "mi enemigo capital" ("my arch enemy"), his only use of this phrase. The guano operation is also mentioned in Letter 14. William Norrlin is mentioned again in Letter 12.

Señor Coronel Don José Castro.
San Diego. 15 de Marzo de 1857.

Estimado Amigo,
El Señor [Guillermo] Norrlin vino en el vapor del [día] 9. Se halla hoy a unas 10 leguas de aquí en un rancho, de paseo. Hoy o mañana lo espero. Me ha autorizado para decir[le] a usted que no tenga cuidado por el asunto del <u>guano</u>, pues aunque es verdad que otras manos quisieron y aún quieren meter en él su <u>cuchara</u>, no hay cuidado, que el negocio está bien calculado y andando.

Me dijo que ya [le] había escrito a usted sobre esto, y para que desechara todo cuidado en el asunto.

Sin más por hoy me repito suyo y buen amigo.
<u>José Matías Moreno</u>

Señor Coronel Don José Castro
San Diego, March 15, 1857

Esteemed Friend,
Mr. [William] Norrlin arrived by steamer on the 9th. Today he is 10 leagues from here on an excursion to a ranch. I expect him today or tomorrow. He had authorized me to tell you not to worry about the <u>guano</u> business, because, although it is true that other hands wanted and still want to stick their <u>spoon</u> in, there is nothing to worry about since the deal is well calculated and underway.

He told me that he had already written you about this, and that you should cast aside all concern regarding the matter.

With nothing more for today I repeat that I am yours and a good friend,
<u>José Matías Moreno</u>

Sor. Coronel d. José Castro.

La Paz, Marzo 31. de 1854.

Muy Apreciable Amigo y Compañero,

Según verá V. por una de las Comunicaciones oficiales que son adjuntas, hé Recivido noticias
ciertas de que los filibusteros han invadido
el Estado de Sonora, y que hay prevenciones
muy vehementes de que se dirijan á ese Territorio con las mismas miras.

Si así fuere, es muy natural que
piensen hacer su desembarque p.r alguno de
los Puertos de la frontera para ir tomando las
poblaciones del tránsito hasta llegar á la Paz.
Es pues necesario que V. esté muy alerta para
impedir cualquiera desembarque, acudiendo prontamente al lugar invadido, p.r que estoy cierto
que las disposiciones acertadas de V. y su acción enérgica que pondrá en uso desde luego,
será suficiente para Rechazar á esos Miserables Aventureros y escarmentar su osadía.

No creo necesario Recomendar á V.
despliegue su celo y patriotismo en una
guerra en que esta empeñado el honor de la

Nación, porque conozco bastante su previsión militar y los deseos q.ᵉ tiene de conservar ilesos
los derechos de la República Mexicana.

Recomiendo á V. muy particularmente
que de cualquiera manera y haciendo los mayores esfuerzos y sacrificios ponga al tanto
de cuanto ocurra sobre este particular, ya
para poderte prestar auxilios y ya también
para comunicar todas las novedades al E. S.
Gral. en Gefe.

El dia 27. del que espira, previo
el juramento de estilo, se recivió del Gobierno político de los Territorios el S. D. Santos
Ruis como primer Vocal Suplente del Consejo
de Gobierno p.ʳ haber sido llamado á Mazatlan el Teniente Cor.ˡ D. Fran.ᶜᵒ Cano que desempeñaba la Gefatura Política. Este nombramiento será muy transitorio, p.ʳ que habiéndose sancionado en la Capital de la República
el dia 4. del corriente la nueva Constitución q.ᵉ
debe regir al País, cuando este Código llegue
al Territorio, se hará la eleccion de las nue-
vas Autoridades con arreglo á lo que ella disponga.

También recomiendo á V. me remi-
ta las noticias que pide el E. S. Gral. en Gefe,
en el Oficio que le incerto; así como las listas de Revista y Presupuestos de lo que pen-
de su guarnicion para ser atendida mensal-

Merino.

Sin otro asunto por ahora, me repito de V. affmo. Amigo y Compañero que
lo Aprecia y Att.º

S. M. B.

León Janes

Letter 10: "I Don't Think It Necessary to Recommend that You Display Your Patriotic Zeal…"

Stationed at the territorial capital of La Paz, León Yáñez was Colonel Castro's temporary superior during the absence of Lieutenant Colonel Don Francisco Castro (no relation). The letter-writer recognizes his appointment as transitory, mentions the drafting of a new national constitution, warns Castro that another filibuster expedition en route to nearby Sonora may attack La Frontera, and concludes by reminding the Vice-Governor to forward overdue paperwork.

Señor Coronel don José Castro.
La Paz. Marzo 31 de 1857.

Muy apreciable amigo y compañero,
Según verá usted por una de las comunicaciones oficiales que son adjuntas, he recibido noticias ciertas de que los filibusteros han invadido el estado de Sonora, y que hay premiaciones vehementes de que se dirigirá a este territorio con las mismas miras.

Si así fuera, es muy asurado[?] que piensan hacer su desembarque por algunos de los puntos de esa Frontera para ir tomando la población de tránsito hasta llegar a La Paz. Es necesario que usted esté muy alerta para impedir cualquier desembarque, recurriendo prontamente al lugar invadido, porque estoy cierto que las disposiciones acertadas de usted y su acción enérgica que pondrá en primera[?] desde luego será bastante para rechazar a esos miserables aventureros y escarmentar su osadía.

No creo necesario recomendar a usted [que] despliegue su celo y patriotismo en una guerra en que está empeñado el honor de la nación, porque conozco bastante su pericia militar y los deseos que tiene de conservar intactos los derechos de la República Mexicana.

Recomiendo a usted muy particularmente que de cualquier manera y haciendo los mayores esfuerzos y sacrificios, [me] ponga al tanto de cuanto reúna[?] sobre este particular y para poder prestar auxilio y ya también para comunicar todas las novedades a Su Excelencia el General en Jefe.

El día 27 del [mes] que expira, previó[?] el juramento al Título que recibió del gobierno político de ese territorio el Señor Don Santos Ruiz como Vocal Suplente del Consejo de Gobierno, por haber sido llamado a Mazatlán el Teniente Coronel Don Francisco Castro que desempeñaba la jefatura política. Este nombramiento será muy transitorio por lo que habiéndose sancionado en la Capital de la Republica el día 4 del corriente la nueva Constitución que debe regir al país, cuando este código llegue al Territorio se hará la elección de las autoridades con arreglo a lo que ella disponga.

También recomiendo a usted que remita las noticias que pide Su Excelencia el General en Jefe en el oficio que le inserto, así como las listas de revista y presupuestos de los que vence su guarnición para ser atendida mensualmente.

Sin otro asunto por ahora, me repito de usted su afectísimo amigo y compañero que le aprecia y atentamente SMB (su mano besa).

[firma de] León Yáñez

La Paz, March 31, 1857

Very Worthy Friend and Comrade,

As you will see from one of the attached official communications, I have received definitive notice that the filibusters have invaded the State of Sonora, and there are persuasive indications that they are headed for this Territory with the same design.

If that is the case, it is very [likely] that they intend to make their landing at one of the points on that Frontier in order to take the settlements along their route one by one until reaching La Paz. It is necessary that you be very alert in order to prevent any landing, heading promptly to the place of invasion, because I am certain that your opportune response and energetic action, which you of course hold as your first priority, will be to repulse those miserable adventurers and make an example of their audacity.

I think it unnecessary to recommend that you unfurl your zeal and patriotism in a war in which the honor of the Nation is at stake because I am quite familiar with your outstanding military qualifications and your will to keep the rights of the Mexican Republic inviolate.

I do recommend to you very particularly that, by whatever means and at the cost of every effort and sacrifice, you keep us informed of everything that transpires relative to these particulars, so that we can lend assistance and also communicate every new development to the Supreme General-in-Chief.

The 27th of this month, before his swearing-in ceremony, Señor Don Sánchez Ruiz was received as Substitute Speaker by the political government of this Territory, since Lieutenant Colonel Don Francisco Castro, who had been Political Chief [Governor], was recalled to Mazatlán. This appointment will be very temporary given that the new Constitution that will guide the Country was announced in the Capital of the Republic on the 4th of this month. When [a copy of] this document reaches the Territory [of Baja California], election of the new authorities will occur according to whatever [procedures] the Constitution prescribes.

I also recommend that you send me the updates requested by His Excellency the General-in-Chief pertinent to the office in which I am replacing him, and likewise the budgetary and review lists for the garrison in order to be attended to on a monthly basis.

With no other matter pending at present, I repeat that I am your most affectionate friend and comrade who values you and attentively kisses your hand.

[signature of] León Yánez

Sn. Franco, Mayo 4 de 1857

Mi apreciable Compadre

Nuestro amigo Gomer pondra
en tus manos esta carta, y te dará una informa-
cion verbal por cuyos motivos su retirada de
aqui se le ha echo indispensable.

Yo no puedo saber de que
modo son estas cosas estoy bastante confundido
y tu formaras el juicio que te parezca.

Nuestro amigo Gomer se muy
bien que no ha muntado á nadie ni ha robado
siertas amistades traidoras en asuntos de honor le
pueden haber conducido á un punto en que su
caracter pudiera tener que sufrir en la sociedad
de sus amigos pero no conozco bien estas circunstancias y por eso omito fundar una opinion sobre
estas causas.

Te deseo mucho bien tu compe.
J. B. Alturado.

Su hijo Estevan se halla aqui en este momento
ya de retirada pa. Monterey por haberse serrado
las secciones de la legislatura su reputacion esta
en el mejor concepto entre todas las clases y todos los
partidos. Por otro conducto te escribire mas larga t

Letter 11: "Certain Traitorous Friendships in Matters of Honor…"

Juan Bautista Alvarado sent this very guarded letter in care of Ambrosio Gómez, who was fleeing American California in response to accusations of robbery and murder. This is the same Ambrosio Gómez who acted as scribe for Modesta in Letter 7 and appended his personal query about life in La Frontera. Although clearly disturbed by the allegations, Alvarado refrains from judgment, pleading ignorance and confusion and inviting Castro to form his own conclusions. The postscript ends the letter on a positive note, reporting once more on Esteban's continuing success. On November 9, 1858, Castro granted Gómez 11 square leagues of land in La Frontera. The "envelope" (opposite page) is addressed to Castro as Governor of the entire territory.

Al Coronel Don José Castro
Gobernador Militar y Político de la Baja California.
Santo Tomás.

San Francisco. Mayo 4 de 1857.

Mi apreciable compadre,

Nuestro amigo **[Ambrosio] Gómez** pondrá en tus manos esta carta y te hará una información verbal por cuyos motivos su retirada de aquí se le ha hecho indispensable. Yo no puedo saber de qué modo son estas cosas. Estoy bastante confundido y tú formarás el juicio que te parezca.

Nuestro amigo Gómez sé muy bien que no ha matado a nadie ni ha robado. Ciertas amistades traidoras en asuntos de honor lo pueden haber conducido a un punto en que su carácter pudiera tener que sufrir en la sociedad de sus amigos, pero no conozco bien estas circunstancias y por esto omito fundar una opinión sobre estas causas.

Te desea mucho bien tu compadre

[firma de] J.B. Alvarado.

Tu hijo Esteban se halla aquí en este momento, ya de retirada para Monterey por haberse cerrado las sesiones de la legislatura. Su reputación está en el mejor concepto entre todas las clases y todos los partidos. Por otro conducto te escribiré más largamente.

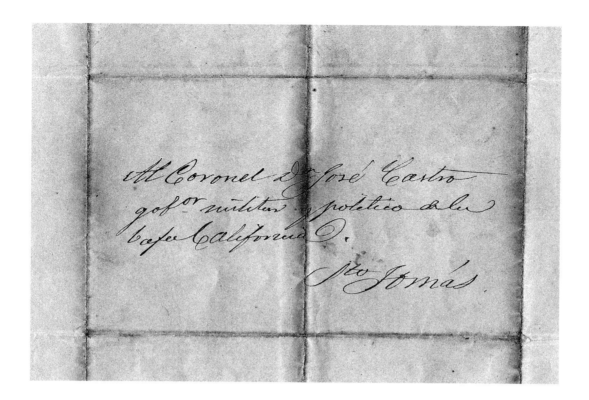

Colonel José Castro
Military and Political Governor of Lower California
Santo Tomás

San Francisco, May 4, 1857

My valued Compadre,

Our friend **[Ambrosio] Gómez** will place this letter in your hands and will give you a verbal explanation of the causes that have made his retreat from here indipensible. I am unable to find out what lies behind these things. I am pretty confused, and you will arrive at the judgment that seems best to you.

I know very well that our friend Gómez has not killed nor robbed anyone. Certain traitorous friendships may have led him to a point in matters of honor in which his character may have suffered in the circle of his friends, but I am not well acquainted with these circumstances and therefore omit forming an opinion about the causes [of this situation].

Your *compadre* who wishes you the best

[signature of] J.B. Alvarado

Your son Esteban is here right now, on his way back to Monterey because the session of the Legislature has concluded. His reputation is the best it can be among all classes and all parties. Via another route I will write to you at greater length.

Letter 12

Sr. Coronel Dn José Castro.   Santo Tomas, Baja Califª Mejico

San Diego Mayo 18, 1857.

Estimado amigo.

Don Sacramento ha puesto en mis manos una carta de Mr. Guillermo Norrlin, escrita á mi de ese punto, en la que pide un credito de alguna importancia de mi tienda, para la orden de vd. Tengo el sentimiento de decir á vd. que no puedo obsequiar la orden del Señor Norrlin, por que este, no tiene acreditada su firma ó responsabilidad con mi casa, y por tanto carece de confianza en mi establecimiento. Siento que el Señor Norrlin haya podido aventurar sus ordenes contra mi á favor de vd. en materias comerciales, sabiendo, como creo, que para girar letras es preciso haber acreditado su responsabilidad. Este es el orden establecido en todo el mundo comercial y con mas razon en este pais tan fecundo en desgraciados acontecimientos. Creo que juzgando vd. esto con la rectitud que le es caracteristica me disculpará y verá que en esto obro mercantilmente. Tengo el honor de repetirme de vd. su muy atento amigo y obediente Servidor.

C. Stransfo & Ca

86

Letter 12: "This Country that Is So Fecund in Unfortunate Occurences…"

*C. Strauss & Company was a San Diego supplier that frequently did business with residents of La Frontera, who routinely relied on San Diego merchants for any necessities that they could not themselves produce. William (Guillermo) Norrlin, mentioned in Letter 9, was apparently an American businessman with Baja California interests and some connection to both José Castro and **José Matías Moreno**. Señor Sacramento, mentioned in Letters 6, 7, and 8, was a trusted friend of the Castro family. Whether Norrlin had Castro's permission to place his order is unclear. Written in impeccable Spanish, this letter is a model of mercantile protocol and tact.*

Señor Coronel don José Castro.
Santo Tomás, Baja California, México.

San Diego, Mayo 18, 1857.

Estimado amigo,

Don Sacramento ha puesto en mis manos una carta de Mr. Guillermo Norrlin, escrita a mí de ese punto, en la que pide un crédito de alguna importancia en mi tienda, para la orden de usted.

Tengo el sentimiento de decir a usted que no puedo obsequiar la orden del Señor Norrlin, porque éste no tiene acreditada su firma o responsabilidad con mi casa, y por tanto carece de confianza en mi establecimiento.

Siento que el Señor Norrlin haya podido aventurar sus órdenes contra mí a favor de usted en materias comerciales, sabiendo, como creo, que para girar letras es preciso haber acreditado en responsabillidad. Este es el orden establecido en todo el mundo comercial y con más razón en este país tan fecundo en desgraciados acontecimientos.

Creo que juzgando usted esto con la rectitud que le es característica, me disculpará y verá que en esto obro mercantilmente. Tengo el honor de repetirme de usted un muy atento amigo y obediente servidor.

C. Strauss & Co.

Señor Coronel Don José Castro
Santo Tomás, Baja California, Mexico
San Diego, May 18, 1857

Esteemed Friend,

Don Sacramento has put into my hands a letter from Mr. Guillermo Norrlin, written to me front that location, in which he requests a rather substantial credit from my store for an order of yours.

It pains me to tell you that I cannot grant Señor Norrlin's order because his signature and authority have not been approved by this house and therefore lack the trust of my establishment.

I regret that Señor Norrlin has risked placing his commercial orders in your favor but against mine, knowing full well, as I believe he does, that in order to send letters of credit it is necessary to have established a guarantee. This is the way things operate in the commercial world, and all the more so in this country that is so fecund in unfortunate occurrences.

Judging this with your characteristic rectitude, I believe that you will forgive me and see that I am simply operating in a commercial manner. I have the honor of reiterating that I am your attentive friend and obidient servant.

C. Strauss & Co.

El Camino Real between La Paz and Santa Ana photographed by Harry W. Crosby.

S. D. Jose Castro

Guadalupe Junio 18 de 1857

Estimado amigo;   Hace ocho
dias que he llegado á esta su casa, y
á pesar de mis continuas dolencias
estaba dispuesto á hir á Sto Tomás para
tener el placer de verme con U.; empero,
como tuve noticia de que se hayaba
U. en S. Quintin y sin determinado
tiempo para regresar, tengo el disgus=
to de volverme sin haver conseguido lo
que deseaba. Si mi imposibilidad fisica
no me impidiera rigorosamente el cami=
no yo hiria hasta donde U. se haya,
mas no puedo absolutamente, y lo siento
infinito y mas particularmente cuando el Juez
D. Egan Mendoza me ha manifestado una
orden de U. por queja de los indios que
se dicen de las rancherias de Guadalupe.

No amigo, es falso que yo sus hijos ó
encargados hayan impedido á los indios las
pixcas de avena, bellota c. que se produce
dentro de los límites del rancho de mi
propiedad, siempre se las he permitido y
aun les he tolerado que los indios cercanos vengan con sus convidados de rancherías distantes, y lo único que les he
exijido y exijiré interin U. no de una ór-
den terminante, que al transitar ó venir á la cosecha pixcas se presenten en el
rancho manifestando donde van ó deben
ir, cuanto numero de personas y quien
es el que los manda para imponerles la
responsabilidad) en que caen si cometen los
robos que continuamente esperimentamos. Creo
S. D José que esto no carece de justicia
y le ruego á U. que no de tanto credito
á los indios por que á mas de que lo
botaran á U. con sus mentiras, le preven-
dran contra los dueños de ranchos, por
que desean conocer los movimientos de ellos:
repito amigo que es falso de lo que se quejan
y si aun dudase U. de mi verdad suplico
mande levantar una información del asun-

vo de la queja á que me contraigo; cuya
orden de U es de fecha 5 de este mes en S.
Quintin, y si fuese tal, falsa como afirma,
castigar á los calumniadores; de esta manera
se corregirá en parte tanto que estan dando
gana de suponer del propietario de Guadalupe por que no consiente que se le robe,
ni se asocia con los criminales.

¡Ojalá pudiera verme con él para
convencerlo de estas verdades!

Soy su afmo amigo

Juan Bandini

Dia 25.

Amigos aun he permanecido en esta
su casa en espera de saber de U hayarse en
Sto Tomas, y como se positivamente q. aun
está U. ausente, me regreso pa S. Diego
por q. tengo necesidad de hacer un viaje
á los Angeles, del q. creo regresaré pronto,
y volveré a este.

Como siempre su afmo

J. B.

Letter 13: "I Have the Displeasure of Returning Without Having Obtained What I Was Seeking…"

Juan Bandini, leading San Diego citizen and owner of prime ranchos on both sides of the border, here lobbies local law-enforcer José Castro to give more credence to the landowners and less to the Indians. Bandini's reference to "your house" echoes the customary Mexican expression of welcome, "Estás en tu casa" ("You are in your own house"). His reference to "Judge" Juan Mendosa is ironic and jocose. Mendosa might have been working for Bandini as a ranch hand at this time; four years later he would be shot in the back by one of Bandini's sons-in-law, Cave Couts. Señor Gutiérrez remains unidentified. After Bandini's death, his enemy José Matías Moreno acquired Rancho Guadalupe.

Señor Don José Castro.
Guadalupe. Junio 18 de 1857.

Estimado amigo,

Hace ocho días que he llegado a esta su casa, y a pesar de unas contínuas dolencias estaba dispuesto a ir a Santo Tomás para tener el placer de verme con usted. Empero como tuve noticia de que se halla con el Señor Gutiérrez y sin determinado tiempo para regresar, tengo el disgusto de volverme [a San Diego] sin haber conseguido lo que deseaba.

Si mi imposibilidad física no me impidiera rigorosamente el camino, yo iría hasta donde usted se halla, mas no puedo absolutamente y lo siento infinito y más, particularmente cuando el Juez Don **Juan Mendoza** me ha manifestado una orden de usted por queja de los indios que se dicen de las rancherías de Guadalupe.

No, amigo, es falso que yo o mis hijos o encargados hayan impedido a los indios las piscas de avena, belota, etcétera que se produce dentro de los límites del rancho de mi propiedad. Siempre se les he permitido y aún les he tolerado que los indios cercanos vengan con sus convidados de rancherías distantes. Y lo único que les he exigido y exigiré interin usted no dé una orden terminantemente, [es] que al transitar a [?] las fincas, se presenten en el rancho manifestando dónde van a situarse, cuánto número de personas [hay], y quién es el que los manda, para imponerles la responsabilidad en que caen si cometen los robos que contínuamente experimentamos.

Creo, Señor Don José, que esto no carece de justicia, y le ruego a usted que no dé tanto crédito a los indios porque a mas de que molestaran a usted con sus mentiras, le prevendrán contra los dueños de ranchos porque desean conocer los movimientos de allá.

Repito, amigo, que es falso de lo que se queja. Y si aún dudase usted de mi verdad, suplico mande levantar una información del [acotador?] de la queja a que me contraigo, cuya orden de usted es de fecha 5 de este mes en San Quintín. Y si fuese tal, falso como afirmo, castigar a los calumniadores. De esta manera se corregirá en parte tanto que están dando gana de suponer del propietario de Guadalupe porque no consiente que se le robe, ni se asocia con los criminales.

Ojalá pudiera verme con usted para convencerlo de estas verdades.

Soy tu afectuoso amigo
[firma de] Juan Bandini

Día 25.
Amigo, aún he permanecido en esta su casa en espera de saber de su regreso[?] en Santo Tomás, y como sé positivamente que aún está usted ausente, me regreso para San Diego porque tengo necesidad de hacer un viaje a Los Angeles. [ilegible] Creo [que] regresaré pronto y volveré a éste lugar].
Como siempre su afectuoso
JB

Señor Don José Castro
[Rancho] Guadalupe, June 18, 1857

Esteemed Friend,

It has been a week since I arrived here at "your house" and, despite continual aches I was prepared to go to Santo Tomás in order to have the pleasure of seeing you. However, I received word today that you are with Señor Gutiérrez and have no set time for your return. I have the displeasure of returning [to San Diego] without having obtained what I was seeking.

If my physical impossibility did not so rigorously block my path, I would go wherever you are, but this is absolutely out of the question and I regret it infinitely, and even more, particularly since "Judge" Don **Juan Mendoza** has shown me an order from you related to a complaint lodged by the Indians who claim to be from the [Rancho] Guadalupe settlements.

No, my friend, it is false that I, my sons, or my employees have prevented the Indians from gathering oats, acorns, and such within the boundaries of my ranch. I have always permitted them to collect them, and have even allowed the nearby Indians to come with their guests from distant settlements. The only thing that I have required of them, and intend to continue requiring in the interim as long as you do not issue a definite order against it, is that as they cross the farms, they stop at the ranch [house] to give notice of where they are going to be located, how many are in their group, and who their leader is, in order to impress upon them the responsibility that will fall to them if they commit robberies like the ones we continually experience.

Believe me, Señor Don José, this policy is not lacking in justice. And I beg of you not to give so much credit to the Indians, because the more they pester you with their lies, the more they will put you on the alert against ranch owners because they want to know the movements there. I repeat, my friend, that what they are complaining about is false.

And if you still doubt the truth of my claim, I implore you to investigate the person who filed the complaint that I am contesting, your order of the 5th of this month at San Quintín. And if it is false, as I assure you it is, punish the slanderers. This way, some part of what they are trying to make people want to believe about the owner of [Rancho] Guadalupe would stand corrected, because said owner does not consent to be robbed, nor does he associate with the criminals.

If only I could see you in person in order to convince you of these truths.

I am your affectionate friend,
[signature of] Juan Bandini

Day 25 –
My friend, I have remained "at your house" awaiting news of your return to Santo Tomás, and since I know for sure that you are still away, I am returning to San Diego because I need to make a trip to Los Angeles [illegible]. I believe that I will return promptly and come back to this [place].

As always, your affectionate friend
J.B.

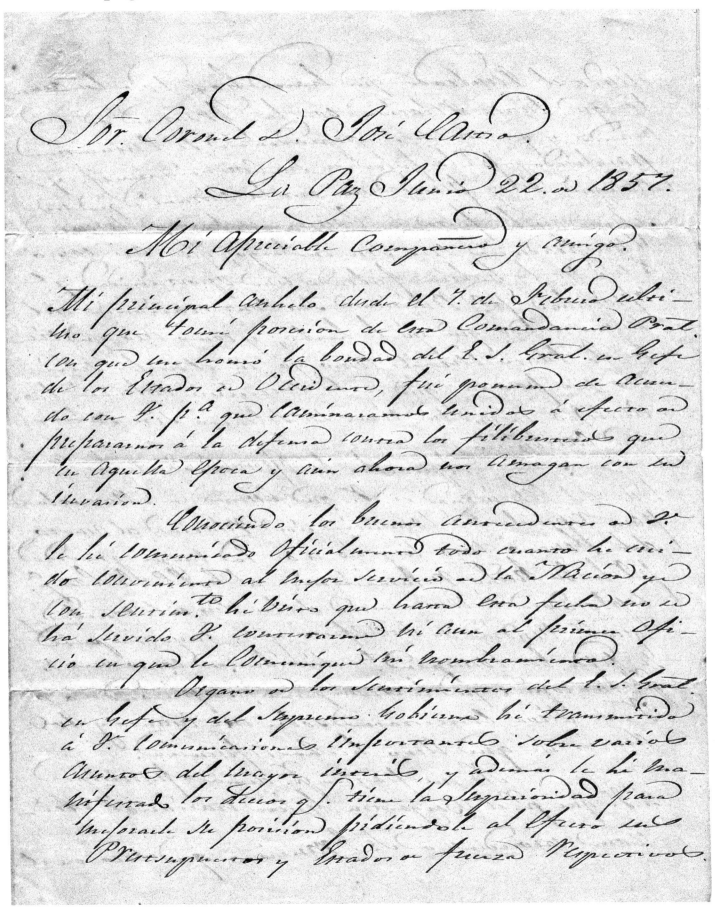

Sor Coronel d. José Alviso.

La Paz Junio 22 de 1857.

Mi Apreciable Compañero y amigo.

Mi principal Anhelo desde el 7 de Febrero ultimo que tomé posición de esta Comandancia Pral.
Con que me honró la bondad del E. S. Gral. en Gefe
de los Estados de Occidente, fué ponerme de Acuerdo con V. S.ª que Camináramos Unidos á efecto de
prepararnos á la defensa contra los filibusteros que
en Aquella Epoca y Aun ahora nos Amagan con su
invasión.

Conociendo los buenos Antecedentes de V.
le he Comunicado Oficialmente todo cuanto he creí-
do Conveniente al Mejor Servicio de la Nación y
con Sentim.to he Visto que hasta esta fecha no se
ha Servido V. contestarme ni Aun al primer oficio en que le Comuniqué mi nombramiento.

Organo de los Movimientos del E. S. Gral.
en Gefe y del Supremo Gobierno he Transmitido
á V. Comunicaciones importantes sobre varios
Asuntos del mayor interés, y además le he Manifestado los deseos q. S. tiene la Superioridad para
Mejorarle Su posición pidiendole al efecto su
Presupuestos y Estado de fuerza Respectivos.

siendo el resultado que trata hoy todos los asuntos que tienen relación con la Provincia de su
mando y que son de su dependencia se encuentran
paralizados p.r la falta o las comunicaciones, y
aunque estoy persuadido que la distancia que nos
separa y la falta de correos embaraza nuestra
correspondencia creo sin embargo, que así como
á mí no le habría faltado una oportunidad q.e
aprovechar p.a recibir sus contestaciones del
mismo modo que yo lo hecho; y como creo que tiene U. tanto interés como yo en el mejor servicio me prometo que en lo sucesivo calmará la
anciedad en que me tiene su silencio sin saber á
que atribuirlo.

      Aprovecho la oportunidad de la la
lida del Comisionado de U. que estuvo en Mazatlan
para reponerle mi comunicación relativa al asunto
del Guano cuyo negocio es de la mayor gravedad
p.r haber hecho reclamaciones al Gob.o la Comp.a
esplotadora á consecuencia de las diez mil toneladas
que U. vendió de los efectos y de cuyo importe
se pide la correspon.te distribución como verá U.
p.r las copias que le acompaño, suplicando á
U. se sirva comunicarme sobre este asunto y los
demás de que llevo hecha referencia.

      No me parece p.r demás participar
á U. que p.r el Bergantin Goleta nacional Arizona procedente de S. Francisco que tocó en el

Cabo de S. Lucas el B. del corriente se anuncia otra nueva Expedición pirática sobre las Frionteros y el Estado de Sonora, y aunque los criminales dicen estar escarmentados con el funesto desenlace de Mr. Crabb y sus complices, nunca será de_ mas Recomendar á V. la Sobe. vigilancia para evitar una Sorpresa

No dude V. del Aprecio que le consagra su Compañero y amigo que es.

B. S. M.

[signature]

Contestada el 15 de Agosto

Letter 14: "It Is Never Remiss to Recommend Super-Vigilance to You in Order to Avoid Surprises"

Three months after penning Letter 10, Interim Governor Yáñez wrote again to Vice-Governor Castro from the territorial capital, reiterating his earlier request for overdue requisitions and giving notice of another filibuster expedition. Apparently feeling slighted by Castro's failure to acknowledge his temporary promotion, Yáñez refers to the export levies pending on Castro's guano shipment and to the fate of filibuster Henry A. Crabb and his cohort (death by hanging), not-so-veiled attempts to prod Castro into line. Yáñez may have reverted to his normal (inferior) rank before Castro's reply, sent two months later, reached La Paz.

Señor Coronel Don José Castro.
La Paz. Junio 22 de 1857.

Mi apreciable compañero y amigo,

Mi principal anhelo desde el 7 de febrero último que tomé posesión de esta comandancia con que me honró la bondad del Supremo General en Jefe de los Estados de Occidente fue ponerme de acuerdo con usted, para que camináramos unidos a efecto en prepararnos a la defensa contra los filibusteros, que en aquella época y aún ahora nos amenazan con su invasión.

Conociendo los antecedentes de usted, le he comunicado oficialmente todo cuanto creí conveniente al mejor servicio de la nación, y con sentimiento he visto que hasta esta fecha no se ha servido usted de contestarme ni aún al primer oficio con que le comuniqué mi nombramiento.

[Como] órgano de los sentimientos del Supremo General en Jefe y del Supremo Gobierno he transmitido a usted comunicaciones importantes sobre varios asuntos del mayor interés, y además le he manifestado los deseos que tiene la Superioridad para mejorarle su posición, pidiéndole al efecto sus presupuestos y estados de fuerza proporcional, siendo el resultado que hasta hoy todos asuntos que tienen relación con La Frontera a su mando y que son de su dependencia se encuentran paralizados por la falta de sus comunicaciones.

Y aunque estoy persuadido que la distancia que nos separa y la falta de control embaraza nuestra correspondencia, creo sin embargo, que así como a mí, no le habría faltado una oportunidad que aprovechar para remitirme sus contestaciones del mismo modo que yo lo he hecho. Y como creo que tiene usted tanto interés como yo en el mejor servicio, le prometo que en lo sucesivo calmará la ansiedad en que me tiene su silencio sin saber a qué atribuirlo.

Aprovecho la oportunidad de la salida del buque comisionado[?] por[?] usted, que estuvo en Mazatlán, para referirle mi comunicación relativa al asunto del guano, cuyo negocio es de la mayor gravedad por haber hecho reclamaciones al Gobernador la compañía explotadora a consecuencia de las diez mil toneladas que usted vendió de los efectos y de cuyo impuesto [importe?] se pide la correspondiente distribución, como verá usted por las copias que le acompaño, suplicando a usted se sirva contestarme sobre este asunto y los demás de que llevo hecha referencia.

No me parece por demás participar a usted que por el bergantín goleta nacional *Arizona*, procedente de San Francisco que tocó en el Cabo de San Lucas, el 3 del [mes] corriente se anuncia otra nueva expedición pirática sobre el territorio de Sonora, y aunque los aventureros dicen estar escarmentados con el funesto desenlace de Mr. Crabb y sus cómplices, nunca está por demás recomendar a usted la sobrevigilancia para evitar una sorpresa.

No dude usted del aprecio que le consagra su compañero y amigo que at. BSM.
[firma de] León Yañez.

[Nota en la mano de Castro: Contestada el 25 de agosto]

Señor Colonel don José Castro
La Paz, June 22, 1857

My Worthy Comrade and Friend,

My principal desire, since the 7th of February last when I assumed the position of this Command with which the goodness of the Supreme General-in-Chief of [illegible] has honored me, was to reach an accord with you so that we could proceed in a united way in order to prepare our defense against the filibusters who, during that period and even now, threaten us with invasion.

Being familiar with your fine record, I have communicated to you everything that I believed to be [relevant] to the service of the Nation, and with pain I have seen that to date you have not taken the trouble to answer even the first official letter in which I advised you of my appointment.

As the organ of the concerns of the Supreme General-in-Chief and the Supreme Government, I have transmitted to you important communications related to various matters of great interest, and have in addition made known to you the wishes of His Excellency to improve your position [by] requesting from you budgetary information and assessments of preparedness. The result has been that to date all the matters under your command and all oversight related to La Frontera remain paralyzed due to your lack of communication.

Although I am persuaded that distance and the lack of contact hinders our correspondence, I believe that just as I have not been without opportunities, so should you take advantage of the same in order to communicate in the way that I have done. And since I believe that you have as great an interest as I do in the best service, I promise that in the future the state of anxiety that your silence produces in me because I do not know to what it may be attributed will be calmed.

Taking advantage of the departure of the [ship] commissioned by you that was at Mazatlán, I repeat my commission relative to the matter of the guano business—a transaction of sufficient magnitude as to have caused the Government to demand compensation from the exploratory company as a result of the ten tons of same that you have sold. Said levy requires the proper distribution, as you will see via the copies that I enclose herewith, petitioning you to take the trouble to answer me regarding this matter and the others referred to herein.

It does not seem at all inappropriate for me to advise you that the Mexican bergantine *Arizona* en route from San Francisco, which dropped anchor in Cabo San Lucas on the 3rd (?), is announcing another expedition against the State and Territories of Sonora. And although the adventurers should have taken warning from the famous dénouement of Mr. [Henry A.] Crabb and his accomplices, it is never out of place to recommend super-vigilance to you in order to avoid surprises.

Do not doubt the esteem dedicated to you by your comrade and friend who attentively BSM (kisses your hand).

[signature of] León Yánez

[note in José Castro's handwriting: Answered on August 25th]

Open air siesta; woodcut by Ernest Freed

6 $ ……

San Diego California
23 de Agosto 1859

Al Señor Don

Jose Castro

Muy Estimado y Amigo

Siempre

vengo como V^m sabe muy apura
do y mas ahora que nunca por
que algunos de los canalles en la
Baja se han opuesto a una or
den de la Compa y como yo
le he aguardado a el en cuanto
podia, tenga miedo que me roba
rian mi autoridad — Escribo to
dos los pormenores al Bulletin, y
creo que el Señor Barruyu lo
enterará a V^m de lo que he pub
licado — Le mando tambien un
pliego de papeles de Esparza y
Vidal y como el tenia Esparza
cuando estuvo en mi casa en la
semana pasada, tenia los papeles

leyendolos, por accidente dejo uno
fuera y eso se le mando en este
sobre — Tengo mucha confianza
en el Señor Esparza, y creo que
es bastante patriotico — Capn.
Colbeis esta cargando su buque en
San Quentin y yo tengo comprado de Esparza casi bastante
para el — Don Sacramento le manda a Vmd. y su familia muchas
espresiones, y dice que todavia no
ha querido entregar los borregos
Don Juan Machado, pero Juan
dice que lo hara mas tarde
Montenegro esta bueno, y tiene
muchos pollitos — Mi familia
esta buena y le manda con su
esposa muchas espresiones
En el Express de Freeman y
compañia le mando los papeles
A su apreciable familia muchas espresiones de mi y los
mios, y quiero que me conteste
con el proximo vapor, contandoles

todas las noticias — Moreno esta
muy enojado conmigo dicie
Juan Mendosa, esta en la Fin
Juana, y dicen que tiene una
pistola nueva que le regalo nues
tro amigo Pedro Serrejos allamamen
Su Amigo
2 B.S.M.
R.K. Porter

Letter 15: "I Have a Great Deal of Faith in Señor Esparza and Believe He is Quite Patriotic…"

*Rufus K. Porter, an American publisher who owned property in La Frontera, is one example of extensive north-of-the-border involvement in La Frontera's affairs. The sentiments expressed suggest that Porter will side with Esparza in the internecine struggle of 1859-61 between Castro's second-in-command and **Juan Mendosa**, one of **José Matías Moreno's** unlikely choices for Castro's replacement. Expressing his fear of reprisals against his Baja California property, Porter also acknowledges ties to the San Quintin salt enterprise as well as to Señor Sacramento (family friend of the Castros, mentioned in Letters 6, 7 and 8), Señor Barragán (same as Señor Berumen, mentioned in Letter 18), Army Paymaster Pérez Vidal, and two other La Frontera neighbors–Juan Machado and Eugenio Montenegro. Porter's final paragraph foreshadows the traumatic events to come when he acknowledges having provoked the ire of José Matías Moreno, and associates Juan Mendosa with a pistol received from one Pedro [Semeguy? Semejay?] (his surname is equally illegible in Letter 17). Here, the writer employs the associated phrase "our friend" ironically. Family references and the request for a reply "by the next steamer" suggest that Porter's letter was directed to San Francisco while Colonel Castro was visiting that city.*

San Diego, California. 23 de Agosto de 1857.
Al Señor Don José Castro.

Muy estimado amigo,

Siempre vengo como usted sabe muy apurado, y más ahora que nunca porque algunos de los canallas en la Baja se han opuesto a una orden del Señor **[Feliciano] Esparza**, y como yo le he ayudado a él en cuanto podía, tengo miedo [de] que me robarían en mi ausencia.

Escribo todos los pormenores en el *Bulletín*, y creo que el Señor [Máximo] Barragán le escribirá a usted de lo que he publicado.

Le mando también un pliego de papeles de Esparza y [Andrés Pérez] Vidal, y como el Señor Esparza, cuando estuvo en mi casa en la semana pasada, tenía los papeles leyéndolos, por accidente dejó uno fuera, y ése se lo mando en este sobre. Tengo mucha confianza en el Señor Esparza, y creo que es bastante patriótico.

[El] Capitán Collins está cargando su buque en San Quintín, y yo tengo comprado de Esparza casi bastante para él [buque].

Don Sacramento le manda a usted y su familia muchas expresiones, y dice que todavía no ha podido entregar los borregos a Don Juan Machado, pero Juan dice que lo hará más tarde. [Captain Eugenio] Montenegro está bueno y tiene muchos pollitos. Su familia está bien y le manda su esposa muchas expresiones.

En el Express de Fireman[?] y Compañía, le mando los papeles. A su apreciable familia, muchas expresiones de mí y los míos. Y quiero que me conteste con el próximo vapor, contándome todas las noticias.

[José Matías] Moreno está muy enojado conmigo. Dicen [que] **Juan Mendosa** [Mendoza] está en la Tía Juana y <u>dicen</u> que tiene una pistola nueva que le regaló nuestro amigo Pedro [Semejay?] últimamente.

Su amigo
QBSM (que besa su mano)
[firma de] R.K. Porter.

San Diego, August 23, 1857
To Señor Don José Castro

Very Valued Friend,

I always arrive, as you know, in a great hurry and more now than ever because some of the scoundrels in Baja have set themselves against an order from Señor **[Feliciano] Esparza**, and since I have assisted him to the degree I've been able, I am afraid that they might rob me in my absence. I am writing all the details in the *Bulletin*, and I believe that Señor [Máximo] Barragán will write you about what I have published.

I am also sending you a bundle of papers from Esparza and [Andrés Pérez] Vidal. Since Señor Esparza, when he was at my house last week, had been reading the papers, he left one of them out by accident, and that's the one I enclose in this envelope. I have a great deal of faith in Señor Esparza and believe he is quite patriotic.

Captain Collins is loading my ship at San Quintín, and I have purchased from Esparza almost enough to fill it. Don Sacramento sends you and your family many expressions [of affection] and says that he has not yet been able to turn over the lambs to Don Juan Machado, but Juan says that he will do it later. [Captain Eugenio] Montenegro is fine and has many chicks. His family is fine and sends your wife many [kind] expressions.

I'm sending you the papers care of the Fireman[?] and Company Express. To your worthy family, many expressions from me and mine. And I want you to answer this letter with the next steamer, telling me all the news.

[José Matías] Moreno is very angry with me. They say that **Juan Mendosa** is in Tía Juana, and they say that he has a brand new pistol, given to him by our friend Pedro [Semejay?] recently.

Your friend
QBSM (who kisses your hand)
[signature of] R.K. Porter

Sr. Subjefe Político de la Frontera
Norte de la Baja California.

Josè Tiburcio Castro Ciudadano
Mejicano y vecino de esta frontera an
te VS. con el debido respeto me presento
y digo, que deseando establecerme con
mis bienes y hallandose un pedazo de
terreno valdio conocido con el nombre de
San Antonio colindante al Oeste con
los limites del terreno de Guadalupe, y
los otros tres puntos con serrania vien
do lo util como un medio sitio de ga
nado mayor.

A VS. Pido y suplico se sirva concederme
el mencionado medio sitio de ga
nado mayor para el beneficio mio
y de mi familia de lo que recibiré
gracia, admitiendome el presente
en papel comun por falta del sellado
que corresponde.

        Juro lo necesario &c.
    Ensenada de Todos Santos
            Febrero 15. de 1858.
        Josè F. Castro

        Sauzal de Camacho
            Febrero 16. de 1858.
        En atención à las razones que
    espone el interesado en su
    terior y satisfecho esta
    tura de mi cargo, de que

que pretende es valdio; estiendaute
el titulo de propiedad y entreguenle
junto la solicitud para su resguardo.

José Couture

Letter 16: "I Request and Beseech Your Excellency to Kindly Grant Me Said Half-lot of Cattle Pasture, for My Own Benefit and that of My Family…"

An example of the many requests for land that Colonel Castro would have granted or denied during his four-year tenure as Vice-Governor, this petition for 2,220 acres adjoining Juan Bandini's coincidentally bears the name of Castro's deceased father and one of his sons (just twelve years old at this time). This coincidence may explain why this document is among the letters saved to posterity. Its ragged state testifies to the ravages of frontier life. Both sections appear to be penned by Castro, suggesting that the petitioner was, like the majority of his Baja California paisanos, illiterate.

Señor Subjefe Político de la Frontera Norte de la Baja California.

José Tiburcio Castro, ciudadano mexicano y vecino de esta frontera, ante usted con el debido respeto me presento y digo:

Que deseando establecerme con mis bienes y hallándose un pedazo de terreno baldío conocido con el nombre de San Antonio, colindante al oeste con los límites del terreno de Guadalupe y los otros tres puntos con serranía, siendo útil como un medio sitio de ganado mayor.

A V[uestra] S[eñoría] pido y suplico [que] se sirva concederme el mecionado medio sitio de ganado mayor para beneficio mío y de mi familia, de lo que recibiré [¿recibirá?] gracia, admitiéndoseme el presente papel por falta del sellado que corresponde.

Juro lo necesario [a] usted.

Ensenada de Todos los Santos
15 febrero de 1858.
[firma de] José T. Castro.

Sausal de Camacho.
Febrero 16 de 1858.

En atención a las razones que expone el interesado en [roto el documento] y satisfecha este [roto el documento] jefatura de mi cargo, de que [roto el documento] sino que pretende que es baldío, extiéndase el título de propiedad y entréguese junto con la solicitud para resguardo.

[firma de] José Castro

Señor Political Sub-Chief of La Frontera Norte, Baja California

[I] José Tiburcio Castro, a Mexican citizen and resident of this Frontera region, present myself before you with due respect and declare:

That wishing to establish myself and my possessions, and having found a vacant piece of land known as San Antonio, bordering on the west with the limits of [Rancho] Guadalupe and on the other three sides with mountain ranges, [and] being useful as a half-lot for cattle [pasture],

Request and beseech Your Excellency to kindly grant me said half-lot of cattle [pasture] for my own benefit and that of my family, from which [grant] you will receive [our] thanks, accepting from me the paper upon which this petition is written due to lack of the required paper [stamped] with the proper seal.

I swear what is required before you.

Ensenada de Todos los Santos
February 15, 1858
[signed] José T. Castro

Sausal de Camacho
February 16, 1858

Attending to the reasons supplied by the interested party in… [missing section] and having satisfied this… [missing section] leadership position in my charge, which… [missing section] but rather claims that it is vacant, let the property title be extended to him along with the request for security.

[signed by] José Castro

San Diego Fbro 2º de 1860

Sr. Don Jose Castro

Muy Sor mio de todo mi respeto.
Ympuesto de la Combocatoria que
la Autoridad de V. hu espedido en el
Rancho de Guadalupe fechada en 20 de
de Enº ultimo, en la qe se digna V. lla
marnos á todos los Vecinos de esa qe
por desgracia estamos fuera de nues
tros hogares y herhandonados todos
nuestros pocos intereses y negocios. Co
yo beo los buenos sentimientos de el
para llebarnos á ese pais des
graciado y yo de mi parte quedo
grabado en mi corason tan justo
deseo y buena fé; pero temo (tal
Vez tendra razon en su temencia
ó no) aunque hehora bine tranq
lo á mi casa á los afanes qe dia
riamte he tenido dia á diesnen el
espacio de diez años qe use que
escoji ese pais para bivir unido
á mi Vara, sin aspirar á mas qe

110

á bibir, pero á la vez que estaba
mas contento fuy perseguido, pertene
ciendo á pena de muerte de tal ma
nera y. se me puso fuera de la ley
como un facineroso, como un Ase
sino, como á un ladron en fin se
me Yuzgo como una semeguy, es co
nu dina y. los hombres de bien sean
perseguidos. En fin son todo esto yo pu
se yo se lo dije á U. antes de su salida
de ese pais.

Por esto no he de temer no á U. por
que le conosco sus sentimientos, pero
una calumnia me hará caer en la des
gracia.

Sor, El Sor Esparza dice y. de
fendia la Autoridad de U. y la Consti
tucion de 57, esta ley el y. la pro
clamaron la debe acatar, El Sor Espar
za ella á barrenado por medio, Esta
dice y. las propiedades son intolva
bles, dice otro Art. que en delitos
Politicos no hay pena de muerte,
pero no hay ley sino la de obediencia, la provi
sion, y nada mas, por ultimo son un
cometido mil tropelias.

sirvase U. tomarse la molesta de decirme en
contestacion de esta si mi Esposa puede

rán á tratar sus intereses particularmente de ella, y si V. tendrá a bien
entregar los títulos de mis terrenos
y papeles particulares, pues si á
si fuere ella misma irá á tralos.

Don José tengo á V. ofrecido un
pedazo de tierra en mi Vecino de San
Marcos, puede V. mandar estender
una Escritura de Venta judicial,
de un año ó para mejor decir una
Cuarta parte del terreno, pues ha
sido y es mi Voluntad hacer á V. tal
presente. Por hacerlos no me
Combiene, irá á vivir á mi Vecino sería despues si las Circunstancias lo permiten, Don Geronimo Hau-
rel dirá á V. prudentemente mis justos motivos, mas Cuando no se nos
dejó sembrar y este es un trastorno y perjuicio por dos años de terreno y.ª buscar que Comer.
Sin mas Asunto por hacerlos
me repito Como siempre su Amigo
q.ª deveras lo ama y At.º b. s. m.

Juan Mendoza

Letter 17: "But I Am Afraid, and Perhaps I Am Right to Be Fearful…"

*As the second replacement proposed to the Governor by **José Matías Moreno** in his campaign to unseat both Colonel Castro and his designated second, **Feliciano Esparza**, **Juan Mendosa** became the latter's adversary in the bloody power struggle of 1859-61. This letter is a bonanza because of the insight it provides into the sentiments of one who by this time was regarded in some quarters as a first-order villain, compared to the same Pedro [?] mentioned in Letter 15. By reproducing spoken language to an extent not seen in any other letter in the collection, Mendosa's style conveys his relative lack of education, making the candid expression of his fears and perceived injuries all the more poignant.*

The writer's stated intention to gift a portion of his Rancho San Marcos, on the San Diego side of the border, to Colonel Castro gives the researcher pause. Was he offering Castro and his devoted family the opportunity for another start, together, on the edge of Mexico?

*The question is moot, since two months and three days after this letter was written, Castro would be shot down, allegedly "by one of his own men" acting on behalf of the enemy band led by none other than Juan Mendosa. (See Part III for the story of Castro's assassination and its traumatic aftermath.) Mendosa would later shot in the back by Cave Couts, San Diegan son-in-law of **Juan Bandini**. After his prompt acquittal in court, Couts would add Mendosa's Rancho San Marcos to his own extensive landholdings.*

San Diego 2 febrero de 1860
Señor don José Castro

Muy compañero mío de todo mi respeto,

Impuesto de la convocatoria que la Autoridad de usted ha expedido en el Rancho de Guadalupe, fechada en el 29 de enero último, en la que se digna usted a llamarnos a todos los vecinos de allá que por desgracia estamos fuera de nuestros hogares y [tenemos] abandonados todos nuestros pocos intereses y negocios.

Compañero, yo veo los buenos sentimientos de usted para acarrearnos a ese país desgraciado, y yo de mi parte queda grabado en mi corazón tan justo deseo y buena fe. Pero temo, y tal vez tendré razón en ser temerario, o no. Y aunque es hora de vivir tranquilo en mi casa en los afanes [que] diariamente he tenido día a día en el espacio de de diez años, que hace que escogí ese país para vivir, único a mi parecer, sin aspirar a más que a vivir.

Pero a la vez que estaba más contento, fui perseguido, sentenciado a pena de muerte, de tal manera que se me puso fuera de la ley como un facineroso, como un asesino, como un ladrón. En fin, Compañero, se me juzgó como a un [Pedro] [Semeguy? Semejay?]. Es cosa de mal que los hombres de bien sean perseguidos. En fin, Compañero, todo esto que pasó yo se lo dije a usted antes de mi salida de ese país. Compañero, esto me hace temer – no a usted, porque le conozco sus sentimientos. Pero una calumnia me hará caer en la desgracia.

Compañero, el Compañero **Esparza** decía que él defendía la Autoridad de usted y la Constitución del [18]57. [Pero] esta ley, el que la proclama, la debe ejecutar. El compañero Esparza la ha berreado por medio[s]. Esta [ley] dice que las propiedades son inviolables. Dice otro artículo que en delitos políticos no hay pena de muerte, pero [en La Frontera] no hay ley sino repudiación, capricho y nada más. Por último, Compañero, hemos cometido mil tropelías [actos ilegales].

Sírvase usted tomarse la molestia de decirme en contestación de ésta: si mi esposa puede, iría a tratar sus intereses particularmente de ella, y si usted tendrá a bien entregar los títulos de mis terrenos y papeles particulares, pues si así fuese ella misma irá a traerlos.

Don José, tengo a usted ofrecido un pedazo de tierra en mi Rancho de San Marcos. Puede usted mandar a extender la Escritura de venta judicial de un [¿dueño?] o para mejor decir una cuarta parte del terreno, pues ha sido y es mi voluntad hacer a usted tal presente.

Por ahora, Compañero, no me conviene ir a vivir a mi rancho. Será después, si las circunstancias lo permiten. Don Gerónimo Laurel[?] dirá a usted fundadamente mis justos motivos, más cuando no se nos dejó sembrar, y esto es un trastorno y un perjuicio por dos años de tener que buscar qué comer.

Sin más asunto por ahora, me repito como siempre su amigo que de veras lo ama y attentamente LBPM [le besa pies y manos].

[firma de] Juan Mendosa

San Diego, February 2, 1860
Señor Don José Castro

My close comrade of all my respect,

Regarding the call to a meeting that Your Authority has dispatched to Rancho Guadalupe, dated last January 29th, in which you are kind enough to invite all the residents of the area: unfortunately we are away from our homes and all our few interests and business concerns [are] abandoned.

Comrade, I perceive your good intentions that we carry that miserable country forward, and for my part that very same desire and good faith remains engraved upon my heart. But I am afraid. Perhaps it will turn out that I am right to be fearful, or perhaps not. And although now is the time to live calmly in my house in the anticipation that I have felt day by day for the past ten years since I chose that place–a unique place in my opinion–with no other aspiration but living my life [there in La Frontera].

But the time that I felt most contented was also the time when I was the most persecuted–sentenced to death in such a way that I was put outside the law, like a habitual criminal, like a murderer, like a thief. In the end, Comrade, I was judged like a [Pedro] [Semeguy? Semejay?]. It is [wrong] that upstanding men should be so harrassed. As I say, Comrade, I told you all these things that happened to me before your [temporary] departure from that country.

Comrade, this [is what] makes me fearful–not of you, because I know your feelings. But any calumny would cause me to fall into disgrace. Comrade, our comrade Esparza used to say that he was defending your Authority and the Constitution of 1857. Whoever proclaims that [code of] law should exercise it. Comrade Esparza has been bellowing it for his own gain. The law says that property [rights] are inviolable. Another article says that there is no death penalty for political crimes. [In La Frontera] there is no law but repudiation and whim–nothing else. So in the last analysis, Comrade, we have committed a thousand illegal acts.

Be kind enough to take the trouble of telling me [your response to the following proposal], when you answer this letter. If my wife is able, she would go to [La Frontera] to take care of her personal business, and if you would be inclined to turn over to her the titles of my lands along with my private papers, if this were possible, she would herself go to retrieve them.

Don José, I have offered you a piece of land on my Rancho de San Marcos. You can have a judiciary deed of sale drawn up as [?] or better yet for one quarter of the terrain, since it has been and continues to be my will to make this gift to you.

For now, Comrade, it is not advisable for me to go live on my [La Frontera] ranch. That will come later, if circumstances permit. Don Gerónimo Laurel[?] will tell you my valid motives, since when we were not allowed to plant our crops, it was an upheaval and a grievance [against us], having had to search out [another source of] sustenance during a period of two years.

With nothing else pending for now, I reiterate that I am as always your friend who truly loves you and who ABPM (attentively kisses your feet and hands).

[signature of] Juan Mendosa

Colonel José Castro died before photography came into widespread use. The image above his signature and rubric is probably not his own; the style of clothing depicted suggests that it belongs to another Alta California Castro, one who outlived the unfortunate Colonel. If the uniformed portrait reproduced on page 8 was done posthumously, a common custom in the early and mid-1800s, its fidelity to Castro's actual appearance is also cast into question.

121   21
10195
205

Con fha 15 de Agosto ultimo manifesté
VS. que el negocio de las Salinas de San Mar
tin habia fracasado por el empresario Don
D. Antonio L. Sosa, y no habiendo otro quien las
quiera tomar por las muchas dificultades que
presentan; me he visto en el Caso de dejarlas libres
por los Ciudadanos que quieran ocuparse de ellas,
y sin embargo de esto nadie emprende; por consigui
ente la unica renta con que contaba la Hacienda
publica ha quedado por ahora en el estado de nulidad.

El ramo de mineria que fué mi objeto des
arrollar desde un principio como unico elemento
que podia dar vida á estos pueblos fronterizos no ha
podido tener su lleno ni deseo, pues las minas
de San Pedro al poco tiempo de su trabajo ela
boracion han dado en borra y las dos que se trabajan
en San Antonio parece que llevan el mismo cami
no.

No obstante esto en medio de la escacez de
recursos en que me he encuentro he podido con
cervar hasta ahora el orden y la tranquilidad
publica manteniendo á mi lado un piquete de
veinte Ciudadanos nacionales que me acompañan
merced á las relaciones de antigua amistad que

tengo con mis compatriotas.

Como es muy natural que el Sr. Beruben
á su llegada á esa halla ido adulteramos las cosas de
lo que son en realidad, tendría un positivo sentimiento
que su autoridad se dejara sorprender por las falsas
noticias que cierto Sr. esparciera ultrajamas malamen
te mi honor como lo ha hecho al salir del país po-
niendose de acuerdo para esto con mi enemigo ca
pital el Sr. Moreno.

V. conoce muy bien que esta clase de hombres hablan
y sirven contra aquella persona que les impide el sariar
sus depravadas intenciones cuando no han podido lle
nar sus ambiciones deseos; y el pensar en el crédito que V. dará les daría
pudiera darles sería hacerle una ofensa á su recto juicio
y buen discernimiento de V. que me es bien conocido

Letter 18: "To Think That You Might Believe Them Would Be an Offense Against Your Upright Judgment…"

Although the actual date of composition is impossible to determine, this letter provides fitting closure to this series because it expresses Castro's failures and frustrations along with his pride in maintaining order, thanks to a band of loyal countrymen, and his perception of the pending threats that, indeed, will shortly take his life and suppress his achievements. A symmetrical complement to Letter 1 (to the President of Mexico), this missive would likely have been addressed to the Governor of Baja California, who in late 1859 and early 1860 was the incoming Ramón Navarro, represented in Part IV by Letters D and E, which set the stage for the expedient disposal of Colonel Castro. The names of some portion of Castro's loyal countrymen can be found on page 177, his future assassin's among them.

Thomas Bona Walker, an Englishman known locally by his middle name, drank to excess and had a poor reputation as mayor of Santo Tomás. Here, Castro turns the surname into a verb apparently connoting failure through incompetence or corruption. Beruben was apparently also known as Máximo Baragom. The fact that Castro has used Antonio L. Sosa as his messenger may be a sign that this letter was written at an earlier date, since in a letter to Juan Bandini on October 22, 1857 (Letter C, Part IV), Castro mentioned having been betrayed by Sosa in his salt extraction enterprise.

Con fecha del 15 de agosto último manifesté [a] usted que el negocio de las salinas de San Quintín había fracasado por el empresario don Antonio L. Sosa, y no habiendo otro quien las quiera tomar por las muchas dificultades que presentan, me he visto en el caso de dejarles libres por los ciudadanos que quieran ocuparse de ellas. Y sin embargo de esto, nadie emprende. Por consiguiente la única renta con que contaba la Hacienda Pública ha quedado por ahora en estado de nulidad.

El ramo de minería que fue mi objeto desarrollar desde un principio, como único elemento que podía dar vida a estos pueblos fronterizos, no ha podido tener su lleno [¿realizarse?] mi deseo, pues las minas de Santiago [?] al poco tiempo de su trabajo [?] bonaíno han dado en bona, y las dos que se trabajan en San Antonio parece que llevan el mismo camino.

No obstante esto, en medio de la escasez de recursos en que me encuentro, he podido conservar hasta ahora el orden y la tranquilidad pública manteniendo a mi lado un piquete de veinte ciudadanos nacionales que me acompañan, merced a las relaciones de antigua amistad que tengo con mis compatriotas.

Como es muy natural que el Señor [A.E.] Beruben a su llegada a esa [¿ciudad?] haya ido adulterando las cosas de lo que son en realidad, tendría [yo] un positivo sentimiento que Su Autoridad se dejara sorprender por las falsas noticias que dicho señor esparciera [para] ultrajarme malamente mi honor, como lo ha hecho al salir del país, poniéndose de acuerdo para esto con mi enemigo capital el **Señor [José Matías] Moreno**.

Usted conoce muy bien que esta clase de hombres hablan y dicen contra aquella persona que les impide saciar sus depravadas intenciones cuando no han podido llenar sus ambiciosos deseos. Y el pensar en que usted les daría crédito sería una ofensa a su recto juicio y buen discernimiento de usted, que me es bien conocido.

[sin firma]

[In my letter] dated last August 15th, I notified you through the empressario Don **Antonio L. Sosa** that the salt enterprise at San Quintín had failed. And since there is no other party desirous of taking it over due to the high number of difficulties entailed, I have had no other option but to open the salt mines to any citizen who wishes to take charge of them. However, no one has come forward. As a result, the only prospective [source of] income for the Public Treasury has been rendered non-existent.

The branch of mining that it was from the beginning my goal to develop as the sole element capable of giving life to these frontier towns has not been able to realize my desire, since the mines at Santiago, worked for just a short time under the Bona regime, have "bona-ed" out, and the two that are being worked at San Antonio seem to be headed in the same direction.

Notwithstanding, [and] in the midst of the scarcity of resources in which I find myself, I have up to now been able to maintain order and public calm by keeping at my side a small party of twenty national citizens who accompany me thanks to the long-standing bonds of friendship that I have with my compatriots.

Since it is very natural [to be expected] that, upon his arrival at that city[?] Señor [A.E.] Beruben has gone about distorting things from what they really are, I have a positive feeling that Your Authority would [not] let yourself be surprised by the false information that said gentleman might be spreading around in order to blatantly offend my honor, as he has done since he left the country, acting in accord with my arch enemy Señor **[José Matías] Moreno**.

You know very well that this kind of individual speaks out and says things against the person who prevents him from satisfying his depraved intentions when he has not been able to realize his ambitious designs. Just to think that you might credit the two of them would be to offend the rectitude of your good judgment, which is well known to me.

[unsigned]

Part III
José Castro in Baja California

Father Alric's Baja California experience symbolically evoked by Mexican artist Carlos Coronado

Abbé Henry-Jean-Antoine Alric at Santo Tomás, from the 1869 Paris edition of his memoir

José Castro in Baja California, 1856-1860

Angela Moyano Pahissa
and Julianne Burton-Carvajal

Barely a month after the US invasion of Alta California in early July 1846, Governor Pío Pico and Military Commander José Castro departed separately for Mexico. There they were received as heroes of the resistance in the war between Mexico and the United States that would continue to be waged on multiple fronts until 1848. Various historians concur that Castro went to the port of Mazatlán in order to be able to make frequent voyages to Monterey, where he could attend to the needs of his wife and numerous children, and from there to San Francisco, where he could oversee his real estate and business interests under the new legal and fiscal dispositions of American rule.

Surviving documents in Mexican national and regional archives suggest that Castro journeyed north with relative frequency. Among the American scholars who endorse this assumption is the eminent Doyce B. Nunis, Jr., longtime editor of the *Southern California Quarterly*. Following information provided by Castro's contemporaries and republished by compiler Florence Shipek, Nunis maintains that the former Commander General of Alta California went to the state of Sinaloa once Alta California passed into the hands of the Americans. He adds that Castro returned to Monterey and San Juan Bautista after the signing of the Treaty of Guadalupe-Hidalgo in 1848 and visited Mexico again in 1853.

Our research indicates that he might have traveled to Baja California in that year, when he also formed a partnership to extract salt from deposits at Cabo San Quintín, on land he had acquired in 1841. This cape lies just south of the northern region of Baja California, known as La Frontera, a semi-desert area where Castro

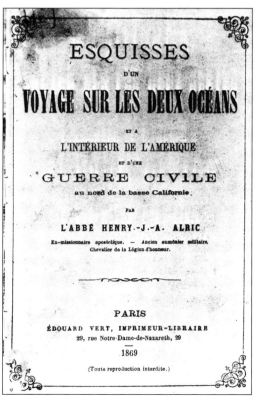

would spend what turned out to be the last four years of his life in service to the government of Mexico.

Nunis's references appear in a recent edition of a principal source for the story of Castro's final years in Baja California. That source is the memoir of a French priest, Abbé Henry-Jean-Antoine Alric, who was sent to La Frontera in 1856 by Bishop Joseph Sadoc Alemany as an apostolic missionary charged with serving the twelve northernmost missions. In this appointment, the Mallorcan-born archbishop of San Francisco was acting on a plea from his Mexico City counterpart, who had been unsuccessful in filling the remote position.

As a sustained account of the northern Baja California region and its affairs between 1856 and 1860, the exact period of Castro's tenure there. Alric's memoir is fundamental to developing a fuller understanding of Colonel Castro's Mexican career. Alric's account has appeared in French in three different versions, under three different titles (Mexico City, 1866; Paris, 1867 and 1869), a composite English translation (Los Angeles, 1971), and a Spanish-language version based on the 1869 French text (Tijuana, 1995). The Mexican edition incorporates much of the exacting scholarshp that editor Doyce B. Nunis, Jr. contributed to the English edition. for which he prepared the preface, introduction and annotations.

Part of the challenge of piecing together José Castro's career in Mexico is the scarcity of primary documents from the 1856-1860 period, and the dispersion of the few that have survived. In addition to the eighteen letters conserved by the Society of California Pioneers in San Francisco and reproduced in the previous section, the following account draws upon half a dozen documents belonging to the Archivo General de la Nación (AGN: Mexican National Archive), copies of which can also be found in the archives of the Institute of Historical Research at the Autonomous University of Baja California in Tijuana (IHH at UABC). Five of these refer to José Castro as Governor (*Jefe Político*) of Baja California; and only one to his position as Vice-Governor of La Frontera (*Sub-jefe Político del Partido Norte de la Baja California*)–an anomaly that will be addressed below.

Research for this essay has also identified a few dozen documents written by and to José Castro that reside in the Bancroft Library at the University of California, Berkeley. Not yet having been able to examine the originals, we have relied upon the summaries provided in the indispensable Spanish-language *Guide to the Manuscripts Concerning Baja California in the Collections of the Bancroft Library*–and hasten to acknowledge our indebtedness to compilers Rose Marie Beebe, Robert Senkewicz, and assistants for their herculean annotation effort.

La Frontera, Two Castros, and the Cleaving of the Californias

The settlement known as Santo Tomás was located at the bottom of a wide *arroyo* (wash) 21 miles inland from the Pacific coast, 105 miles south of San Diego, and some 700 miles north of La Paz. Founded by Dominican priests in 1791 as Santo Tomás de Aquino, it was abandoned in 1849 after the long and depleting campaign to remove American filibuster William Walker from the region.

On May 22, 1851, Santo Tomás became the seat of government (political subprefecture) for the 30,000 square mile section of northern Baja California officially known as *El Partido Norte*, the Northern Section. More commonly referred to as La Frontera, this region stretched from a few miles below San Diego to Mission San Vicente in the south, and from the islands off the Pacific coastline eastward to the lower Colorado River delta that empties into the Gulf of Cortez. Comprising some 750,000 acres, La Frontera had a population density of only 1.15 per square mile. In 1855, when Baja California was administratively reorganized, La Frontera became the Municipalidad de (township of) Santo Tomás. (See map on page 39.)

Father Alric offers the following general description of the region:

The poverty and misery that one meets almost everywhere are most striking. The soil is usually arid, water from springs and rivers is very scarce, and it rains only a few days in the whole year…[which] is why sowing can be done only in irrigable land [and] since this is very rare, the population constantly emigrates to more favored regions. … The mountains, of which the greater part is covered with wild oats, give enough pasturage for the numerous herds, which are the principal riches of the country. (90-93)

From the 1840s to the 1860s, La Frontera was the site of a prolonged and increasingly ruthless struggle for supremacy involving a host of players: Mexicans from both sides of the border, Baja Californians and relocated Alta Californians, American filibusters and fortune-hunters, venture capitalists of several nationalities, countless tribes of Indians, including several groups driven across the border, and whichever local residents managed to retain their often precarious foothold. Beyond the mining of gold, silver, copper, salt, lime, talc, and guano, the most coveted prize was the disposition of the repeatedly contested lands stretching north to the newly defined border. In the opening paragraph of his introduction to the English translation of Father Alric's memoir, Nunis offers this eloquent summary:

In the wake of the Mexican[-American] War, Baja California was plagued with recurring problems. Isolated from mainland Mexican development, the remote peninsula suffered one political outburst after another. The explosive atmosphere was exploited on every hand by self-seeking elements, both native and foreign. Greedy American filibusters and expatriates cast a long shadow over a rugged landscape. Lawless refugees from across the border provided a willing reservoir of opposition–guns ready for hire. Never a prosperous land or people, within two decades, 1848-1868, the territory was reduced to abject poverty and desolation. Twenty years of post-war hardship left a dreadful historical legacy to those few who survived. (1971: 19)

The first demarcation between Lower and Upper (or Old and New) California was established by Dominican and Franciscan friars in 1772 to divide responsibil-

Arthur Schott's 1854 drawing of Kumeyaay Indians near San Diego echoes the Holy Family's flight into Egypt

ity for their respective missions, south and north. José Joaquín de Arrillaga, who governed the two Californias as a single unit from 1800 to 1804, separated the "old" and "new" for administrative purposes at the end of his governorship. Forty-four years later, in February of 1848, the Treaty of Guadalupe-Hidalgo concluding the Mexican-American War (begun in 1846 over a border dispute in Texas) retained Baja California for Mexico and established a new boundary just south of San Diego. This decision, ratified several months later, rent asunder long-standing ties, for the sparse and isolated population of northern Baja California had been perennially dependent upon San Diego for necessities as well as amenities.

The borderline stipulated in the treaty was physically defined by Ricardo Ramírez, a Mexican topographer who undertook to perform the task across La Frontera between March and June of 1851. As attested by documents relating to Baja California in the Bancroft collections, Ramírez requested and received a military escort for his labors from the captain in charge of the Santo Tomás colony, Manuel de Jesús Castro (letters #4511, 4517, 4529, 4531, 4556, 4890). The son of José Nepomuceno (Simeón) Castro and Josefa María Cota de Castro, Manuel was a native-born Montereyan who, like his elder cousin José. resisted the American take-over of California and relocated to Mexico. His story, outlined in the sidebar that begins on the facing page, turns out to be connected to Castro's Baja California career to an extent never before recognized.

A very brief biographical sketch by Rose Marie Beebe and Robert Senkewicz states that Manuel Castro "supported Pico against [José] Castro" (1996: 321). Our findings do not support that assertion. In *California Conquered*, Neal Harlow writes that on July 7, 1846, upon receiving news of the raising of the American flag at Monterey, the Commander General of Alta California sent his cousin Manuel southward as his emissary *"to make a reconciliation with [Governor Pío] Pico, who had set out from Los Angeles to oppose [Commander José Castro]"* (143). Robert R. Miller notes that when the latter departed for Mexico, he delegated his command to his cousin Manuel (124) while Castro's rival Governor Pío Pico left his to the Mexican José María Flores. Historians often conflate the "flight" of military leader José Castro and that of his political counterpart and southern rival Pío Pico. Harlow maintains that "*Both*

the governor and the general left the capital [Los Angeles] in the night" while making clear their divergent paths:

> *Disbanding his military force, Castro crossed to Altar in Sonora, where he vainly petitioned the central government for assistance. Pico (…) stayed the night at Teodosio Yorba's rancho (in Orange County), then lived in concealment until September 7, when he escaped into Baja California. From Mulegé [in southern Baja California] and Guaymas [on the mainland coast of Sonora], Pico repeatedly importuned the Minister of Foreign Relations for aid in the recovery of California, and for his own relief, to no avail.* (Harlow, 150)

The next record of Manuel Castro places him in southern Baja California. As officially designated captain of a troop of soldiers, Manuel Castro led a 700-mile march north from La Paz to Santo Tomás, beginning in mid-1849. He became the first captain of the La Frontera military colony, initially established at Rosario, where he would have been camped with his troops when he received word of his father's death in late June of 1850 (#4285). In October of the same year, assisted by Sergeant José Antonio Chaves, he moved his troops to Santo Tomás, the military colony's permanent location. Captain Castro stayed on there as military commander until his return to Upper California in 1852.

Whether routine or atypically substantive, the scores of documents relating to Manuel Castro in the Bancroft Library collection are very illuminating. First and foremost, they establish beyond question that Castro and Chaves had the ongoing support of officials in both Mexico City and La Paz as they struggled long and hard first to establish and then to sustain the officially mandated military colony. Although Captain Castro requested permission to resign from his post in early 1851, he continued to discharge his duties until mid-1852, notwithstanding a number of letters from family members urging his immediate return to Upper California in order to testify in the US Land Commission hearings regarding the legality of pre-American property titles (#4478, 4495, 4532, 4616, 4630 *et al.*).

The military colony established by Manuel Castro in the former mission buildings at Santo Tomás was one of eighteen ordered in 1850 by President José Joaquín

Herrera to protect the 1200 miles of Mexico's newly adjusted northern border from additional land grabs. Fifteen years later, command of the westernmost of what turned out to be nine military colonies located between the Pacific and the Gulf of Mexico would be offered to Captain Manuel Castro's elder cousin. Colonel José Castro brought solid military and political experience to the challenge of administering the post and the neglected, often lawless region surrounding it.

The selected Bancroft Library documentation on Manuel Castro, summarized below, suggests the extent of the documentary record that would have been associated with José Castro's tenure in Baja California, had more of it survived. It also suggests that, before deciding to accept the governorship of Baja California when it was first offered to him by the Mexican government, José Castro would have sought a thorough briefing from his cousin, whose official reports document persistent efforts to meet the responsibilities of his office.

As senior military official of the colony, Captain Manuel Castro was expected to: properly supply the troops, contend with a disorganized administration, establish a system of reliable communications and transport from the capital, distribute wages, discipline unruly soldiers, keep troublesome Indians at bay, recapture horses, mules and other stray domestic animals, provide aid to ships in distress, investigate and prosecute murders, allocate vacant land, regulate egress and exit from the region, host visiting dignitaries, investigate suspicious foreigners, resist filibusters and pirates, control the large number of *vile individuals who are part of the colony and should be jailed* (#4278), and prepare the countless official reports, lists and copies that, having survived, permit the following outline of his activites.

Summary of Bancroft Library Sources Related to Manuel Castro in Baja California

Manuel Castro's co-commander in the resistance to American takeover, José Flores, eventually attained the rank of general in the Mexican army. Among Bancroft Library's extensive Baja California materials, Flores is represented by a single undated document (#4880) relating to property at Punta Banda, Ensenada. In contrast, one of the richest caches of documentation for any one of the more than 1,000 individuals listed in the index to the Beebe-Senkewicz bibliography comprises over 200 communications written between 1847 and 1852 to, from, and concerning Manuel de Jesús Castro.

On February 3, 1848, he is mentioned in a letter from the Secretary of War in Mexico City. On May 21, 1849, Baja California Governor Colonel Rafael Espinosa sent him twenty pesos to defray his expenses to Guadalajara (#4041). At the territorial capital of La Paz between July 24th and August 1st, Manuel Castro was one of four signatories on the enlistment documents for seven soldiers (#4046-4049, 4051, 4053, 4054) and the sole signatory on the eighth (#4055). During the month of August, he submitted the following lists: projected expenses (#4056), soldiers in review (#4057), inventory of resources (#4061, 4064, 4066) and clothing needed for the troops (#4062). His report on the desertion of one soldier, along with the horse allotted to him, also explained that heavy rains had halted the march of his troops (#4069, 4070). On August 31st he submitted a voucher for funds received and distributed (#4072).

Continuing to receive instructions from Governor Espinosa and, through him, the central government (#4068, 4073), Castro laboriously worked his way up the long, desolate, generally arid peninsula, reporting from Loreto in early September (#4079-4082) and from Mulegé in early October (#4090, 4093, 4095-4097, 4099, 4105, 4106, 4113-4116, 4118-4125). His communication of October 5th (#4095) noted the persistence of heavy rains and illness among the soldiers, on whose behalf he stressed the need for "housing and regular wages" (#4095). The following day, he wrote to the local *alcalde* indicating that he was not authorized to get involved with elections or political appointments but merely to maintain order.

Governor Espinosa wrote to him on November 12th (#4120), enclosing a copy of a communiqué from the Minister of Foreign Affairs regarding the high number of foreigners arriving in Baja California without appropriate documentation. Given the American military takeover of the peninsula just two years before, the authorities were understandably wary. Under the terms of the 1848 treaty of Guadalupe-Hidalgo, Mexico had agreed to cede nearly half its territory–comprising today's states of California, Texas, Arizona, New Mexico, Nevada and portions of Colorado and Utah–to the Americans. Manuel Castro's communications to the Governor in November of 1849 reported increased illness among the troops, insufficient food supplies, lack of funds, and uncertainty about whether he should continue the march under such circumstances.

Manuel Castro and his troops arrived at San Ignacio in early December. He was joined there–if only temporarily–by the long-awaited Sergeant José Antonio Chaves with additional troops and supplies (#4149, 4169). On January 11, 1850 Governor Espinosa sent Captain Castro instructions as to what he should do upon arriving in La Frontera (#4166). Four days later, Manuel Castro authorized three unnamed *mexicanos de Alta California* to establish themselves in Baja California as long as they fulfilled the requirements stipulated by the central government (#4171). On February 1st Governor Espinosa wrote Castro urging him to do whatever he could to create a permanent colony and assuring him that, once he arrived at his destination, funds would be relayed on a more regular schedule (#4182).

On October 15, 1850 Governor Espinosa petitioned the Supreme Government to name a *subjefe político* (vice-governor) for the Northern Section, La Frontera. Lieutenant Colonel Francisco Del Castillo Negrete eventually received the appointment, which Mexican historians have concluded was rejected and resisted by Castro and Chaves (Alric/Moyano Pahissa 15). However, correspondence in the Bancroft Collection delineates a fuller timeline and suggests a more cooperative working relationship, at least initially.

On December 26, 1850, Governor Espinosa sent Manuel Castro a copy of his letter to Del Castillo Negrete noting the need to attract settlers to the colony (#4394). A letter from Del Castillo Negrete that same month, datelined Santo Tomás, requests a secretary. An exchange of letters between Del Castillo Negrete and Manuel Castro, written on January 23rd and 24th and datelined Santo Tomás (#4450, 4451) respectively request and supply information on the secularization of the California missions. On February 5, 1851, again from Santo Tomás, Del Castillo Negrete submitted a receipt for his pay (#4471).

On February 12, 1851, Governor Espinosa wrote from La Paz that he had named Del Castillo Negrete provisional Vice-Governor, pending approval from the central government (#4479). On the very same day, writing from Santo Tomás, Manuel Castro petitioned Governor Espinosa for permission to retire from the service (#4481, 4482, 4485) and also prepared a separate communication requesting that paymaster Andrés Pérez Vidal entrust funds to Del Castillo Negrete (#4480, 4484). Given the notoriously slow transit of letters, Captain Castro's request to resign would have certainly crossed with the notice of Del Castillo Negrete's pending appointment. Although Manuel Castro expressed his intent to return to Northern California from early 1851, he continued to serve the Baja California military colony for another year. Perhaps as an inducement to remain, on August 10th Governor Espinosa sent him a copy of a letter informing Vice-Governor designate Del Castillo Negrete of Castro's official appointment as Captain of the Military Colony at Santo Tomás (#4618).

Manuel Castro's "order of the day" on May 28, 1851 was naming Andrés Pérez Vidal as ensign of the colony (#4574). Barely two months later, on July 31st the ensign sent a letter to Captain Castro protesting the order to march to Mulegé (#4613). In an undated draft response (#4892), Castro explained his reasons.

Writing from San Ignacio in March of 1851, Del Castillo Negrete gave notice of his appointment as Vice-Governor in a letter to an unidentified correspondent that also describes his arduous march and mentions difficulties caused by a brutal mule-driver and the desertion of a soldier (#4515). On June 3, 1851 Governor Espinosa notified an unidentified correspondent, probably Captain Castro, that Del Castillo Negrete was on his way to the colony, adding a warning about the pending threat from American filibuster Joseph Moorehead (#4570).

The next communication in the Bancroft collection closes a ten-month gap. Writing from San Diego on April 13, 1852, en route to attend to pressing affairs in Northern California, Manuel Castro instructed **Father José María Suárez del Real** regarding the imminent arrival and treatment of Del Castillo Negrete (#4718). Sometime in 1852, Manuel Castro had written to the Minister of War, enclosing certified documents pertinent to the case of one Manuel F. de Córdoba, who had allegedly brought foreign troops into the territory. His letter mentioned Del Castillo Negrete's role in the matter, which is not specified in the published summary (#4741). On February 4, 1853 Del Castillo Negrete wrote to Captain Castro regarding the absence of documents in the colony's archive (#4744), enclosing under separate cover the Minister of War's request for Captain Castro's accounts (#4743).

Even upon meticulous re-examination of all these communications, it may prove impossible to tell when the rift occurred between the military commanders of the colony and the incoming Vice-Governor, but two other letters seem especially relevant. Writing to Manuel Castro from Santo Tomás on October 12, 1851, Lieutenant Chaves expressed concern that, despite his own repeated requests, Del Castillo Negrete had remained at San Felipe for nearly three weeks, holding back the awaited supplies and funds for the colony. Chaves declared his intention to report Del Castillo Negrete's *"trampas"* (tricks) to the authorities unless Captain Castro returned soon (#4626). The other pertinent communication has clearly been mis-dated by the heroic bibliographers who summarized and indexed the Baja California holdings at Bancroft Library. Andrés Pérez Vidal's letter from Baja California to one José Serrano, petitioner for land near Rancho Tia Juana, is dated November 19, 1831 (#3780). It should be reclassified as 1851 in light of its content: information about a conspiracy to murder [Manuel] Castro and [José Antonio] Chaves.

A letter in the Mexican archives (IIH 1852.10 8.30) from **José Matías Moreno,** hero of the resistance to the American takeover of Baja California in 1847-48 and sometime secretary to Colonel Del Castillo Negrete, alleged an annexation conspiracy spearheaded by Captain Castro, Sargeant Chaves, the prominent Peruvian-born San Diegan **Juan Bandini,** and Father Suárez del Real, formerly at Carmel Mission and Monterey. Moreno accused Bandini of fomenting disorder as a means of financing his ex-Misión de Guadalupe concession, a property transfer that Moreno regarded as illegal. Moreno prompted the central government to annul all previous concessions of territory and credited Del Castillo Negrete with frustrating the conspiracy to annex Baja California to the United States—a conspiracy dependent upon *"fomenting internal disagreements under the most unscrupulous Machiavellian system."* (Moyano Pahissa in Alric 1995, 15-17). As this summary amply confirms, letters in Bancroft Library promise to reveal other interpretations of the delayed hand-over of political authority in La Frontera to Del Castillo Negrete.

Retracing the Trail of José Castro's Letters and Documents

Baja California materials in the Bancroft Library number much fewer for Colonel José Castro than for his cousin Manuel.* The first pertinent item is an i.o.u. (*pagaré*) for 3000 pesos/dollars from José Antonio Castro to his cousin Manuel de Jesús Castro, sent from an unspecified point of origin and dated October 20, 1851 (#4629; C-B 483:1, 102). On November 16, 1851, again from an unspecified location, José Castro sent a letter to his cousin and returned an unspecified document.

More significantly, the Bancroft collection includes an accord relating to the salt flats at San Quintín, Baja California signed on May 4, 1853 by José Castro and Manuel de Jesús Castro, **Juan Bautista Alvarado,** and **J.A. Moerenhout,** (#4747; C-B 52:226-228). By this date, Del Castillo Negrete was in place as Vice-Governor of La Frontera and Manuel Castro was again residing in Northern California. In addition to establishing the identity of the partners in the salt mining enterprise referred to in letters 1, 5, and 14 from the Society of Pioneers collection, this document also confirms an ongoing relationship between Castro cousins José and Manuel.

On April 1, 1854, **José Matías Moreno** wrote to José Castro requesting *expedientes* (legal documentation) in order to confirm the latter's claim to the San Quintín property, noting that he had discussed the matter with Vice-Governor Del Castillo Negrete, for whom he was presumably acting as secretary (#4756; C-B 483:1, 219). In July of that year, the same correspondent sent José Castro a letter detailing the current state of affairs in Baja California (#4758; C-B 52:234-235). On December 13, 1855, during the Baja California governorship of Colonel José María Oñate, Moreno would acquire fifteen leagues (about thirty square miles) encompassing Mission San Vicente and the port of San Quintín (Nunis in Alric 100 n.2).

* Listing #4763 is a letter from one José Priani de Castro written on October 19, 1855. On April 13, 1850, one Vicente Sotomayor writes to one José Castro to reclaim a mule (#4234; C-B 483:1, 45). On December 25 of the same year, one Tomás Antonio Soberanes wrote a letter to one José Castro for which the compilers provide no annotation (#4393; C-B 483:1, 57); the point of origin is unspecified and the content apparently trivial.

After a gap of some three years, the next pertinent document in the Bancroft collection dates from 1857, the second year of Castro's term as Vice-Governor of La Frontera, and consists of his description of that region's administrative organization (#4770; M-M 21:662-671). On March 11, 1858, Castro sent his cousin Manuel copies of documents relating to land holdings, which confirms their continuing contact. The Beebe-Senkewicz bibliography identifies just eight other miscellaneous documents in the Bancroft collections relating to José Castro between 1858 and 1860, most of them part of property dossiers too complicated to summarize here.

The earliest document in Mexican collections pertinent to José Castro outside Alta California is to be found in the archives of the University of Baja California's Institute for Historical Investigation. Written by Castro to the Secretary of State in Mexico City, the letter confirms receipt of his official appointment as Governor (*Jefe Político*) of Baja California and places him at the mainland port of Mazatlán on the date of composition, February 22, 1855. Castro mentions having received the letter of appointment on December 7, 1854, while at Monterey. In his letter of acceptance sent on January 21, 1855, he reiterated his intention to proceed to La Paz in order to assume his new position *"full of the most patriotic enthusiasm, delighted to be able to consecrate my final days to the service of my country, and profoundly grateful for the confidence shown to me by His Excellency President Comonfort"* (AGN 1550 27, 7.68; UABC IIH 7.68).

Colonel Castro then expresses his confusion after having learned indirectly that the Supreme Government reportedly intended to allow General José María Blancarte to retain his post as Governor of Baja California. Pending receipt of orders to the contrary, Castro inicates that he is suspending his march to La Paz. Should official reconfirmation of his appointment not be forthcoming, he states his readiness *"to return calmly to the bosom of my family in order to await the occasion of being of some use to my country"* (IIH 1855.16, 9.8).

In December of 1855, a year after the first letter of appointment, the State Department in Mexico City sent a second official letter of appointment to Castro in Monterey, naming him Governor of Baja California (again) and informing him that his predecessor General Blancarte was to be sent to Guadalajara to await reassignment (IIH1389, 1696, 2). Castro accepted the appointment on January 20, 1856, indicating that he would sail on the next ship for La Paz *"in order to meet the obligation about which your communication gives me notice"* (IHI 1389, 1696, 3).

It is apparent that this reply crossed in transit with a document signed at La Paz by one José María Gómez. Addressing his letter to the Secretary of State in answer to the latter's note requesting that he turn over the command to Colonel Castro, Gómez laid out his reasons for refusing to do so. Indicating that the Ministry should by then have received the "Organic Statute of the Baja California Territory" dispatched on December 2, 1855, Gómez wrote: *"I suppose that your order will have already been revoked since it not only impinges on Article 5 and Article 6 [of the Statute] but also stands in contradiction to the Plan de Ayutla on which it is based"* (IIH 1856.1 9.24).

It is likely that Gómez was correct in his refusal to follow the mandate that he turn over the command of Baja California to Castro. Under the Plan de Ayutla issued after General Juan Alvarez's successful rebellion against General Santa Anna, the Territorial Assembly had been reinstituted. That body had in turn expedited the Organic Statute, which called for popular elections to elect a governor on December 3rd–the day after the new set of statutes had been dispatched to the authorities in Mexico City. According to the *Historia de Baja California* by Pablo L. Martínez, the successful candidate was José María Gómez himself (2003: 462).

It can be inferred from this information that Colonel José Castro, impeded once more from assuming the high command offered to him, may have proceeded to La Frontera in order to look after personal interests, perhaps foremost among them the aforementioned San Quintín salt extraction enterprise. Martínez accuses Castro of not having presented himself at the territorial capital of La Paz. Obviously, his sources were unaware of the document that we have just summarized indicating Gómez's refusal to relinquish command–a communication that Castro may have received while stopping at San Diego, visiting La Frontera, or changing ships at Mazatlán.

To reach La Paz overland from the north involved a long and grueling journey over desert terrain. The more desirable sea route required sailing the length of the peninsula from San Diego, rounding Cabo San Lucas, crossing the wide mouth of the Sea of Cortez to Mazatlán, then recrossing the mouth of what is also known as the Gulf of California to La Paz, located in an inlet facing the mainland some 100 miles north of Cabo San Lucas.

Given the remoteness of the territorial capital of Baja California and the impediments to timely communications, it was patently more convenient for Castro to remain at La Frontera, where he would be that much closer to his family and to his Northern California obligations. From Santo Tomás, he could conveniently oversee the salt enterprise to the south as well as journey northward to San Diego when he needed to board a steamer for San Francisco or Mazatlán.

José Castro as Vice-Governor of La Frontera

We can determine the date of José Castro's appointment as Vice-Governor of La Frontera only indirectly, thanks to a petition to and a letter from José María Esteva, General Inspector of Taxes, noting that Colonel Castro was in place as Sub-Governor in the month of August of that year. The tax Inspector was dispatched in answer to a petition from settlers requesting an audit of territorial finances. Referring to José Castro, the petition mentioned that he had replaced Sub-Prefect Francisco de Paula Ferrer as of August 1856.

Esteva's report to the Ministry of State concluded that the region's biggest problem was the result of recently organized American companies that were buying up lands with the intention of annexing them to the United States. Esteva implicated the new Vice-Governor along with **José Matías Moreno**, suspecting them both of belonging to the American concerns "perhaps without knowing their true purpose" (IIH, exp. 185617, 9.40). Placing Castro and Moreno together in this particular boat becomes highly ironic in light of subsequent events that aroused an intense mutual aversion between two men whose initial contact seems to have been cooperative.

On April 7, 1856 Castro addressed himself to Mexican President Ignacio Comonfort (Letter 1) summarizing his situation from the time of the American takeover of Alta California in 1846 and alluding to the disappointment of finding General Blancarte unwilling to vacate the promised territorial governorship. He explains that the demotion to Second Lieutenant would prevent him from meeting his financial obligations and from advancing his goal of facilitating the relocation of his Alta

California compatriots. This letter may be a de-facto petition to be appointed Sub-Prefect of La Frontera, since that is the region to which Castro would be most able attract settlers–a goal that he believed would serve the needs of the central government, as well as those of his compatriots and family members.

In Letter 4 (undated) Castro declares dejectedly to his eldest son Esteban in Monterey: *"Believing that I might remedy my position and yours, I seem to find myself in even greater difficulties"* and expresses his hope *"to be in Baja California next month, from there cross to La Frontera, and from there [sail north] to see all of you"* no later than September. Since it alludes to the withholding of his promised appointment as Governor of the Baja California territory, this undated letter may have been written from Mazatlán in early 1856.

The dates of the surviving letters in the Society of California Pioneers collection confirm that Castro remained in Baja California. Writing from Santo Tomás and Sausal de Camacho near Ensenada, he held on to his vice-governorship despite voyages north to visit family and to testify in the ongoing US Land Commission hearings.

Doyce Nunis, Jr. summarizes the situation when José Castro took office at La Frontera as follows:

> *A series of petty tyrants held office as sub-prefect for La Frontera in the interval prior to 1856. Their administrations can hardly be labeled peaceful. However, hopes for stability brightened with the appointment of Colonel José María Castro to the chief administrative post in late 1856. With his arrival on the scene, a semblance of tranquility prevailed.* (1971: 20)

Arriving at San Diego in February 1856, Father Alric was escorted to Santo Tomás by **Juan Bandini.** Doyce Nuniz Jr. believes that **José Matías Moreno** was probably also a member of this party, which was met two kilometers from town by the officers of the garrison. Father Alric described Santo Tomás as a "ruined city." Apparently, it still bore the scars of both the American military takeover of 1846-48 and the campaign to repel American filibuster William Walker, who had finally been driven over the border in early May of 1854. In descriptive detail unmatched in any other source, Fa-

ther Alric conveys the scene that would have also greeted José Castro upon his arrival a few months later:

> *The town was then occupied by about 200 soldiers, with their wives and an equal number of civilian residents. There were shops, cafes, and bars as well as gambling [dens] where men went to lose their money and often their health. There were only twenty houses, all badly built… of reeds and brushwood …covered with a thick coating of mud. They had only a ground floor without flooring or ceiling. Doors, windowpanes, and shutters…were replaced by skins of animals or by screens made from young tree branches.* (71-72)

The missionary found that *"the church was occupied by the artillery, and the mission's living quarters by the troops."* For lack of other accommodations, he was taken to the home of **Juan Mendosa,** *"who later made himself famous for various crimes"* (71).

Father Alric stated that he himself received three land grants while Castro was Vice-Governor and that he established successful farming and milling operations on the virgin lands of El Chocolate and Rancho Viejo. He reported that his wheat and corn yielded at the phenomenal rate of 900 to 1, with *"grains of wheat as large as beans"* and several shoots on each stalk of corn (77). The missionary complained that Castro, following in the footsteps of his unpopular predecessor Francisco de Paula Ferrer, requisitioned these crops for his troops in exchange for a promise of 10,000 francs that was never redeemed. *"This forced loan put me in difficulties and discouraged me,"* Father Alric wrote. *" I left the district, firmly resolved never to return"* (78). After eight months as military chaplain at Yuma on the California-Arizona border, however, the French cleric let friends from Santo Tomás lure him back.

Nunis notes that Castro sold guano and granted land to whomever had money to buy, a practice that violated Mexican government orders not to sell property to people with foreign (non-Mexican) surnames. Castro's compatriots from Alta California would not have been considered foreigners. Yet instead of *"mexicanos alti-californianos,"* a term that appears in documents from 1851, they were commonly referred to as *"ex-mexicanos,"* presumably because their formerly Mexican territory had been taken over by the Americans. This unwelcoming usage between fellow *mexicanos*, suggestive of either having rejected or been rejected by Mexico, both denoted and exacerbated the formidable internal

"Father Alric Touring La Frontera;" engraving from the 1869 Paris edition of his memoir

resistance to settling the underpopulated northern region with emigrant families of Mexican ancestry from Upper California. It can be argued that the dearth of settlers encouraged greater lawlessness in La Frontera. In the years immediately following José Castro's death, the inverse was also true.

Castro's expressed goal was to create colonies of settlers in La Frontera. Governor Espinosa had articulated this same goal to Manuel Castro and Francisco Del Castillo Negrete five years earlier. Mexican historians emphasize that Colonel Castro made concessions to foreigners: seven leagues at Jacume to Baron Mörner (also known as **Jacques A. Moerenhout**); ex-mission Santa Gertrudis to Antonio Milatovich, an associate of Mörner/Moerenhout's; three leagues at Sausal de Camacho near Ensenada to Rufus K. Porter of San Diego; plus the aforementioned grants by special dispensation to Father Alric (Moyano Pahissa in Alric, 22). Before judging his tenure in this regard, it will be necessary to survey available documents for additional grants.

In this context, it would also be pertinent to acknowledge that Mexico experienced no less than 50 presidents in the two decades between 1848 and 1868. (General Comonfort assumed office twice, General Santa Anna no less than 12 times.) Abrupt changes in political orientation–from liberal republican to conservative monarchist–determined who held office, how briefly, and which laws they chose to enforce, ignore, or replace. With this in mind, a balanced judgment must weigh Castro's sales to foreigners (three Europeans and one American) against the number made to Mexicans and "ex-Mexicans." Ironically, the primary avenue for salvaging this information is the series of reports written by Castro's avowed enemy, **José Matías Moreno**, a year after the former's death (Shipek 17-67; portions quoted below).

Because of the proximity of La Frontera and the still very recent imposition of a border *line*, many San Diegans continued to hold property on both sides and to travel frequently between the two regions. In light of La Frontera's ongoing instability, San Diego residents were understandably avid for news and information from the region. The *San Diego Union* newspaper attempted to meet that need in 1870 by publishing a series of articles written up to a decade earlier. Article #9 begins with a facetious reference to grants made by Castro during his tenure as Vice-Governor of La Frontera a decade earlier:

Castro disposed of 268,00 acres and, thinking then peradventure [that] there was no more to grant, yet [still] in his most genial mood, [he] gratified his old friend Don Juan Machado of Descanso [Baja Cali-

fornia]…with eleven leagues of the Sierra Nunca Vista–literally "the mountain [range] never seen." … Don Juan has not yet "surveyed" his prize,… thought to be hardly as substantial as the mirage above the Coronados. (Shipek 65)

Without even pausing to indent a new paragraph, the same source, now identified, is quoted in an altogether different tone:

Of [Castro's] land sales in general, Moreno observes, sourly, "Some are of vacant lands; others are grants shingled over grants. In some cases, there is no such land as that named, the names used being imaginary. The greater part are to foreigners, or to Mexicans become aliens, who never intended to live in La Frontera, but got these titles to sell for small sums at San Francisco, in the dream then indulged by both buyers and sellers that Lower California would soon be sold to the United States." (Shipek 65)

Letters 6 and 7, sent from Modesta Castro in Monterey via scribe, indicate that February and March of 1857 found her husband still at Santo Tomás. Using as his source the *Pioneer Notes* written by Judge Benjamin Hayes of San Diego, Doyce Nunis tells us that Castro at this juncture was dedicated to *"waging a campaign to impose law and order and searching assiduously for signs of filibusters."* (Hayes 93 n.31)

No account of this place and period would be complete without addressing this latter phenomenon. The term "filibuster," like "freebooter," refers to a person waging unauthorized war against a foreign state. In the mid-1800s, the hunger for new frontiers to conquer, and the desire to extend slavery's sphere in the face of northern abolitionism, prompted many brash Americans to lay claim to territory wherever they thought they could get away with it. With Congressional support, the young nation's expansionist impulse persisted throughout the 19th century–separating Panama from Colombia for the sake of building a transoceanic canal, and intervening in Spain's colonial war to make neocolonies of Cuba, Puerto Rico and Guam.

The most infamous of the American filibusters was sometime lawyer and journalist William Walker. After unsuccessfully invading mineral-rich Sonora in 1853, he returned to San Francisco to recruit for a second ex-

pedition late than same year. In November, after taking La Paz and arresting Governor Rafael Espinosa, Walker proclaimed himself President of the Republic of Lower California.

After capturing Espinosa's incoming replacement at Cabo San Lucas, Walker and his followers established a more northerly base of operations at Ensenada de Todos Santos on the Pacific Coast of La Frontera, from which he issued another proclamation in January 1854 declaring the Republic of Sonora. His proclamations heralded law, order, protection of property, and the advent of energetic individuals capable of replacing indolence with prosperity, all of which played very well in the American press.

Walker's forces began to dwindle as local opposition grew, eventually forcing him across the border to San Diego, where the only charge brought against him was failure to observe the laws of neutrality between nations. His absolution was thanks in part to the good offices of US Army Captain **Henry S. Burton**, a fact that led **Juan Bandini** and other still-prominent Californios to conclude that the American government supported filibusters even while officially condemning the practice.

Vice-Governor designate Del Castillo Negrete arrived at San Diego a month before William Walker, ostensibly to await sufficient aid to enable him to assume command at Santo Tomás. The long-awaited removal of Walker left La Frontera open for renewed internecine conflict. Juan Bandini reported that General Blancarte, then Governor of Baja California, named Juan Meléndrez military commander of La Frontera after Castillo Negrete abandoned the territory. Antonio Chávez, former second to Castillo Negrete, coveted Meléndrez's position and went to Santo Tomás with intent to kill the "usurper." Finding himself a prisoner, Meléndrez pardoned Chávez and sent him back across the border, where he continued his scheming, enlisting armed men to his cause and importuning Blancarte by letter.

On June 26, 1855 Lieutenant José Pujol, arriving in Ensenada as emissary of Blancarte, lured Meléndrez to Santo Tomás on the pretext of granting him a commission. Instead, Meléndrez found himself face to face with a firing squad and executed as a traitor, allegedly for *"having intended to sell the region to the Americans for 2,000,000 pesos."* (Moyano Pahissa in Alric, 19). This intricate power struggle–with its deceptions and betrayals, hot-button accusations, and deadly outcome

–anticipated to an uncanny degree the one to come between **Juan Mendosa** (former comrade-in-arms of Meléndrez) and **Feliciano Esparza** (former aide to José Castro) in which Colonel Castro would lose his life.

Colonel José María Oñate enjoyed a typically brief interlude as Vice-Governor, followed for part of 1856 by Captain Francisco de Paula Ferrer, who soon decamped for San Diego, as had Del Castillo Negrete before him. A section of Ferrer's report to his superiors illuminates like no other the disincentives to retaining the post of political chief (vice-governor) of La Frontera:

> *From San Ignacio to Rosario is little more than a desert and it takes ten days to cross it without cargo. Foodstuffs are not to be had anywhere. There were only four families left at the ex-Mission, to whom I had to give barley [meant for the horses] that they might not die of hunger. Eighteen leagues distant is the Port of San Quintín where the employees live who work for the foreign concern that contracts the salt production, along with a small military detachment and the administrator of the salt quarry. Six leagues further on is Rancho San Ramón, where one family lives [and] … from that town to the [border] line there is not a single inhabitant who knows how to read and write or even sign his name. …*

> *The misery of this frontier is so general that I have not seen my way clear to assign even a small monthly sum to fund a school. Whenever someone is arrested it is necessary to put him in the garrison and feed him from the soldiers' mess. Wheat flour, corn, coffee, rice and … whatever is needed for food and clothing is imported through San Diego, although in insignificant quantities... since among all the inhabitants of this frontier not 100 pesos in cash can be collected. … Today in Santo Tomás absolutely nothing can be found for sale and the families trade with one another for what they need most to nourish themselves.* (Valadés 54-57)

In early April of 1857, Castro received news from acting Governor at La Paz León Yáñez (Letter 10) that a group of filibusters had invaded the state of Sonora and were headed for the mines there. The interim official believed that the invaders might make their landing in the northern section of the Peninsula before directing themselves to La Paz. His letter urged Castro to halt the invaders at La Frontera.

Former Governor of Alta California **Juan Bautista Alvarado** addressed his letter of May 4, 1857 (Letter 11) to José Castro as Military and Political Governor of Baja California at Santo Tomás. This title echoes the contradictions manifest in the six documents from Mexican archives. These consist of one letter from 1855 and two from 1859 naming José Castro territorial Governor (*Jefe Político*); one from 1856 in which José María Gómez explains that he cannot turn over the governorship to Castro, having himself been elected to the post; one from 1859 that authorizes Governor Castro to name a Vice-Governor (*Subjefe* or *Subprefecto*); and only one–written at Sausal de Camacho near Ensenada de Todos los Santos on November 3, 1858–in which Castro as Vice-Governor (*Subjefe Político del Partido Norte de la Baja California*) rules in favor of an earlier grantee of the Valle de las Palmas concession (Pablo Herrera Carrillo Collection, IIH.1.84).

Letters from María Amparo Ruiz de Burton and José Matías Moreno

Other letters addressed to Castro at Santo Tomás in the spring of 1857 indicate that he was in residence there at that time. A communication from a private citizen, sent from San Diego on April 23, begins:

> *My Dear Sir Whom I Esteem,*
> *Various people have arrived from Santo Tomás in recent days and, although I continue to trust in the promise that you made to me, I was hoping that each one of them would deliver to me Judge Lucero's written decision regarding Gastélum's suit against me. I have been disappointed, so it seems that you have forgotten the promise you made to me about sending it on, or else the Judge forgot to do it, which I do not think probable.* (Sanchez/Pita 140-142)

In a rather imperious tone, this correspondent goes on to request that Castro write to the President of Mexico endorsing her petition for "two properties on the Colorado River" and that he back-date his endorsement to October of the preceding year(!). Making wordplay on the Judge's surname and probably his complexion as well, she asks that Castro "enlighten the dark little Lucero" on behalf of her personal interests. The letter concludes enticingly that upon performing all she requests of him and *"Above all, by forwarding a copy of the judgment, you can be sure of my gratitude and the sincere recognition of your affectionate servant – M.A. de Burton."* (Ruiz de Burton, 142)

María Amparo Ruiz de Burton was a Baja California native who married Captain **Henry S. Burton**, the US Army officer in charge of the American occupation of Baja California during the US-Mexican War. She would become important to cultural history as the author of *Who Would Have Thought It?* (1872) and *The Squatter and the Don* (1885), novels composed and published in English. According to Rosaura Sánchez and Beatriz Pita, she was the first person of Mexican origin to publish fiction in the United States. Sánchez and Pita have painstakingly assembled Ruiz de Burton's correspondence and articulated its historical context in their book *Conflicts of Interest: The Letters of María Amparo Ruiz de Burton*. Although only two out of the 200 missives from the prolific Señora de Burton are addressed to José Castro, this pair of letters suggests the range of requests that would have routinely come his way as he attempted to govern a large territory with minimal staff and support.

In her second letter, written on May 2 from San Diego, Señora de Burton begins peevishly and is quick to generalize her sense of outrage:

> *I have been informed that one of our servants, called José, is now somewhere in La Frontera, where he took refuge after running away from us, taking with him a horse with saddle and bit, all stolen. Since my husband is absent, I am compelled to write to you about this matter, confident that you will do whatever you can to apprehend this Indian rascal and take away from him what he stole.*
>
> *Unfortunately, La Frontera has for some years now been the refuge of rascals and thieves who, crossing the line, feel confident of their impunity… Do not therefore permit, Mr. Castro, this evil to continue unabated–at least while you find yourself in command, since too much as already been said in discredit of that unhappy region, and it is high time people see that it is not den of thieves.* (142)

Mrs. Burton's extensive correspondence is an unusual resource. Few women of her era in the Spanish-speaking Californias were literate, let alone sufficiently emancipated to carry on sustained correspondence with a number of prominent gentlemen. In her case, these included Mariano Guadalupe Vallejo, the most prominent of the Alta Californios during the American period, and José Matías Moreno, most influential of the Baja Californios.

Mrs. Burton was inclined to sarcasm, if not cruel slander, as when she asked Moreno in her letter of December 18, 1858: *"What do you think about our* paisanos bajacalifornianos [Baja California countrymen] *who have requested as their governor the illustrious and worthy Castro? Poor, poor us. Truly, if this is the case, I will be ashamed to be from 'Baja'"* (106). In a letter written on February 21, 1860 the aspiring society matron refers derisively to *"the annexation plans suggested to Castro's brutified head by bad whiskey and the shenanigans of that monkey Esparza"* (124). Her letter of December 28, 1858 expressing relief that Castro's appointment to the Goverrnorship of Baja California was not recognized La Paz, due to the onset of civil war in Mexico, is mentioned but not included in the Sánchez-Pita collection (123).

On June 18, 1857 Interim Governor León Yáñez sent Castro a second missive (Letter 14) from the territorial capital of La Paz reiterating his previous request for budgetary information and notifying the Vice-Governor somewhat obliquely that he will be required to pay taxes on the ten million tons of guano he had just sold out of Mazatlán. The ostensible motive of this many-layered communication, with its not-so-subtle shifts in tone was to sound the alarm regarding yet another group of filibusters who had recently departed San Francisco on a southern course.

On February 15, 1858 one José Tiburcio Castro of Ensenada, a "resident of this territory," petitioned José Castro as Political Sub-Chief of La Frontera to grant him a piece of grazing land in nearby San Antonio (Letter 16), a request that Castro approved. Despite sharing his name with Colonel Castro's deceased father and young son, this Castro was apparently no relation. (As already noted, Bancroft Library sources indicate that there were other Castro families in the region.)

A significant portion of 1858 seems to have been occupied in an ongoing dispute with **José Matías Moreno** over a petition for land that Castro had denied. In 1853 General Santa Anna had voided grants of Baja

California mission lands made by Pío Pico when he was Governor. President Porfirio Díaz would subsequently void land concessions made under his predecessors, including those allocated by President Benito Juárez. The practice of calling into question grants made by predecessors would occasion bitter disputes and prolonged court battles on both sides of the border.

Given that Moreno would succeed Castro as Vice-Governor of La Frontera, it is significant that the written record he left to history is much more extensive than Castro's. As already mentioned, many of the period newspaper articles about La Frontera collected by Shipek were written by Moreno. In addition, eighteen of Señora de Burton's collected letters, penned between 1857 and 1867, are addressed to him. Although none of his replies to her are included in her collected letters, two of his letters to other correspondents do appear (portions reproduced below). The annotated Beebe-Senkewicz bibliography indicates that Bancroft Library holds a packet of 31 letters by **José Matías Moreno** written between 1859 and 1863, and another six to him from **Juan Mendosa**, a person of importance to this account.

Two letters written by Moreno in late 1851, five years before Castro's appointment as Vice-Governor of La Frontera, shed light on the writer's attitudes and subsequent actions. The first of these was written at San Diego on November 29th to the Supreme Government of Mexico and entrusted to Don Rafael Espinosa, Governor of Baja California at the time, who was about to depart for the Mexican capital (#4639). This communication evinces Moreno's hostility toward the incipient attempt by Alta Californians to establish colonies of their displaced compatriots in Baja California. Writing from his home on the newly American side of the border, Moreno hastens to distinguish between "good Mexicans" and evil interlopers. Manuel Castro, the Alta California cousin of José Castro introduced in the opening section of this essay, apparently heads up the latter category.

Most Excellent Sir:

The undersigned, deeply interested in peace and order for his fellow citizens, the good Mexicans, as well as in the good name of the Supreme Government, does not waiver an instant in his vigilance regarding the aberrations that are committed against the legitimate authority or [in his willingness] to denounce them before the relevant party in

order that the evildoers may receive the appropriate punishment in an opportune manner.

A year and a half ago, a band of soldiers calling themselves a military colony arrived on the Baja California frontier, under the command of Captain Don Manuel Castro and Lieutenant Don José Antonio Chaves. Since this fatal incursion, the border region has been the theater of innumerable evils and grave consequences [transcendencias], both for the unfortunate inhabitants of that remote country and for the Supreme Government. And in spite of having continually written about the wrongs that have transpired and those confusedly awaited, I have never seen one measure taken to stem the impetuous torrent of these evils. It is true that I have always attributed this apathy on the part of the superior government to the enormous distance that separates the frontier region from both the national capital and that of this territory, without even a mail service to enable us to communicate effectively.

Last August we were awaiting a new authority in the guise of Political Sub-Chief and Sub-Inspector of the so-called military colony, and with this expectation our hopes for the remediation of so many evils grew. But at the same time rumors were spread by the then-chiefs of the colony that whomever the new chief turned out to be, he would not be admitted but instead thrown out on whatever pretext. To realize this pernicious goal, Captain Castro deserted Mexican territory, relegating himself to Monterey in Alta California, where he remains today, having left the command of the colony to Lieutenant Chaves.

Finally, at the beginning of October, the awaited chief arrived in the border region, he being Lieutenant Colonel Don Francisco Del Castillo Negrete. After he had delivered to Santo Tomás all the resources that he had brought for the colony, they refused to recognize his authority, injuriously casting him out on the frivolous pretext that he intended to introduce foreign troops into the region. That region, therefore, continues to be governed by a mere alcalde (combined mayor and magistrate)–English by nationality, drunken by daily custom, Tomás Bona by name–as well as by Lieutenant Chaves, both of whom have reassumed authority over everything [omnímodas facultades]. (Ruiz de Burton, 160-61; Bancroft M-M 21, box 2)

Moreno's letter goes on to accuse Lieutenant Castro of running La Frontera's affairs from Monterey, enclosing as evidence an intercepted a letter written by the latter to his delegated second ten days earlier (#4636, November 18, 1851). That letter allegedly contains instructions in "encoded sketch." Towards the conclusion of his customarily long-winded letter, Moreno offers a de facto census of the "bad Mexicans:"

I should not fail to add that, from its initial incursion to the present, the California military consists of one captain, one lieutenant, two sargeants, two corporals, and four soldiers – the latter group equivalent to Indians from the countryside since only their names, not their dress or manners, distinguish them" (Sánchez-Pita in Ruiz de Burton 162).

Like his bi-cultural friend Señora de Burton, Moreno indulges racial slurs. She calls Feliciano Esparza a *macaco* (monkey) while Moreno's reinforces a racial hierarchy in which Indians occupy the lowest rung.

His follow-up letter of December 7, 1851 (#4642), addressed to the same Governor Espinosa who was entrusted with the last letter, acknowledges Espinosa as a cousin by marriage. After registering receipt of Espinosa's letters of November 18th and 21st, Moreno turns his attention to the "unhappy Frontera region," stating with vehement indelicacy:

You will recall that my nostrils are tiny, but they can smell things from very far away, and you will also remember that my predictions have proved correct. [Manuel] Castro and Chaves have decided that the frontier region is their patrimony, and there is no doubt that for some time to come they will continue causing many and great wrongs, backed up by the extremely poor and insignificant force of that colony, as well as the influence of the pernicious Father [Suárez del] Real, who stands beside them.

Señor [Del Castillo] Negrete's authority has been formally rejected, and he has been taken prisoner based on an insidious and subversive accusation made by the colonists who, having no enemies, believe their triumph to be secure. They deceive themselves, and you will soon see their crime punished. The Proclamation that Señor Negrete made is now in print, and likewise a communiqué signed by various Mexicans, a copy of which I enclose. [With these and other documents sent to the relevant re-

cipients], I am waging silent warfare against these unsuspecting scoundrels.

… It is not possible for me to gratify the request you make in your letters that I cross the border at this time…since you know that no reason, law, or God exists there, and that justice is an exotic species grafted onto arbitrariness and whim... Aware of those evils, who would want to subject himself in cold blood to the insults and ill-treatment of those scoundrels?

In order to go to La Frontera, I would have to go armed. There are several Mexicans here who have volunteered to put themselves under my orders, armed to punish the dissidents, but I have not wanted to and shall not do so, because Señor Negrete is no longer there, and because the matter is in the hands of the Superior Government, which legally must judge everything and determine the punishment for those who are at fault…

Let us not rush or spoil things; let them instead fall from their own doings… Be patient and try to remain calm in order to stay clear of surprise attacks by those shits [carajos].

Here the Indians are threatening us, and we all go about with a rifle on our shoulder. Many folks from here and from Los Angeles have gone out to battle with them. Give my best to my cousin… (Ruiz de Burton, 163-164; Bancroft M-M 21, box 2)

Colonel Castro's "Arch Enemy"

Seven years after these hostile ruminations, **José Matías Moreno** seized the opportunity to turn his considerable energies, rhetorical and otherwise, against another Castro of Alta California origin. Letters in The Huntington Library indicate that Moreno was in Monterey as early as 1846 while serving as secretary to Governor Pío Pico. The notorious and longstanding animosity between Pico and Castro may have shaped Moreno's hostility to the latter, whom he would have known from that early date.

The sparse record of correspondence between the two men begins with a letter written on April 1, 1854, already alluded to in the opening Bancroft Library summary, in which Moreno tells Castro that he has spoken to Del Castillo Negrete regarding Castro's claim to property at Las Salinas and San Quintín, and requesting that Castro send the *expedientes* so that his property rights could be confirmed.

The Society of California Pioneers collection (Letter 9) contains a perfunctory note from Moreno to Castro dated March 15, 1857. Given the intensity of the enmity that developed between the two, however, it should not be assumed to be as innocuous as it appears on the surface. In the last lines of Letter 18 (undated and written to an unnamed superior), José Castro refers to Moreno as *"mi enemigo capital"* ("my arch enemy"). Although he refers in Letter 2 to *"enemies on all sides who have wished to confound me,"* this is the only instance in which he identifies an individual adversary.

In 1858, Moreno managed to have the Governor at La Paz authorize the removal of José Castro from his post and name José Sáenz, suggested by Moreno, as his replacement. Following what seems to have been common practice in Baja California Territory, Castro refused to vacate the post.

Whenever pressing business called him north, Vice-Governor Castro customarily named his second and sometime secretary, **Feliciano Ruiz de Esparza**, as Interim Vice-Governor. During Castro's absence in 1859, **Juan Mendosa** attempted to displace both Castro and Esparza by claiming that *he* had been named Vice-Governor of La Frontera, creating a field with four contenders: Castro, Esparza, Saénz and Mendosa. (Letter F in Part IV provides an example of how Moreno subsequently directed Mendosa's pursuit of Esparza from San Diego.)

We know that Colonel Castro was back in La Frontera in November of 1858 because of a document he prepared at Sausal de Camacho reaffirming his refusal to re-grant a piece of land in El Valle de las Palmas and commenting that *"It continues to surprise me how the Supreme Government can grant land concessions not only to the disadvantage of the people currently holding them… but also to that of the nation itself, which should be given the direct protection [of a settler population] because its geographic location requires it* (AGN 15314; IHH 18.4 1858).

Nunis credits Judge Benjamin Hayes of San Diego with the information that Castro fined José Sáenz $10,000 and George Ryerson $2000 for *"their role in the recent revolution."* In San Diego, this fine was considered *"a very arbitrary and oppressive act"* on Castro's part (104,

note 16). By this juncture the friction between Esparza and Mendosa was intensifying. In his introduction to Father Alric's memoir, Doyce Nunis summarizes "what might be called the Esparza-Mendoza affair [of] 1859-60" as follows:

The bitter animosity between these two men, both leading rival factions, commenced and ended in utter confusion. When Castro assumed command of La Frontera, he refused to honor former land grants meted out by Pío Pico in the year preceding the Mexican War…

But Castro's action, although compatible with national governmental policy, challenged lands claimed by his patron, José Matías Moreno. Furious over this affront, Moreno asked Manuel Amao, jefe político [governor] at La Paz, to remove Castro… Apparently acting on Moreno's recommendation, José Sáez [Sáenz, Saiz] an elderly [and] illiterate landowner, was designated sub-prefect. Castro bluntly refused to comply. Delay and a change in authority in the south compounded the situation. … Amao's replacement… elevated Juan Mendoza, a man of dubious reputation, but quite acceptable to Moreno.

In the meantime, because of delayed communication and confusion, Castro assumed the title of Jefe Político, in effect governor, of all Baja California [on] July 1, 1859 and appointed Feliciano Ruiz de Esparza as Subjefe Político of La Frontera, granting to him "all governing powers…during his [Castro's] absence."…Not long after, Castro left to serve as witness in land cases pending before the United States District Court in San Francisco, [where] he was an essential witness because of his long residence and official position in Alta California prior to 1848.

[Upon escaping imprisonment by Mendoza's men]…Esparza sought to legitimize the situation, …called for a popular junta to decide, …and was duly elected by acclamation… Mendoza demanded Esparza's submission to his authority. On the latter's outright refusal, the struggle for La Frontera was joined… Mendoza… launched the offensive, aided by an ill assortment of reputed criminals and supported by Californios who were desirous of repossessing their abrogated land titles… (Nunis in Alric, 26-29)

In the list of relevant documents housed in the University of Baja California Archives, a communication from August 1859 gives notice that the Supreme Government at Veracruz had named José Castro Governor of Baja California once more (IIH, 1860, 9, 16.57). Another in the National Archive, from the Interim President of the Mexican Republic in 1860, grants extraordinary powers to Governor of Baja California José Castro. No evidence has come to light indicating that Colonel Castro was formally invested in that office.

In his *Pioneer Notes*, Judge Benjamin Hayes states that on January 9, 1860 Castro arrived at San Diego on the ship *Senator* from San Francisco, ready to resume his command at La Frontera and, despite being informed of imminent danger, set forth immediately with a single servant (193). According to Father Alric, Castro arrived at La Frontera on January 14th to find that his delegated surrogate, **Feliciano Ruiz Esparza**, refused to hand over the military command (111 and n.19).

Esparza proceeded to relocate "his" troops to the former Mission Santo Domingo, 73 miles south of Santo Tomás and five miles inland from the Pacific coast, according to Alric, who continues:

> Before his departure, he recommended strongly to Castro not to release the twelve prisoners whom he [Esparza] had taken at Grulla… Castro, remaining nearly alone with few provisions [and] anxious to make friends with these individuals, soon released them on their simple promise to come to his aid in case of need. But they had scarcely left before they secretly turned against him, until finally one of them, Manuel Márquez, killed him on April 5, 1860 and fled to Sonora, where he found hospitality he did not deserve. (111-112)

Other sources erroneously give the date of Castro's death as April 14th.

The Death of José Castro

Number nine in the series of *San Diego Union* articles provides the fullest account of the death of José Castro, depicting it as the kind of wild west shoot-out that would be restaged in a thousand American pulp novels, stage plays and movies:

> In an unhappy hour of festivity at the Mission Vieja, he fell into a quarrel with Manuel Márquez. The latter returned to get arms, followed by the Governor [Castro], pistol in hand. It was the work of a few seconds. They faced each other. Castro fired twice; Marquez then fired. (Shipek 67)

Judge Hayes refers to the event as an assassination. In Spanish the verb *asesinar* means "to murder, to kill with premeditated intention" while in English it connotes the politically motivated disposal of a leader. Most English-language accounts, ignoring Hayes, echo the same ignominious refrain, maintaining that José Castro was *"shot in a drunken brawl by one of his own men."*

Like the *vox populi* circulating in Castro's native Monterey to this day claiming that he abandoned his family to start another in Baja California, this tawdry drunks-at-the-saloon scenario is more likely an instance of slander masquerading as historical fact.

Castro's declaration of the loss of California to the Americans, written to the Mexican Minister of War in September of 1846 and published in the Mexico City press a month later (reproduced in Part V), includes the names of the Alta Californians who accompanied him to Mexico in his quest for official support to mount a counterattack. Lieutenant **Manuel Márquez** ranks second in that list of sixteen men, establishing that Castro had indeed been his commanding officer in 1846. However, both Father Alric and Judge Hayes concur that in 1860 Manuel Márquez de León belonged to the camp of Castro's would-be replacement José Saénz (Moyano Pahissa in Alric 25), who for reasons already explained can be viewed as a delegate of **José Matías Moreno**.

The *San Diego Union* article (apparently not in this instance penned by Castro's "arch enemy") goes on to praise the deceased Vice-Governor with dubious effusiveness and to exonerate Márquez:

> The loss of Governor Castro is justly regretted as a calamity to the frontier. He possessed superior executive qualities, his plans were indisputably pure and patriotic, and his disposition personally toward all men was kind and amiable. Without doubt he had revolved in his mind the project of getting rid, by summary blow, of the outlaws that thronged around him, but it must have originated with Esparza. For such a thing Castro really was, to use a simple word, too good-natured; all who knew him will recognize this trait in him… His design had

been to organize a military guard, for which purpose had had [brought] with him [from American California] twenty uniforms… Esparza was ever ready and urgent; the Governor, dubious and dilatory… The secret heart of Castro revolted from the bloody act, and so it was delayed from day to day. It is understood among near friends of the Governor that he thought well of and trusted Márquez, who in turn was a strong partisan of Castro, and this relation between them, coupled with the actual circumstances of their difficulty, tends to relieve the unfortunate man from the change of assassination. (Shipek 67-68)

Father Alric states that upon Castro's death, *"civil authority passed immediately into the hands of Esparza, who had already reserved to himself the military command and had only relinquished the civil with regret."* Just two weeks later, on April 20th, Esparza called an urgent meeting for the election of a provisional Governor (112-113). The results of the election surprised no one. As Father Alric explains:

The soldiers whom he was paying, at the expense of local residents, having the greatest interest in keeping him voted first, and naturally gave their votes to Esparza; it would have been very imprudent of the rest of the electors not to follow their example. (113)

Esparza avenged Castro's death with the capture and execution of a dozen men. Although Father Alric *"[made] it very clear how very criminal [Esparza and his henchmen] were in my eyes,"* his entreaties only managed to save one life (114-116). From the previous November, according to Father Alric, Esparza had *"become unrecognizable–he who, before his arrest at Santo Tomás [by Mendosa's forces] was endowed with an excellent character and a probity which would have met any test, suddenly becomes cruel as a tiger, no longer respect[ing] the welfare of others and dream[ing] only of vengeance"* (111).

Juan Mendosa and José Sáenz reportedly recruited a number of Indians to their faction, then divided into groups and began taking prisoners and plundering ranches along their separate ways to track down Esparza. Alric mentions the family of one Don J.M. Castro from Santo Tomás who fled with *"a cart on which were his wife, two suckling infants, and his father, eighty-five years of age."* Along with a neighbor family named Díaz, the group *"were all leaving for Upper California"* until Juan Mendosa reportedly confiscated the goods,

arrested the men, and left the remainder of the party *"to continue on foot for the forty miles still to go to San Diego, with no provisions whatever…"* (123)

Arriving at Padre Alric's house, Mendosa's men *"seized or destroyed everything they could get their hands on. They looked for me carefully, but fortunately I had been warned in time by a wild Indian who had left the band, and I escaped on horseback, taking the road to San Diego"* (129-130).

When he fired the bullet that killed José Castro, Manuel Márquez was already under indictment for murder at Los Angeles (Nunis in Alric 112 n.22). According to Clelland's classic history of southern California, *The Cattle on a Thousand Hills*, in 1862 a "desperado" of the same name was the leader of a band of "robbers and murderers [who] infested the region between San Juan Capistrano and Santa Ana." (71)

Feliciano Ruiz de Esparza reportedly fled to Guadalupe Island with his family and another in-law family in March 1861. He died there under mysterious circumstances some time before the rest of the group, clad only in goatskins, were rescued as castaways by a passing ship.

Juan Mendosa, leader of the anti-Esparcistas, would eventually be gunned down on the other side of the line by the son-in-law of his former employer. Colonel Cave Johnson Couts was a prosperous cattle rancher who had acquired Rancho Guajome as a wedding gift from Abel Stearns upon his marriage to **Juan Bandini**'s daughter Ysidora. His profits from selling beef to the Forty-niners enabled him to acquire the Buena Vista and Vallecitos de San Marcos ranches. Known for his explosive temper, Couts was twice indicted for violence to Indians and twice more for the murder of Californios. In October 1865, he was exonerated by the San Diego court, Judge Benjamin Hayes defending, for shooting Mendosa in the back the preceding February (Alric 136-132 n.23; Sánchez and Pita 127). Rufus K. Porter wrote the report for the *San Francisco Evening Bulletin*.

La Frontera After Castro

Once José Castro was permanently removed from the scene in 1860, La Frontera exploded in an orgy of violence, rapacity, and terror that by some accounts resulted in an 80% reduction in its population by the end of the following year. It is no small tribute to this staunch, politically liberal Californio to conclude that, when called to Baja California to preside over a roiling cauldron of conflicting interests and passions, he managed to keep the lid on during four long years.

Among the far-flung fragments comprising the puzzle of José Castro's Baja California years, many of the retrievable ones seem to have been shaped by his enemies, particularly the energetic and conniving **José Matías Moreno**. Having at first assisted but later determined to oppose and undermine Castro, this "loyal Baja Californian" would not only assume his enemy's office but also manage to conduct the affairs of La Frontera "long-distance" from his home base in San Diego.

In March 1861, Moreno was named Vice-Governor of La Frontera. President Benito Juárez not only made the appointment but sent troops to enforce the installation. Moreno's term turned out to be very brief. Lack of support from the central government–a complaint endemic to the colony at least from the era of its founder Manuel Castro a decade earlier–was the unconvincing explanation offered for his resignation one year later.

Father Alric's summary of Moreno's term invokes a familiar litany of complaints:

> *His partisans hastened to return to support him as best they could, but their satisfaction did not last long because, following in the footsteps of almost all of his predecessors, he seemed to take despotism as the rule of conduct. In fact, he…consumated the despoliation of a great number of lawful [land] owners, then seized and sold a treasury of silverware, all that remained of what had belonged to the border missions. In a word, he overwhelmed all the honorable part of the population with vexations, and aroused great animosity toward himself, until finally a* pronunciamiento [public declaration] *forced him to take flight.* (135)

On June 19, 1861 Moreno was arrested in San Diego by the US Marshall. Charged with violating international laws of neutrality during the conflict between Esparza and Mendosa, he was placed under a $10,000 bond and tried three days later (Nunis in Alric 135-36 n.20). Set at liberty possibly by negligence, a bitter Moreno turned his back on the city of San Diego where he had resided for so many years and relocated with his family to Rancho Guadalupe in La Frontera.

As previously stated, this desirable property had formerly belonged to one of Moreno's declared enemies, **Juan Bandini** of San Diego. Moreno had been instrumental in prompting the Juárez regime to declare all previous allocations of land in Baja California null and void. A direct beneficiary of this ruling and the opportunities available in its aftermath, he purchased Bandini's former rancho for $3000 in 1863.

The man who reviled Bandini and Santiago Argüello, another prominent *altacaliforniano* based in San Diego, for allegedly having welcomed the US takeover himself became the agent of American capitalists barely fifteen years later. In this capacity, Moreno would also revisit the salt quarries at San Quintín held earlier by partners José and Manuel Castro, **Juan Bautista Alvarado**, and **Jacques Moerenhout**, helping Grisar Byrnes and Company acquire (or re-acquire) the concession in 1866. The name Grisar appears in Letter 2, suggesting that the company's involvement dated from the Castro years.

A contentious era predictably breeds opportunism. However, José Matías Moreno and his longtime correspondent María Amparo Ruiz de Burton–who shared roots in La Paz, loss of their fathers at an early age, a relentless drive to transcend the genteel poverty that dogged them, and an acid disdain for José Castro –would have been contenders of note no matter how crowded the field. Masters of manipulation, they were not above the unscrupulously self-serving deployment of their considerable writing skills and assiduously cultivated personal contacts.

In 1857, as noted above, Señora de Burton instructed Vice-Governor José Castro to backdate her presidential petition for property along the Colorado River. Her machinations subsequently lured two other Mexican officials, Presidents Benito Juárez and Porfirio Díaz, into validating an early land title on which she had brazenly altered the quantity of parcels awarded from "2" to "5" (Sánchez/Pita 403).

Rosaura Sánchez and Beatriz Pita, who dedicated immense scholarly effort to understanding Mrs. Burton's life and epistolary-literary output, judge her rationale for such actions as "specious." They conclude, *"Seen even in the most generous of lights [she adopted] a squatter's mentality"* (404) as she *"navigated between dodging creditors and pursuing claims, learning to use even debts for her own interest"* (140). Her unchecked opportunism even prompted her own mother to bring suit against her. As the same authors note, having *"rejected any political intervention of the United States in Mexico [she] was only too willing to introduce foreign capital to produce 'progress'"* (126).

According to Judge Benjamin Hayes, Moreno was *"celebrated for intrigue and management and… always had considerable influence in Mexico"* (236, cited in Sánchez/Pita 125). Judging Father Alric's assessment of both Moreno and Judge Hayes as tinted by favoritism toward Juan Bandini, Sánchez and Pita prefer to view Moreno as *"an intelligent, well-read Californio, a progressive thinker,…without capital and therefore ill-equipped to see his projects through"* (128) while acknowledging *that "like María Antonia Ruiz de Burton, [he] was not above securing, out of the spoils of contested lands and questionable grants, lands for himself"* (133).

Sustained scrutiny of the roles played by Ruiz de Burton and Moreno prompts the following question: Can Castro's contention that in working to populate the border region he was also benefiting the interests of the Mexican nation be dismissed as similarly self-serving?

Conclusion

The recorded history of Nueva California settlement is generally traced to the simultaneous missionary and military campaigns of 1769, respectively led by Father Junípero Serra and Captain Gaspar de Portolá. Intrinsic to the writing of history is the pursuit of more remote beginnings. The history of Upper or New California, properly reconstructed, must be traced backward and southward to La Paz and to 1533, when the designation "California" was first applied. As W. Michael Mathis asserts in his foreword to the bibliographical guide by Beebe and Senkewicz, *"An accurate, cohesive, and complete history of California … must be evolved chronologically from its foundation in Baja California"* (xi).

Since 1851, an arbitrary line of demarcation has divided peninsular from mainland California, but the overriding reality is that the lived history of the region, in both human and natural realms, has been conjoined for hundreds if not thousands of years. This investigation into the life and career of Colonel José Castro inevitably brings the two Californias into convergence once again.

Having rejected American citizenship, Castro accepted the positions offered him in Baja California at considerable cost to self and loved ones. Showing uncommon forbearance in the face of two countermanded appointments, he brought with him to the "other California" a patriotic zeal to rebuild war-battered Mexico, still vulnerable to opportunistic forces without and within. He also brought seasoned leadership and administrative skills, civic as well as military, and a vision of resettlement arguably beneficial not only to repatriating Alta Californians but also to the territorial needs of the peninsula and the broader welfare of the Mexican nation. Castro could hardly have foreseen that, in the decade between 1858 and 1868, Mexico would undergo a wrenching period of civil war (as would the United States) followed by an invasion by the imperial army of France that would place Austrian-born Prince Maximilian at the helm of the nation.

History is written by the victors–and by those who manage to survive a little longer. Even historians removed from their subjects by a century or more are not immune to partisan motivations. What is striking about Colonel José Castro and his predecessor Manuel de Jesús Castro is that, in the nearly 150 years since the former's death, no researcher has been inclined to reconstruct either's (hi)story. The void has remained unfilled even after the challenges posed by such eminent historians as Bancroft in 1886 and Nunis in 1971.

Having resisted the US takeover, and deploring the treatment to which their compatriots were subjected at American hands, Alta Californios José and Manuel Castro opted at different junctures to relocate to "the other California." Both Californias derived their population from the same roots: soldiers from the Mexican mainland, principally the villages of Sonora and Sinaloa, who accompanied the Spanish priests–Jesuit, Franciscan, or Dominican–in their missionary endeavors, mixing here and there with Native populations.

Manuel Castro served in Baja California from 1848 to 1852, returning north well before his cousin José departed for his first, unfulfilled appointment in early 1855. Manuel lived out a long life in the land of his birth while José met an early death in a second homeland far from family. In choosing the Mexican option when he did, each man demonstrated nationalist loyalty–as José Castro expressed more than once in his surviving writings. When he proudly agreed to "consecrate my final days" to serving the nationality he had chosen to reaffirm, one wonders if he had any inkling of how that decision risked cutting short his final days.

The Castro cousins would presumably not have been surprised by disregard or distortion on the part of American chroniclers, but they might have hoped for a more sympathetic hearing from Baja Californians and fellow Mexicans. Yet the pair were viewed as northerners from an unfamiliar province, relocating to Baja California at a time when colliding waves of contending forces were engulfing not only the isolated peninsula but also the vast Mexican mainland. (Against the tally of 50 heads of state in a span of 20 years, Baja Californians could claim 56 territorial governors during the same period.) As much or more than the sectionalized United States of America, mid-19th century Mexico was a nation undergoing construction/destruction/reconstruction in a vertiginous, contradictory struggle. Under such precarious circumstances, the Castro cousins would have been naïve to hope their conduct and achievements might be regarded by either *mexicanos* or *bajacalifornianos* with an unjaundiced eye.

The ancient Nahuatl language of central Mexico has a term for the in-between space in which the pair of cousins found themselves, literally and figuratively. *Nepantla* means the land of neither-nor. Among those displaced by the conquering Americans and the almost immediate influx of avid gold-seekers from around the world, Manuel and José Castro would be self-servingly perceived by the newcomers to Alta California as part of an "indolent," "unenterprising" past that was being justifiably superceded. As citizens of Mexico who dedicated themselves to the settlement and protection of one of that country's most underpopulated regions,

they would be perceived in Baja California as scheming outsiders beholden to the very same American and European capitalists who were so avidly displacing them. Nowhere at home on either side of the border, they could scarcely have hoped for benign regard from posterity.

By assuming the military and political posts offered to them in La Frontera, the pair consigned themselves to a location that, although a coveted pawn in a number of competing geopolitical games, was also *peripheral* to the fourth degree: peripheral to the center of power in central Mexico as both northwesterly and peninsular, peripheral to the United States as under-endowed in comparison to their recent Alta California acquisition, peripheral to Southern Californians as their unruly flank, and peripheral to the territorial capital at La Paz as the peninsula's most remote administrative unit.

Since the wrenching events of the 1960s involving mass protests and harsh repression in both the United States and Mexico, the focus of scholarly inquiry has significantly shifted from the mainstream to the marginalized, from center to periphery, from the privileged to the disempowered. Overlapping waves of scholarship in Chicano/Latino letters, leaders, and antecedents, as well as in the history of the Californias and the American Southwest, have immensely expanded available knowledge. This attempt to reevaluate José Castro and his cousin Manuel may be construed as a "local" phenomenon, having originated in their long-ago hometown of Monterey, but its goal is to reestablish their place in a broader, more nuanced scope of history and binational dialogue.

Dr. Angela Moyano Pahissa is the author of twelve books and numerous essays on the history of the United States and on US-Mexican relations in the 19th century. During her 21-year tenure at the National University in Mexico City (UNAM), she held a Fulbright Fellowship to the University of Chicago (1985-86) and a four-year research appointment at the University of Baja California in Tijuana. Since 1998 she has been a member of the faculty of the University of Querétaro, one of the magnificent colonial-era cities along Central Mexico's "Silver Route."

Dr. Julianne Burton-Carvajal translated Professor Moyano's contribution and expanded it with additional research and writing. The two scholars have been in contact since 2003, when they met in Querétaro through the intermediary of Montereyans Yve and José Rafael Ramos, who also enjoy a home there. After producing sixteen issues of **Noticias de Monterey** *since 2003, Burton-Carvajal relinquishes the editorship with this 50th anniversary volume.*

Traditional Baja California construction provides maximum shade while inviting refreshing breezes

Sources for José Castro in Baja California

Letters written to and by Colonel José Castro:
Alice Phelan Sullivan Library, Society of California Pioneers, San Francisco; Bancroft Library at the University of California, Berkeley; Archivo General de la Nación, Mexico City; Instituto de Investigaciones Históricas, Universidad Autónoma de Baja California, Tijuana.

Abbé Henry-J.-A. Alric. *Sketches of a Journey on the Two Oceans and to the Interior of America and of a Civil War in Northern Lower California*. Translated from the French by Norah E. Jones. Edited with introduction and notes by Doyce B. Nunis, Jr. Los Angeles: Dawson's Book Shop, 1971. Baja California Travel Series #24.
--*Apuntes de un viaje por los dos océanos, el interior de América y de una guerra civil en el norte de la Baja California*. Translated from the French by Tomás Segovia. Prologue by Angela Moyano Pahissa. Notes by Doyce B. Nunis Jr., selected by Aidé Grijalva. With an appendix of 21 documents related to José Matías Moreno. Mexico City and Tijuana: Secretaría de Educación Pública and Universidad Autónoma de Baja California, 1995. Colección Baja California: Nuestra Historia #9.

Ellen C. Barrett, compiler. *Baja California: 1535-1956*. Los Angeles: Bennett and Marshall, 1957.

Rose Marie Beebe and Robert Senkewicz, compilers. *Guía de manuscritos concernientes a Baja California en las colecciones de la Biblioteca Bancroft / Guide to the Manuscripts Concerning Baja California in the Collections of the Bancroft Library*. Berkeley: University of California Library, 2002. (The Foreword by W. Michael Mathis and the Introduction by the compilers appear in both English and Spanish; listings appear in Spanish only.)

María Amparo Ruiz de Burton. *Conflicts of Interest: The Letters of María Amparo Ruiz de Burton*. Edited with commentary by Rosaura Sánchez and Beatrice Pita. Houston: Arte Público Press, 2001.

Harry W. Crosby. *Last of the Californios*. San Diego: Copley, 1981.
-- *Gateway to Alta California: The Expedition to San Diego, 1789*. San Diego: Sunbelt Publications, 2003.

Robert Glass Clelland. *The Cattle on a Thousand Hills*. San Marino: The Huntington Library, 1941, 1990.

Neal Harlow. *California Conquered: The Annexation of a Mexican Province, 1846-1850*. Berkeley: University of California Press, 1982.

Ulíses Urbano Lasépas. *Historia de la colonización de la Baja California y decreto de 10 de marzo de 1857*. Tijuana: Universidad Autónoma de Baja California. Colección Baja California: Nuestra Historia #8.

Pablo L. Martínez. *A History of Lower California*. Mexico: Editorial Baja California, 1960. Republished as *Historia de Baja California*, 2003.

W. Michael Mathes. "Incunables Peninsulares: Los primeros impresos bajacalifornianos." *Calafia* VII: 37, 1992.

Robert Ryal Miller. *Juan Alvarado, Governor of California, 1836-1842*. Norman: University of Oklahoma Press, 1998.

Angela Moyano Pahissa. *La resistencia de las Californias a la invasión norteamericana (1846-1848)*. Mexico: CONACULTA. 1992.
--*Mexico y Estados Unidos: origenes de una relacion, 1819-1861*. Universidad Autonoma de Nuevo Leon y de Quéretaro, 2nd ed. 2002.

Antonio María Osio. *The History of Alta California: A Memoir of Mexican California*. Translated, edited, annotated and biographical sketches prepared by Rose Marie Beebe and Robert M. Senkewicz. Madison: University of Wisconsin, 1996.

Andrew F. Rolle. *An American in California: The Biography of William Heath Davis, 1822-1909*. San Marino: The Huntington Library, 1956, 1980.

Florence C. Shipek, ed. *Lower California Frontier: Articles from the* San Diego Union, 1870. Los Angeles: Dawson's Book Shop, 1965. Baja California Travel Series #2.

Adrián Valadés. *Historia de la Baja California 1850-1880*. Mexico: National University (UNAM) Instituto de Investigaciones Históricas, 1974.

Msgr Francis J. Weber. *The Missions and Missionaries of Baja California*. Los Angeles: Baja California Travel Series, 1968.

Marjorie T. Wolcott, ed. *Pioneer Notes from the Diaries of Judge Benjamin Hayes, 1849-1875*. Los Angeles, 1920.

Montereyana
in typical dress

Part IV
Letters from the Huntington Library

José Matías Moreno, successor to Colonel Castro in La Frontera

Eight Letters from the Huntington Library, 1853-1868

The letters in this section were discovered during three intensive days at the Huntington Library in San Marino, California. Placing them in a separate section recognizes their different provenance and enlarged time frame. It is also appropriate because they were discovered after the conclusions to Part III had been formulated. Representing the key players in the Baja California saga, these letters substantiate those conclusions. However, because this publication is the first to map the Baja California chapter of José Castro's career, it is impossible to predict how many other pertinent sources remain to be located. It therefore seems fitting that the different sections of this first Castro monograph recapitulate the trajectory of the discoveries made and conclusions drawn—findings that future researchers may corroborate or dispute.

*As transcribed and translated here, with kind permission from The Huntington Library, letters from Colonel Castro's predecessor Francisco Javier Del Castillo Negrete, his associates **Feliciano Ruiz de Esparza**, **Juan Bandini** and **José Matías Moreno**, his incoming superior Governor Ramón Navarro, his cousin Manuel de Jesús Castro, along with one penned by Castro himself, are presented in chronological order. As in Part II, a phrase from each letter serves as title, and a brief commentary precedes the modernized Spanish transcription and English translation.*

Letters A, D and E are written in opaque "officialese." Rather than smoothing over their nearly impenetrable syntax, the translations endeavor to be as faithful as possible to the style of the writer, thereby acknowledging their linkage between obfuscation and power.

San Diego in 1850; lithograph by G.C. Conts

Letter A: "You Will Provide without Excuse or Pretext the Assistance that Is Asked of You, Both Now and in the Future…"

(Abel Stearns Collection, Box 15, #49)

*This requisition from Francisco Javier Del Castillo Negrete, Military and Political Commander of the Northern Region (La Frontera), to the administrator of Rancho Valle de San Rafael, the Baja California ranch belonging to **Abel Stearns** of Los Angeles, was written a year after **Captain Manuel de Jesús Castro** returned to Upper California and nearly three years before his elder cousin José Castro assumed his post as Military and Political Sub-Chief (Vice-Governor) of La Frontera. Finding the situation there untenable–due to the presence of William Walker and his fellow filibusters, among other factors–Castro's predecessor Del Castillo Negrete later withdrew to San Diego, where he could await re-enforcements from México in comfort if not in confidence. This communication, written at San Rafael B.C., exemplifies how La Frontera residents and property owners were routinely taxed with supplying one fighting force or another. The involuted syntax, a sign of Del Castillo's superior educational level and social status, stands in marked contrast to Colonel Castro's direct, unembellished style.*

---

17 diciembre de 1853

Esta Frontera ha sido invadida por una expedición piratical precedente de San Francisco, y necesitándose algun auxilio de bestias para montar la fuerza que ha de representar a fin de conservar el honor nacional y defender los intereses nacionales y extranjeros existentes en el país, y siendo usted encargado de la administración de los bienes de este rancho propio del Co[mpañero] americano don Abel Stearns, que como buen súbdito americano debe procurar sostener la opinión de la nación y proseguir a los malvados que desacreditan el buen nombre que goza aquella gran República. Cumpliendo también con lo que tiene prevenido el Excelentísimo Señor Presidente de los Estados Unidos, dará usted sin excusa ni pretexto los auxilios que se le pidan, tanto ahora como en lo sucesivo, para dicho objeto pues redunda en beneficio común y soseniente del decoro de ambos gobiernos. Advirtiendo a usted desde ahora que el comisionado para recibirlos se presentará con orden escrita de este Gobierno al pie de la cual firmará el recibo de los que usted imparta cuando él la presente.

Dios y Libertad.
San Rafael.
Del Castillo Negrete.

Baja California scene drawn by H. Rimbault in the late 1840s.

December 17, 1853

This Frontier has been invaded by a piratical expedition originating in San Francisco, and being in need of some assistance [in the form of] beasts upon which to mount the force that is destined to represent [this region] with the goal of preserving the national honor and defending the national and foreign interests that exist in this country, and being that you are charged with the administration of the assets of this ranch belonging to the American Comrade Don Abel Stearns, who as a good American subject should try to maintain the [good] opinion of the nation and prosecute the evil-doers who discredit the good name enjoyed by the Republic. Following also what His Excellency the Lord President of the United States has foreseen, you will provide without excuse or pretext the assistance that is asked of you, both now and in the future, for the sake of said goal, since it redounds upon the common benefit and maintains the decorum of both governments. Advising you from now on that the [individual] commissioned to receive [the requistioned items] will present himself with a written order from this Government, which he will sign on the bottom in receipt of [what you will] grant whenever he may present it.

God and Liberty
San Rafael
Del Castillo Negrete

Letter B: "The Only Thing that Moves Me to Convey These Guidelines to You Is [the Goal of] Avoiding Difficulties" (Abel Stearns Collection, Box 7, #38).

*Baja Clifornia property owner **Juan Bandini**, writing from his home in San Diego, offers advice and words of caution to the newly arrived José Castro in La Frontera. Castro's avid investigation of the region's mining potential, consistent with his era's obsession with discovering deposits of minerals and gems, was presumably motivated by the need to replenish official coffers.*

Señor don José Castro
Subjefe Político, Santo Tomás

S[an] Diego
1 diciembre de 1856

Querido amigo,

Tengo a la vista la aplicable de usted fechada en Santo Tomás el 3 del corriente [*sic*] y que recibí ayer. Mucho me alegro del buen resultado que le ha dado la mina del Corralito en San Antonio, y yo siempre tenía esta presunción no obstante el mal éxito de dos ensayos mandados [a] hacer en San Francisco. Como deseo que las minas se trabajen y que éste es el principal motivo de mi establecimiento en [La] Frontera desde el año 1845, tendré mucho placer ver al fin que esta empresa tome el impulso que yo por desgracia, a pesar de mis esfuerzos, no he podido alcanzar, no obstante haber consumido bastante capital para conseguirlo.

Pero amigo, por la misma razón que estoy interesado en que se fomente el ramo de minería, me tomo la libertad de indicar a usted que es preciso prever para lo futuro. Ese mineral fue denunciado y trabajado, y si llega a ser bueno, no faltará cómo introducirse los antiguos poseedores, porque es verdad que el país ha presentado inconvenientes que no se han podido superar.

No crea usted que yo soy interesado, pues nunca quise asociarme por no tener inclinación al trabajo de minas de plata, y lo único que me mueve a dirigir a usted estas indicaciones es evitar dificultades. Las ordenanzas de minería dicen el modo y [la] forma a que se ha de proceder para denunciar vetas minerales, ya sea en cerro virgen, ya [sean] las vetas muchas y abandonadas, y faltándose a los requisitos que exige la ley, condena el derecho de adquisición.

Aún hay más. Creo que usted debe tener cuidado de no figurar como denunciante por razón de su carácter público hoy en su distrito, porque entiendo que es un inconveniente. Quiero copiarle parte del Artículo 2º y el 3º del título 7 de la ordenanza publicada el año 1846. [El] artículo 2º también prohibe a los regulares de ambos usos el que puedan denunciar ni de alguna manera adquirir para sí ni para sus conventos o [ni] comunidades minas algunas. El artículo 3º dice [que] tampoco podrán tener minas los Gobernadores, intendentes, conseguidores, alcaldes mayores, ni otros cualquiera justicias de los reales o asiento[s] de minas, ni menos los escribanos de ellos, pero [se] les concede el que puedan tenerlas en distinto territorio del de su jurisdicción.

Por esto verá usted que mi presunción no deja de fundarse en pruebas que, puestas en acción, pueden dar un resultado en contra de sus deseos e intereses. Yo si lo digo a usted es para que del mejor modo posible obre usted sobre el particular para evitar los disgustos que pueden sobrevenir.

Mucho empeño tengo en que se trabajen las minas, pero es cierto que deseo [que] sea sin tropiezos, para que cada uno disfrute de su trabajo con toda libertad y paz. Cuando hablo a usted con tanta seguridad de la mina del Corralito, cuyo nombre está registrado bajo el… [elipsis en el original] es porque tengo en mi poder documentos que lo acredita.

Y repito a usted que no tengo ni he querido tener parte en ese mineral que hoy llama usted la esmeralda. Dios quiera que su riqueza corresponda a la brillantez de su nuevo nombre. Todo lo que hay es que está dentro de los límites de mi rancho y muy inmediato al jacal y corral que establecí en San Antonio. Esto siempre será más favorable a la persona de usted por las consideraciones y aprecio que le profesa su [abreviación ilegible].

JB

Señor Don José Castro
Vice-Governor, Santo Tomás

S[an] Diego
December 1, 1856

Dear Friend,

I have in front of me yours dated from Santo Tomás on the 3rd of this [*sic*] month, which I received yesterday. I am very happy about the good result you have gotten from the Corralito mine at San Antonio, and I always had this supposition despite the bad outcome of the two assays sent to San Francisco for analysis. Since I wish for the mines to be worked, because this is the principal motive of my establishment in [La] Frontera since 1845, I will take considerable pleasure in seeing this enterprise at last assume the momentum that unfortunately, despite my efforts, I have not been able to obtain—even though I have consumed quite a bit of capital in attempting to achieve it.

But Friend, for the same reason that I am interested in the promotion of the mining branch [of the local economy], I take the liberty of reminding you that it is essential to look out for the future. That mineral [deposit] was [already] claimed and worked, and if it turns out to be good, the former claimants will not fail to find a way to reintroduce themselves, because it is true that [this] country has presented insurmountable obstacles.

Don't think that I am an interested party, since I never wished to associate myself [with that branch of mining] because I lacked the inclination for working silver mines, and the only thing that moves me to convey these guidelines to you is [the goal of] avoiding difficulties. The mining regulations indicate the mode and manner according to which one has to proceed in order to claim mineral veins, whether they be in virgin mountain ranges or in already mined and abandoned areas, and the right of acquisition shall be refused if the requirements demanded by the law are not met.

Furthermore, I believe that you should be careful not to figure as a claimant due to your public role in the district today, because I understand that this is an obstacle. I want to copy for you the 2nd and 3rd articles of Title 7 of the 1846 public ordinance. Article 2 also prohibits the possibility of claiming–or in any manner acquiring for oneself or one's community, religious or secular–any mines whatsoever. Article 3 also prohibits governors, commanders, procurers, mayors, magistrates [as well as] members of mining tribunals and their scribes from acquiring mining interests, but it does concede that they may have them in another territory outside of their own jurisdiction.

Thus you see that my supposition does not fail to base itself on actual proofs which, put into action, can produce a result contrary to your wishes and interests. And if I say this to you, it is so that you might proceed in the best possible way in this matter in order to avoid any unpleasantness.

I am very determined that the mines should be worked, but it's true that I want this to happen without any slip-ups, in order that each person may enjoy the fruits of his labor in liberty and peace. When I speak to you with such certainty about the Corralito mine, a name that is registered under the … [ellipses in original], it is because I have in my possession the documents to prove it.

And I reiterate to you that I do not have, nor have I wished to have, any part of that mineral that you are now calling "emerald." God willing, may its brilliance correspond to that of its new name. All [that you have found] is within the boundaries of my ranch and very near the barn and corral that I set up at San Antonio. This will always be more favorable to your person due to the special consideration and regard that your [illegible abbreviation] professes toward you.

JB

Lithograph of San Francisco in 1849 based on a drawing by Henry Firks

Letter C: "I Want to Work, But in Order To Do So, I Need an Additional Favor from You" *(Abel Stearns Collection, #60, Box 15)*

*This communication from Colonel Castro to **Juan Bandini** demonstrates that in the first several months of his assignment to La Frontera, Castro invested a good deal of effort and expense in various mining enterprises—among them silver, emeralds, and salt—and provides a partial explanation of why the latter enterprise failed. Antonio L. Sosa reappears in Letter F as an agent of Jose Matias Moreno and his delegate ,Juan Mendosa.*

E[nsenada] de Todos los Santos
October 22, 1857

Señor don Juan Bandini, San Diego

Amigo y Señor,

Habrá usted sabido que cinco meses trabajé personalmente en las Salinas de San Quintín y el resultado fue quedar endrogado en más de tres mil pesos. [Antonio L.] Sosa me engañó y yo perdí diez yuntas de bueyes que tenía fletadas. Se me murieron y entre ellas la de usted. (Arreglaremos esto.)

Quiero trabajar, pero para esto necesito de un favor más de usted y es el siguiente. Sé que tiene usted muchos burros y si me vende veinte a bien precio y plazo para pagárselos, o me los presta, entonces yo podré acarrear trescientas toneladas de sal que tengo fuera de las lagunas. Veinte burros le suponen a usted muy poca cosa y con ellos salgo yo de apuros.

Vamos a otra cosa: estoy en este punto establecido y he habilitado el Puerto provisionalmente. Estamos ahora más cerca y espero que me escriba.

Toda mi consideración a su apreciable familia y usted mande a su Servidor y amigo.

[signed] José Castro

E[nsenada] de Todos los Santos
October 22, 1857

Señor Don Juan Bandini, San Diego

Friend and Sir,

You are probably already aware that I myself worked in the salt flats at San Quintín for five months and the result has been to fall 3,000 pesos in debt. [Antonio L.] Sosa deceived me and I lost ten team of oxen that I had hired. They all died on me–yours among them. (We will work this out.)

I want to work, but in order to do so, I need an additional favor from you, and it is as follows. I know that you have many burros, and if you can sell me twenty of them at a good price with a long term for repayment, or if you lend them to me, then I will be able to transport the 300 tons of salt that I now have out of the lagoon. Twenty burros are but a small matter to you, and with them I can get out of these straits.

Moving on to the next matter, I have now established myself in this location and have provisionally outfitted the Port. We are now nearer to one another and I hope that you will write to me.

[I send] all my consideration to your worthy family, and please direct your Servant and friend

[signed] José Castro

Letter D: "The Simplest Thing Is to Remove the Cause in order to Put an End to the Effects" (CT 1686, Author's retained copy, A.L.S.)

Although the handwriting in this letter to incoming Governor of Baja California Ramón Navarro is inconsistent with other examples of **José Matías Moreno**'s *correspondence, the overblown diction and syntax are characteristic of his style of expression. Frequent grammatical errors suggest that this copy was made by someone who was unfamiliar with correct Spanish, but also—to judge by several words scratched into the paper as if in frustration or anger—deeply engaged with the effort. The transcription renders the letter into grammatically correct Spanish. The translation respects the run-on sentences of the original as well as the curious elision of personal agency (ambiguous verb forms, omission of personal pronouns) that is equally characteristic of Moreno's writing style.*

This letter exemplifies Moreno's ongoing efforts to manage the affairs of Baja California Territory. In this chilling example, he ingratiates himself with the newly named Governor of Baja California Territory (or his successor), predisposes the Governor against Colonel Castro by quoting the latter's alleged (invented?) attacks on the new official, mocks Castro's authority and accuses him without basis of engineering the American takeover of La Frontera. Moreno urges the Governor to expand his own political and military powers in order to dispose of Castro without the inconvenient obligation of transporting him to the capital for trial, followed by an unrealistic request for fifty troops—preferably led by a "native son" (like himself).

Jefe Político don Ramón Navarro, La Paz
29 julio de 1859

Muy Señor mío y de mi respeto,

Aunque no tengo el honor de conocer a usted personalmente, me basta el justo elogio que de usted se hace para creerme disculpado al dirigirme a usted confidencialmente por la presente carta, más cuando ella no lleva otro fin que el de hacer a usted una explicación verdadera de la situación que guarda esta pobre y desvalida frontera, ya como a Jefe Superior que es usted del territorio y ya como un ciudadano distinguido interesado en el bien público.

No sé si al recibo de esta [carta] aún permanecerá usted al frente de los destinos del país, y si así no fuera, suplico a la bondad de usted que la presente al que le haya sucedido en el mando, porque mi objeto es dirigirme al jefe político para que el Jefe Político tome pronto y eficazmente las medidas convenientes para evitar la corriente del mal que se desploma sobre este lejano suelo víctima del abandono.

Por las comunicaciones oficiales que dirijo a usted en esta fecha se supondrá del estado de rebelión en que el Coronel Castro ha puesto a una parte de estos habitantes, haciéndoles creer que él es el único Jefe Superior legal que existe en el territorio, acusando a usted y al resto de la península [de] sublevados y anarquistas, con la singular circunstancia de que este hombre se titula defensor y redentor de la Constitución del 1857, fundándose para darse tal investidura en una nota que le puso don Santos Degollado con fecha 5 de septiembre desde "Sayula."

Para dar a usted los antecedentes de esto, le diré que Castro había escrito al Señor Degollado como a Ministro de la Guerra, asegurándole que él con las tropas permanentes que tenía a su mando, con los cuerpos de guardias nacionales que había organizado, y con una gran porción del pueblo, había atacado a las fuerzas conservadoras o de la causa clerical, que los había escarmentado, poniéndolos en completa fuga, y que así continuaría haciendo en el resto del territorio hasta dejar bien puesto el orden constitucional.

En esta virtud, el Señor Degollado que tanto ha trabajado y trabaja por la misma causa, al ver una parte tan rumbosa y halagüeña a favor a su causa, no vaciló en dar a Castro las gracias, y sin más ni más, lo nombró Jefe Superior Político y Comandante General del Territorio, estimulándolo para continuar en su obra.

De este malvado engaño resulta que Castro haya recibido ese pliego y ni el Dios ni el Diablo [le] hace creer que no es el Jefe del Territorio (aunque él bien sabe la verdad de las cosas, pero que con este embuste ahincó a los incautos), en igual sentido que ese Señor Degollado ha escrito al Gobierno de Miramón o de los frailes, bajo estos principios [Castro] trata como rebeldes a todos los que no le reconocen la Superioridad de sus empleos.

Así es que ha reasumido en la frontera los poderes legislativo[s], ejecutivo[s] y judicial[es] en grado [?] Supremo. Sin embargo, habiendo sospechado que pronto será relevado por disposiciones de la Superioridad del Territorio, y no estando seguro en el pequeño partido con que cuenta en la frontera, se largó para San Francisco de la Alta California el 20 de junio último, dejando el mando distribuido en la forma siguiente: **Feliciano Esparza**, Subjefe Político; José Luis, Comandante Militar; **Andrés P. Vidal**, Alcalde General en toda La Frontera; Pedro E. Duarte, Juez de 1ª Instancia–a todos con facultades extraordinarias para obrar según las circunstancias. Estas circunstancias son relativas a oponerse a toda disposición que emane de la Capital del Territorio y aún del Gobierno Supremo que [no] tienda [a] confirmar el nombramiento de Castro y probar cuánto él ha hecho.

Mirando dicho Castro y sus colaboradores que todos sus ensueños de ser funcionario legal superior venían por tierra, trata de independizar la frontera de la unidad nacional para en seguido anexarla a los Estados Unidos mediante una suma de personas que cree [que] le darán por su trabajo. En este plan están iniciados **Máximo Barragón, Feliciano R[uiz] Esparza, Manuelote [Manuel de Jesús] Castro, Andrés P. Vidal, Juan Julio Mörner [Morenhout],** Solomón Pico, Mariano Valaivia[?] y otros por este estilo, con la pretensión de hacer una cobeta de gente de la raza española que en clase de vagos abunda en la Alta California.

El Señor Don Felix Gibert, que hace poco estuvo en estos puntos, se halla muy bien impuesto de estas intentonas y probablemente las habrá puesto en conocimiento de usted. Con tales motivos y contando yo con una mayoría de los habitantes de esta Frontera, he resuelto dar [varias palabras ilegibles] plan porque no hay otro medio de dar respecto a la ley, porque careciendo de tropas y de toda clase de recursos para conducir los reos a La Paz con una distancia tan enorme de cuatrocientos leguas, lo más sencillo es quitar la causa para que cesen sus efectos.

Así mismo, [le] suplico a usted el que tenga la bondad de renovar los despachos de un [mi] empleo, y explicando en ellos si el mando militar de esta frontera como aún a los más adictos a las disposiciones el La Paz, les cabe la duda de si se me ha conferido dicho empleo por el hecho de ser nombrado Subprefecto.

Si las circunstancias lo permitieran, sería muy conveniente que dispusiera usted el envío de una sección de cincuenta infantes o para caballería que aquí se mentaría en caso necesario que pudieran venir por mar a demarcar [desembarcar] en la Ensenada de Todos Santos, siguiera por algunos pocos días, porque con esto se vería que había energía en la Capital del Territorio y para detener cualquiera mira de invasión que trate de hacer <u>Castro</u>. Si el Jefe que tal mandara fuera hijo del país, sería más conveniente.

Deseara [yo desearía] que por una orden oficial me indicara usted lo que debo hacer con una porción de criminales y cándidos que hay en esta frontera solorándose a la sombra de la impunidad, los que con frecuencia se introducen de la Alta California y que después regresan a robar caballadas y otros objetos para disfrutarlos aquí, y esto que ha tolerado Castro nos mantiene en un duro conflicto con los americanos que a cada paso nos amenazan con [una] invasión, con lo que quedo expuesto creen [varias palabras ilegibles] bien impuesto a usted de los males que aquejan este país y mientras espero sus providencias, quedo de usted su muy atento y humilde servidor QBSSM [que besa su suprema mano].

JM

Governor Ramón Navarro, La Paz
July 29, 1859

My very respected Sir,

Although I do not have the honor of being personally acquainted with you, the justified praise that circulates regarding you is sufficient to make me feel excused for addressing myself to you in this confidential manner via this letter–all the more so when it has no other goal than that of offering a truthful explanation of the situation that this poor and unprotected frontier endures to you–both as the Superior Chief of the territory, which indeed you are, and as a distinguished citizen interested in the public good.

I do not know whether upon receipt of this letter you will still be at the helm of the destiny of this country [territory] and, should it not be so, I beseech of your good-heartedness that you present this [letter] to the one who has succeeded you in command, because my object upon addressing the governor is that said governor rapidly and efficiently take the appropriate measures in order to stem the stream of evil that engulfs this distant soil, victim of abandonment.

Via the official communications that I direct [deeply scratched word] to you on this date, one can deduce the state of rebellion into which Colonel Castro has put a portion of these inhabitants, making them believe that he is the only legal Superior who exists in the territory, accusing you and the rest of the peninsula of [being] rebels and anarchists, with the singular circumstance that this man gives himself the title of defender and redeemer of the Constitution of 1857, basing himself in order to give himself said investiture on a note sent by Don Santos Degollado dated September 5th from "Sayula."

In order to provide you the background of this [situation], I will tell you that Castro had written to Señor Degollado as to the Minister of War, assuring him that the permanent troops whom he had under his command, along with the corps of national guard that he had organized and a large proportion of the people, had attacked the conservative or pro-clerical forces and made an example of them, putting them completely to rout, and that he would continue to do so in the rest of the territory until he had put constitutional order back in its rightful place.

In this manner, Señor Degollado, who has worked and continues to work so hard on behalf of the same cause, upon seeing such a magnificent and flattering counterpart [working] in favor of his cause, did not hesitate to thank Castro [by] promptly naming him Superior Political Chief and Commander General [Governor] of the Territory, [thus] stimulating him to continue his labor.

From this nefarious deceit has Castro received his portfolio, and neither God nor the Devil can make him believe that he is not the Territorial Chief (although he knows full well the truth of things, but with this imposture he brought the unwary to their knees), in the same manner that Señor Degollado has written to the Government of Miramón or of the priests, according to these [same] principles [Castro] treats as rebels everyone who does not recognize the Superiority [official mandate] of his strategies.

Thus it is that he has reassumed to the Supreme degree the legislative, executive and judicial powers of La Frontera. However, having suspected that he will promptly be relieved by orders of the Territorial Superiority, and not feeling confident of the little party on whom he counts in the frontier, he took off for San Francisco in Upper California on the 20th of this past June, delegating his command in the following manner: **Feliciano Esparza** as [interim] Vice-Governor, José Luis as Military Commander, Andrés P. Vidal as Mayor-Magistrate of the entire frontier, and Pedro E. Duarte as Judge of the First Instance—all with extraordinary powers in order to act as circumstances [require]. Said circumstances involve opposing every order that emanates from the Territorial Capital and even from the Supreme Government that does not tend to confirm Castro's appointment and affirm all that he has done.

Said Castro and his collaborators, seeing that all his [their] dreams of legally holding superior office are crumbling, are attempting to make La Frontera independent of the national union in order to immediately annex it to the United States in exchange for a sum [of money] that he believes will be given him [by certain] people for his effort. The initiates of this plan are Máximo Barragón, **Feliciano R[uiz] Esparza, Manuelote [Manuel de Jesús] Castro,** Andrés P. Vidal, **Juan Julio Mörner [Morenhout],** Solomón Pico, Mariano Valaivia[?] and others of their ilk, with the pretension of assembling a bunch of people of the Spanish race [scratched in hard] who abound in Upper California in the capacity of vagabonds.

Señor Don Felix Gibert [customs officer], who not long ago was in these parts, is very well informed regarding these grand schemes and probably will have already made you aware of them. With these motives, and being myself able to count on the majority of the inhabitants of this frontier, I have resolved [upon the following?] plan because there is no other way to ensure respect for the law, because lacking troops and all necessary supplies in order to conduct the prisoners to La Paz, given the enormous distance of 400 leagues, the simplest thing is to remove the cause in order to put an end to the effects.

So I beseech you to kindly reissue the [my] orders, explaining in them whether the military command of this frontier [is delegated to me] since even those most addicted [faithful] to orders from La Paz have room for doubt regarding whether or not said office has been conferred upon me by virtue of [my] being named Sub-Prefect.

If circumstances permit, it would be very convenient that you order the dispatching of a force of fifty infantrymen or cavalry that are lacking here, who if necessary could come by sea, disembarking at Ensenada de Todos Santos, even just for a few days, because with [their arrival] one would see that there was energy in the Territorial Capital and [it would also serve] to put a stop to any attempt at invasion that Castro might try. If the chief [officer] were a native son, it would be more appropriate.

Desiring [I would desire] that via official order you indicate to me what I should do with the bunch of criminals and simpletons that there are in this frontier basking in the shade of impunity, who frequently slip into Upper California and then return to steal herds of horses and other objects in order to enjoy [their loot] here, and this [situation], which Castro has tolerated, keeps us in a tough fight with the Americans, who at every step threaten us with invasion, which leaves me exposed [unintelligible phrase]. [Now that you have been] well informed of the evils that torment this country [territory] and while I await your disposition, I remain your very attentive and humble servant who kisses your Supreme hand.

J.M. [initials of José Moreno]

*El Camino Real
between Santa Gertrudis
and San Ignacio; photograph
courtesy of Harry W. Crosby.*

Letter E: "In Order to Satisfy His Ambition to Rule and the Abuses to which He is Accustomed…" *(CT 1728, contemporary copy)*

*This response from Ramón Navarro, incoming Governor of Baja California Territory, to the preceding letter from Sub-Prefect **José Matías Moreno**, indicates that the writer subscribers to Moreno's condemnation of Castro. Within six months of this exchange, Castro would be assassinated by **Manuel Márquez**, reportedly in the service of **Juan Mendosa**, who was in turn under orders from Moreno (See Letter F). The vague reference to Castro's private life remains unexplained, while the Governor's reference to Moreno's own imprisonment testifies to other operative channels of information—if not to their timeliness or reliability.*

República Mexicana
4 de noviembre 1859

Se ha impuesto detenidamente este Gobierno de la comunicación de usted fechada 29 de julio último en la que manifiesta el desacato a las órdenes que se han remitido por este mismo gobierno al Sub-Jefe Político Don José Castro para que entregue a usted el mando de ese Partido, contra las que no sólo se han rebelado este Señor y los satélites que lo rodean, desconociendo a la autoridad de que imanan, sino que además se han finopaseado a abusar Castro la persona de usted poniéndolo preso el intruso de **Feliciano R[uiz] de Esparza** [durante] la ausencia del precitado Castro.

Ya este gobierno tiene dada cuenta al Supremo de la nación de los desórdenes cometidos en esa parte de la península con los demás hechos que atestan la conducta pública y privada del Señor Castro, a reserva de las disposiciones que ha dictado ya y seguirá dictando en lo sucesivo hasta restablecer el orden que por desgracia ha sido alterado para Su Superior conocimiento y resolución.

Tanto por esto como por estar informado [por] usted impero dice [palabra ilegible] de San Francisco llegado en estos días a esta capital el que han sido reducidos a prisión los promovedores de tales escándalos, entre las que figura el susodicho Esparza, y hallarse en camino para esta [ciudad] con carácter de prisioneros, a la vez que Castro [ilegible] principal se halla fuera del país, quizá en demanda de otros medios que le aseguran volver a satisfacer la ambición de mando y los abusos a que está acostumbrado, cree [¿?] este gobierno estará reestablecida a la fecha en ese [ter-ritorio] la tranquilidad pública, y terminada felizmente la discordia que ha causado tantos males a sus habitantes.

Y para que en lo de adelante no volviesen [?] a repetirse los mismos escándalos, a más de confiar este gobierno en el celo de usted para mantener a todo trance el orden público, [tenga] cuidado que se administre pronto y cumplidamente la administración [¿?] de la justicia, persiguiendo a los vagos, promoviendo la instrucción pública, y cumpliendo en fin con todos los deberes que le impone el Superior cargo que ejerce, se autoriza ampliamente a esa Sub-Prefectura para que abra y resuelva en todos casos [de] difícil resolución del servicio aún cuando sean de aquellas de exclusión.

Como cimiento[¿?] de este gobierno y que ese [territorio] no se pueda allanar por la inmensa distancia que [¿lo?] separa cuanto crea [usted] prudente y necesario al sostenimiento del orden [y la] seguridad de esa frontera y todo lo que concierna al respeto debido a leyes y a las autoridades sin más sujeción que a lo dispuesto por aquellas leyes y de acuerdo con lo que resuelva la mayoría de los vecinos más notables de ese partido, a quienes reunirá y consultará en [¿punta de?] los casos extraordinarios que puedan ocurrir.

Principalmente y de toda preferencia procederá usted tan luego como reciba esta [carta] a organizar la Guardia Nacional de [ilegible] usted es el Jefe nato[¿?] por la ley, así como al nombramiento de los oficiales que deben mandarle, y deberán ser dentro [?] aquellas personas que por su honradez, patriotismo y conocimientos le merezcan la mayor confianza, siendo tan importante esta medida al orden y reposo público, que se admite el encarecérsela [¿?] pues en ella estriba además de todos [los] bienes mencionados, las garantías de las sociedades, y aún la independencia de los estados en caso de invasión.

Dios y L[ibertad].
Ramón Navarro
[firma con rúbrica]

Mexican Republic
November 4, 1859

This Government has carefully studied your communication dated June 29th in which you make manifest the disregard of the orders transmitted by this very same government to Vice-Governor Don José Castro indicating that he hand over to you the command of that section, against which orders not only has this gentlemen and the satellites who surround him rebelled, refusing to recognize the authority from which said orders emanate, but also [this same] Castro [and company] have [dared to?] abuse your person when the interloper **Feliciano R[uiz] de Esparza** had you taken prisoner during the absence of the aforementioned Castro.

This government has already informed the Supreme [Government] of the nation regarding the disturbances committed in that part of the peninsula along with the other deeds that attest to the public and private conduct of Señor Castro, in exception to the commands that have been and will in the future continue to be dictated until the order that has been so disgracefully upset is reestablished for the knowledge and satisfaction of His Superior [Authority].

As much for this purpose as in order to be informed [by] you, however, in recent days from San Francisco has arrived [the news] that the promoters of said scandals have been reduced to prison, foremost among them the aforementioned Esparza, and that they are on their way to this [capital] as prisoners, [and] that meanwhile Castro, the leading actor, finds himself out of the country, perhaps in search of other means that will guarantee his return in order to satisfy his ambition to rule and the abuses to which he is accustomed. [illegible abbreviation] [T]his government will have reestablished public tranquility in that [territory] by said date, and the discord that has caused its inhabitants so many ills will have ended.

And in order [to ensure] that in the future the same scandals are not repeated, in addition to the government's trust in your zeal to maintain public order at any price, [take] care that the administration of justice is performed rapidly and thoroughly, persecuting the vagrants, promoting public instruction—in sum, performing all the duties which the Superior office that you exercise imposes upon you, that Subprefecture being broadly authorized to open and resolve all problematic cases, even those that are outside its jurisdiction.

As a means of establishing a strong foundation for this government, and because that territory cannot be pacified due to the immense distance that separates it [from the territorial capital], [do] whatever [you] believe prudent and necessary to the maintenance of order and safety of that frontier, and everything regarding due respect of the laws and the authorities without further subjection beyond what is laid out by said laws, and in accordance with whatever the majority of the more notable residents of that section [advise], whom you will convene and with whom you will consult [regarding] any extraordinary cases that might arise.

Principally and preferably you will proceed as soon as you receive this [letter] to organize the National Guard [illegible abbreviation] [of which?] you are the Chief [illegible] by law, as well as the naming of the officials [unclear] and they should be [chosen from] among those persons who on the basis of their honorable nature, patriotism, and knowledge warrant your greatest confidence, being this measure so important to public order and repose that it cannot be over-emphasized [?] since in addition to all [the] benefits already mentioned, upon it depend all social protections and even the very independence of the states in case of invasion.

God and L[iberty]
Ramón Navarro
[signature and rubric]

Letter F: "I Charge You to Energetic Activity in Your Operations"
(File CT 1685)

*From **José Matías Moreno** to **Juan Mendosa**, the last of three letters written within to Mendosa within a single month–one of which is addressed:* "A don Juan Mendosa / Donde se halle / La Frontera. BC" (To Don Juan Mendosa / Wherever He May Be Found / La Frontera, BC). *The file contains copies made by someone unfamiliar with Spanish and consistently prone to errors, as well as the fragile originals in Moreno's handwriting. This example suffices to demonstrate how Moreno managed to pull the strings of the civil war in La Frontera from his safe haven in San Diego. First he attemps to kindle Mendosa's ire by repeating (or perhaps fabricating) rumors against him, then he exhorts and instrucs him on how to pursue Esparza, and finally he puts into the mouth of Mendosa's wife or child (Moreno's diction is characteristically ambiguous) the gruesome instruction to deliver Esparza's ears. "Give them their passports, Rivera style," clearly a code phrase, carries an ominous ring. All three letters were certified by the Pendleton County Clerk on July 9, 1861–possibly in connection with their author's trial in San Diego for interfering in the affairs of a sovereign nation–those of Mexico.*

Muy querido amigo,

Su apreciable del 2 está a la vista, la que con ansia esperábamos, porque aquí se contaban millares de mentiras. Siendo la principal que usted y su gente andaban huyendo derrotados por **Esparza**. Deberá usted entender que estas noticias son dadas [se dan] con repetición por los Argüellos-**Bandiníes** y los españoles Rivas-Escajadillo y [José Maria] Necoechea. Todos estos publican que los poblanos que están allí con usted son unos cobardes y que estos mismos lo han de entregar a usted con [a] Esparza.

Escajadillo dice públicamente que usted es un ladrón y asesino, que en su tierra era usted un bandido. Los mismos dicen que cuando usted y los poblanos que están ahí vengan a éste [lado] los van a tomar prisioneros para mandarlos a la prisión del Estado. En fin, cuentos y más cuentos.

Observe usted los movimientos y la conducta de don Rufino Porter, que se dice que está con alma y cuerpo defendiendo a Esparza, y que cuando todo mal les vaya, se embarcarán a su Sancha o Goletita que tienen en la Costa. Si Don Rufino está ahora neutral o contra Esparza, tenga cuidado. Anda mal. Procure cogerlo y ver cómo se remite a la [ilegible] le toque por ahora de sus intereses y en todo caso, respete mucho a su familia.

Algunos Yankees aquí son esparsistas porque dicen que éste hizo el bien de matar a los ladrones y asesinos y que tal vez usted los protegía, pero esto dicen porque así lo dicen los Argüellos y los Bandinis. Por ahora ceñirse usted a tomar a Esparza y sus secuazes y déles sus pasaportes a lo Rivera. Lo demás se hará después.

Doña Cornelia le manda una poco de ropa y dice que don Reyes Rodrigo le manda más pantaloneras para que las use. [Antonio L.] Sosa le dirá y le llevará cuanto se pudo comprar con las cosas que trajo para vender. Reloj de dos tapas no se pudo conseguir. No hay ya pólvora aquí. Todo se acabó y sobretodo el juez ha dado orden en las tiendas de que no se venda pólvora ni otros pertrechos de guerra a nadie.

Sin embargo, avise usted más adelante para poderla encargar a San Francisco, pero para esto es fuerza [preciso] tener aquí algunas mulas para vender con anticipación y no andar apurados el día necesario que viene el enviado. Procurando que dichos animales sean de los que eran los mulijas de don Rufino [Porter]. Procure usted economizar la pólvora y [las] balas porque aquí ya no hay.

Como su amigo lo digo todo lo arriba referido y le encargo igualmente la mucha actividad en sus operaciones. No se retire de Esparza. Cérquelo eternamente. No lo deje ir más abajo. Si sale de su encierro, atáquelo y déle duro hasta cogerlo.

Sosa le dirá todo lo demás. Arnaban lo saluda y toda la familia. Doña Cornelia [está] buena y su niño creciendo–y le encarga las orejas de Esparza. No nos deje tanto tiempo sin noticias; aquí nos desesperamos.

Walker el filibuste no ha sido fusilado en Centro América. En México los liberales han derrotado a Miramón.

Suyo
J.M.M.
San Diego, 23 octubre de 1860

More than a century after the events revisited in this volume, the all-leather dress and modest housing of these Baja California vaqueros *offer a visual echo of the region as experienced by the Castro cousins, Moreno, Mendosa and their contemporaries.*

Very dear friend,

Your worthy [letter] of the 2nd of this [month] is in front of me, the one that we were anxiously awaiting because here thousands of lies were being told–the main one being that you and your people were on the run, defeated by **Esparza**. You must understand that these claims are made repeatedly by the Argüello-**Bandinis** as well as by the Spaniards Rivas-Escajadillo and by Necoechea. All these people broadcast that the settlers there with you are a bunch of cowards and that they will be the very ones to hand you over to Esparza.

Escajadillo says publicly that you are a thief and a murderer, that in your [his?] land you were a bandit. The same people say that when you and the settlers who are there [with you] come over to this [side of the border] they will arrest you in order to send you to the state prison. Oh well, stories and more stories.

Observe the movements and conduct of Don Rufino Porter who, it is said, is defending **Esparza** body and soul, and when they have dispelled every evil, they will set sail for that Sancha or little Goleta that they have on the coast. If Don Rufino is now neutral or against Esparza, be careful. He's up to no good. Try to grab him and see how he changes his tune[?]. For the time being [avoid?] touching his interests, and in any case, be very respectful of his family.

Some of the Yankees here are on Esparza's side because they say that he did well to kill the thieves and murderers, and that perhaps you were protecting those men, but they say this because that's what the Argüellos and Bandinis say. For now, limit your efforts to taking Esparza and his followers, and give them their passports Rivera-style. The rest can be done later.

Doña Cornelia is sending you a little clothing and says that Don Reyes Rodrigo is sending you more side-buttoned trousers in order that you use them. [Antonio L.] Sosa will tell you and will bring you what he was able to purchase with the things he brought in order to sell. A pocket watch could not be found. There is no [gun] powder left here. It has all run out and, furthermore, the judge has ordered the stores not to sell powder or other defensive supplies to anyone.

However, give more advance notice so that it [gunpowder] can be obtained from San Francisco, but in order to do this it is essential to have some mules here to sell in advance so as not to go around in a rush the day that the shipment arrives. Arrange for said livestock to come from those little mules that used to belong to Don Rufino [Porter]. Try to economize powder and bullets; there are none here anymore.

As your friend I tell you what is recounted above and by the same token charge you to energetic activity in your operations. Do not retreat from Esparza. Surround him eternally. Do not let him head further south. If he gets out of the encirclement, attack him and give it to him until you take him.

Sosa will tell you all the rest. Arnaban[?] sends you greetings and all the family [*sic*]. Doña Cornelia [is] good and her [or your, plural] male child [is] growing–and she [or he] asks you to bring home Esparza's ears. Do not keep us waiting so long for news; here we get desperate.

Walker the filibuster has not been shot by firing squad in Central America. In Mexico the liberals have overthrown Miramón.

Yours, J.M.M.
San Diego, October 23, 1860

Letter G: "If Only the Governments of Our Nations Had Looked after the Security of Our Respective Frontier Populations…" (CT 1961)

*Colonel José Castro's second-in-command (and delegated replacement when Castro was required to give testimony before the United States Land Commission in San Francisco on behalf of numerous Californio families) writes to an American supporter in San Diego eleven months after Castro's assassination. The addressee, husband of one of **Juan Bandini's** daughters, would subsequently win prompt acquittal after fatally shooting **Juan Mendosa** (his father-in-law's former employee and José Matias Moreno's agent of warfare) in the back. Cave Couts would acquire Mendosa's Rancho San Marcos on the American side of the border–the same ranch that Mendosa offered to deed in quarter portion to Colonel Castro (see Letter 16).*

El Descanso.
Enero 9 de 1861.

Mr. Cave Couts.

Muy Senor mío,

Recibí su apreciable [carta] fechada el 24 del [mes] pasado y por ella veo que no faltan buenos y solícitos amigos a un hombre de bien, enemigo de los ladrones y asesinos. No puedo explicar a usted con palabras cuán grande es mi gratitud y reconocimiento hacia mis buenos amigos de San Diego y principalmente hacia usted.

¡Ojalá que los gobiernos de nuestras naciones hubiesen mirado más para la seguridad de sus respectivos pueblos fronterizos, acordando tratados de extradición de los criminales que se escapasen de ambas partes!

Sin embargo yo, por mi cuenta, estoy resuelto, aunque sin tal requisito, estoy decidido a entregar a cualquiera que venga de ese lado, o a castigar severamente al que de aquí haya ido a causar males allá, y a mi Gobierno yo responderé con la justificada [e] imprescindible necesidad de la seguridad de mi pequeño pueblo.

No sé qué leyes tenga establecidas la Unión Norteamericana con respecto a esas vandálicas expediciones que salen de su seno a país extranjero, como la [filibustera] reciente que vino aquí; pero me parece que de cualquier manera que sea, bien que haya leyes especiales para el caso o bien que no las haya, [se] deben castigar con severidad; pues dejarlas impunes sería la más flagrante violación del Derecho de Gentes, o internacional; sería degradarse al estado salvaje.

Por tanto yo espero que la corte especial de Los Angeles (la Marshall Court) procederá de acuerdo con estos principios y dará su merecido a tanto[s] malvado[s] facineroso[s] que asesinaron y robaron a los inermes habitantes que desgraciadamente cayeron a sus garras.

Los indios están aquí alzados todavía y en un estado amenazante y siguen todavía comunicándose con [José] Sáenz, [José María] Necoechea, y Arnabar y recibiendo sus malignos consejos. No sé cómo hacer con todo esta canalla. Mi autoridad aquí no tiene un sólo centavo de renta y los proprietarios son unos egoístas malentendidos y malagradecidos para ayudarme. Sin embargo, no desespero.

Soy su afectísimo amigo y seguro servidor QBSM [que besa su mano].

[signature and rubric of] Feliciano R. de Esparza

El Descanso,
January 9, 1861

Mr. Cave Couts
My Very Dear Sir,

I received your worthy [letter] dated the 24th of last month, and thanks to it I see that a respectable man [who is the] enemy of thieves and assassins does not lack for good and solicitous friends. I cannot convey with words the scope of my gratitude and appreciation toward my good friends in San Diego–and to you most of all.

If only the governments of our nations had looked after the security of our respective frontier populations, drawing up extradition treaties for criminals who escape from either side!

Even without a requirement to do so, I am for my part resolved and determined to turn in anyone who comes over from that side, or to severely punish whoever may have left here to cause problems over there, and I will answer to my Government based upon the justifiable and indispensable necessity of my small settlement's security.

I do not know what laws the North American Union may have established with regard to those vandalizing expeditions that depart from its bosom for foreign soil, like the [filibustering] one that recently came here, but it seems to me that, whether or not special laws exist, [such expeditions] should be severely punished no matter what, because leaving them unpunished would be the most flagrant violation of the rights of nations, or international law, reducing ourselves to a savage state.

I therefore hope that the special Marshall Court in Los Angeles will proceed according to these principles, giving what they deserve to all those wicked rascals who robbed and murdered those defenseless and unfortunate inhabitants [of La Frontera] who fell into their grasp.

Here Indian uprisings persist in their threatening state, and the Indians continue to communicate with and to receive the pernicious counsel of [José] Sáenz, [José María] Necoechea and Arnabar. I don't know what to do with all those rascals. My office here does not have a single cent of income and the property owners are a selfish, uncomprehending, ungrateful bunch, [ill-disposed] to help me. However, I do not give up hope.

I remain your very fond friend and sure servant who kisses your hand.

[signature and rubric of] Feliciano R. de Esparza

Manuel de Jesús Castro circa 1870; courtesy of Monterey Public Library

Letter H: "…So that He Can Move Forward with his Enterprise"

(Abel Stearns Collection, Box 60, #62)

*This letter from **Manuel de Jesús Castro** in San Francisco to **Abel Stearns** in Los Angeles confirms that the writer maintained contact with Baja California eight years after his cousin José Castro was killed there. Although the business to be conducted remains unspecified, this brief message suggests that it may have been through Manuel Castro's efforts that the final correspondence of Commander Castro found its way back to his family and, eventually, to Library of the Society of California Pioneers.*

---

18 de febrero de 1868

Muy Señor mío y amigo:

Mi primo el Capitán don José Ramón Pico sale allí con dirección a la Frontera de la BC [Baja California], donde su presencia dará probablemente un buen resultado respeto a los asuntos de que hablé a usted en nuestra última entrevista. Lleva todas las instrucciones necesarias sobre el particular, y agradeceré mucho de usted que en caso necesario y él lo solicite, le auxilia usted con algunos caballos y otros recursos que se le ofrezcan para ir adelante con su empresa.

Sin otro particular le desea su mejor salud, atentamente SSQBP atentamente [palabra repetida en el original]

Manuel Castro
[firma y rúbrica]

February 18, 1868

My esteemed Sir and friend,

My cousin Captain Don José Ramón Pico is leaving there headed for La Frontera of BC [Baja California], where his presence will probably produce a positive result regarding the affairs that I spoke to you about in our last interview. He is carrying all necessary instructions regarding the matter, and I will be very grateful to you if, in case it should be necessary and he should request it, you come to his aid with some horses and other supplies that might be offered to him so that he can move forward with his enterprise.

With nothing else pending [and] wishing you the best of health, I attentively SSQBP [kiss your hands and feet] attentively [repetition in original].

Manuel Castro
[signature and rubric]

Part V
Supplementary Material

1856 Republican Presidential campaign cartoon featuring Jessie Benton Frémont and John Charles Frémont

Californio kitchens like this one, sheltered by a ramada *or branch roof, survived into the early 20th century*

José Castro Timeline

1807 Born at Monterey

1808 Baptized at Mission Soledad

1828 Appointed Secretary to the Monterey *Ayuntamiento* (Town Council), a post he would hold for three years

1829 Briefly jailed at the Monterey Presidio by soldiers brought by Governor Solís

1830 Establishes otter-hunting enterprise with former classmates Juan Bautista Alvarado and Mariano Guadalupe Vallejo; the three are temporarily excommunicated for reading books forbidden by the Catholic Church

1831 Marries Modesta Castro at Mission San Carlos Borromeo del Río Carmelo; appointed Commissioner of Mission San Miguel

1835 Becomes Interim Governor for six months after successful rebellion against Governor Figueroa; named Comisionado at San Juan Bautista

1836 With Alvarado and Vallejo, leads successful revolt against Governor Chico; overthrows Governor Gutiérrez with help from Isaac Graham and his American mountaineers; becomes President of the *Diputación* (Assembly); elevated to rank of Colonel; renames San Juan Bautista "San Juan de Castro"

1839 Becomes Prefect of the Northern District with his headquarters at San Juan

1840 Escorts Isaac Graham and some 100 other foreigners arrested for plotting against the government to the northern Mexican supply port of San Blas, where Castro is himself taken prisoner, accused of mistreating his charges, and sent to trial in Mexico City

1841 Absolved of the charges thanks to his defense attorney Micheltorena; acquires title to Cabo San Quintín on the Pacific coast of northern Baja California with its unexploited salt deposits. Returns to San Juan Bautista to find a new Prefecture headquarters and adjacent 2-story adobe home for his growing family overlooking the mission, both built in his absence by his father José Tiburcio Castro; death of the latter

1842 Named Chief of the Presidial Company at Monterey despite lack of formal military training

1843 Relocates his family residence to Casa Castro on the Monterey Mesa overlooking the Presidio

1844 Participates in revolt against Micheltorena, who had been sent from Mexico as Governor of the Californias

1845 Treaty of San Fernando ends the revolt, but is immediately breached; Castro is named Comandante General of Alta California on February 22nd, and southerner Pío Pico as Governor; the rivals try to undermine and supplant one another as tensions between the US and Mexico over Texas continue to mount

1846 Castro challenges the unauthorized visit of American topographer Captain John Charles Frémont and his men, who defiantly raise the American flag at Gavilán Peak before fleeing under cover of darkness; the Californio leadership meets at Rancho Alisal to discuss the future of Alta California; both Pico and Castro gather troops to fight one another; American immigrants stage the Bear Flag revolt and take Sonoma, seeking support from Frémont. After days of hesitation, Commodore Sloat raises the American flag at Monterey on July 7th, declaring the annexation of California by the US Navy. Castro and Pico lead troops in opposition but, outnumbered 3 to 1, depart separately for Mexico in early August; Castro's declaration of the loss of the Californias is published in Mexico City in mid-October, and in Washington DC in early December

1847 Castro remains in Mexico, unsuccessfully seeking support for the reconquest of California

1848 Castro returns by March to his large family in Monterey when the Treaty of Guadalupe-Hidalgo brings an end to the US-Mexican War by granting half of the latter's territory to the former; Territorial Governor Richard B. Mason grants Castro's request to keep the San Juan Mission orchard property; Castro offers his family's house at San Juan to the destitute Breen family, survivors of a snowbound winter in the Sierra; gold discovery at Sutter's Mill greatly accelerates the displacement and outnumbering of the Californios; gold strike by one of his sons allows Patrick Breen to purchase the Castro home and turn it into the United States Inn

1849 Jessie Benton Frémont and daughter Lily arrive in San Francisco via Panama; her husband John Charles Frémont rents them two rooms at Casa Castro in Monterey, home of José, Modesta and their children; Jessie and Lily remain there from October through December, with occasional visits from Frémont; they all depart Monterey on New Year's eve, sailing for New York on the news that Frémont will be one of the first pair of Senators from the proposed 31st state of California

1850-1854 Castro continues to seek ways to support his growing family in lieu of governmental and military opportunities, in light of US legal challenges to all Californio land holdings, and in the face of mounting financial pressures; receives first letter of appointment from Supreme Government of Mexico on December 7, 1854

1853 Travels to Mexico, possibly visiting the salt flats at San Quintín, Baja California for the exploitation of which he forms a partnership with his cousin **Manuel de Jesús Castro**, just returned from four years of military service in Baja California, his lifelong friend Juan Bautista Alvarado, and French Consul at San Francisco and Monterey Jacques **Moerenhout**

1855 Journeys to Mazatlán to accept his appointment only to find that the incumbent refuses to vacate the post; returns to his family in Alta California; in December receives another official letter of appointment to the same position

1856-1860 Accepts reappointment on January 20, 1856 and journeys again to Mazatlán only to learn that a civilian has been elected Governor of Baja California under a new governmental dispensation; writes to the President of Mexico requesting to be named Vice-Governor of the northern region of Baja California, La Frontera. Fulfills this mandate from August **1856** with occasional trips to American California to visit his family and appear as expert witness in the ongoing US Land Commission hearings at San Francisco. Returns from a trip north in late **1859** to find his delegated surrogate, **Feliciano Esparza**, refusing to relinquish control of the troops. Ongoing efforts to unseat Castro and Esparza result in the former's assassination on April 5, 1860 and a year of internecine bloodshed that reduced the population of La Frontera by 80%

1861 During the year that he holds the Vice-Governorship of La Frontera, **José Matías Moreno**, the man whom Castro identifies in Letter 18 as "my arch enemy," (re)writes the history of the four-year Castro regime, having survived all the principles in the fierce struggle for power that erupted upon Castro's death

1899 Modesta Castro de Castro, widowed thirty-nine years, dies at the home of José Castro Jr. in Alameda and is buried in the Catholic Cemetery at Monterey opposite Casa Castro

1957 The Society of California Pioneers acquires five letters pertaining to José Castro's final years in Baja California from his descendant Mrs. Modesta Castro Smith, possibly the daughter of Castro's son and namesake.

Mission San Carlos Borromeo del Rio Carmelo, where Jose and Modesta were married on September 12, 1831; William Rich Hutton sketch from 1847 courtesy of The Huntington Library.

Hubert Howe Bancroft on José Castro

…Thus, José Castro was the most prominent of his name as a public man. No Californian has been so thoroughly abused as he in what has passed for history. It should be stated at the outset that nine tenths of all that has been said against him by American writers has no foundation in truth. Of his conduct in the sectional quarrels of '45-46, there is not much to be said in his favor, except that it was somewhat less discreditable than that of his opponent, Pico; but with his acts in the contest with the settlers and the US, little fault can be justly found. He did not mistreat the exiles of 1840, as charged by [Thomas Jefferson] Farnham and others. He did not break his pledge to [John Charles] Frémont in the spring of '46, nor did he do any of the absurd things attributed to him in connection with the Gavilan affair; but his conduct was far more honorable, dignified, and consistent than that of Frémont. He did not threaten to drive the immigrants back into the snows of the Sierra, but treated them with uniform kindness; nor did he incite the Ind[ians] to burn [John] Sutter's grain-fields. In the southern negotiations of August he bore a much more honorable part than did Com[modore] Stockton. Indeed, his record as a public man in Upper Cal. was, on the whole, not a bad one. He had much energy, was popular with most classes, was true to his friends, and as a public officer fairly honest. About his private character there is great difference of opinion among competent witnesses, native and foreign, who knew him well. He must have had some good qualities, yet it is clear that he had some very bad ones. He was addicted to many vices, and when drunk, especially in the later years, was rough to the verge of brutality; yet a kind-hearted man when sober. Of commonplace abilities and education, in most respects inferior to such men as [Mariano Guadalupe] Vallejo, [Juan] Bandini, [Juan Bautista] Alvarardo, and [José Antonio] Carrillo, he was yet by no means the cowardly, incompetent braggart that he has been generally painted.

"Pioneer Register and Index" in *History of California,* Volume XIX. San Francisco: The History Company 1886, page 752.

The Conquest of the Californias:
Notifying Mexico and the World

José Castro's letter to the Mexican Minister of War provided the first official word that the United States had taken California. Written from northern Mexico on September 9th, five weeks after Castro had delegated his command to his cousin Manuel de Jesús Castro and headed into Sonora accompanied by sixteeen officers and soldiers, his letter did not appear in print until six weeks later.

For its American publication six weeks after that, the letter was translated by Jessie Benton Frémont, wife of John Charles Frémont, and her elder sister Eliza Benton Jones, wife of William Carey Jones. Both husbands were involved in the conquest of California. In 1849, before hers drew the straw to become one of the first two senators from the proposed 31st state, Jessie Frémont and daughter Lily resided for several months in Monterey, at the home of former Commander General Castro and as guests of his wife, Modesta Castro de Castro.

Digital photographs of the 1846 newspaper columns were provided by Zachary W. Elder, Research Services, Duke University Libraries in Durham, North Carolina. Minor modifications have been made by this Editor.

"LIBERTY, THE UNION, AND THE COISTITUTION."

WASHINGTON CITY, FRIDAY NIGHT, DECEMBER 4, 1846.

Letter from Commander José Castro to the Mexican Minister of War
September 9, 1846
Published in the *Diario del Gobierno*, Mexico City, October 16, 1846
Translated and reprinted in the *Daily Union*, Washington DC, December 4, 1846

To His Excellency the Minister of War and Marine

Most Excellent Sir:

On conveying to Your Excellency the enclosed documents #1-8, I feel regret at not having been able to make greater sacrifices in defense of the Department [of Alta California] that was under my command at the time when the American squadron took possession of it.

A chain of events prevented me from preserving it any longer. The extreme scarcity of supplies of every nature, and particularly of arms and munitions, compelled me to retire. For three months I was able, with arms in hand, to maintain myself against the enemy. Finally I resolved to place myself at the disposal of the Supreme Government, which I have the honor to address, hoping that its deliberations on this important subject will result in restoring this beautiful country to the enjoyment of its rights and liberties.

From this place [probably in Sonora], I await the order of the government, as I am not able to continue my march for want of supplies.

I behold for a single day the usurpers of our territory with inexpressible regret. Your Excellency will permit me to say that if speedy measures are adopted, a victory over the enemy will not cost much. His force consists now of from 2,000 to 3,000 men. The greater part of them are on duty in the [naval] squadron and cannot be employed half a league from the seacoast.

The only force that can be employed at present in the interior of the country consists of from 400 to 500 mountain men, together with the [American] individuals who have settled in it [inland near Sutter's Fort]. They are daily expecting a large number of emigrants for Oregon in support of the land forces, but in my opinion these cannot be in any great number until the coming year, according to the information that I received upon leaving the Department.

The inhabitants of all that country, Most Excellent Sir, await with anxiety a remedy for their misfortune. All possess sentiments of fidelity and constancy to the Supreme Government. Coronel Don Juan Bautista Alvarado, Senior Prefect of the Second [Northern] District, Don Manuel Castro, Captain of the Auxiliary Forces, and Captain Don Joaquín de la Torre, accompanied by various citizens, are at present concealed in neighboring parts of the country, whence they make overtures to visit the towns for the purpose of destroying the infernal intrigue of our oppressors.

The Governor, Don Pío Pico, by agreement with me, left the Department for this place, but I am yet ignorant of his whereabouts. On the 10th of last month, I commenced my march from the camp of La Mesa, near the city of Los Angeles, where the number of [my] troops did not amount to more than 100 men. I was accompanied by the officers and soldiers mentioned in the list below. These gentlemen are worthy of the consideration of the Supreme Government.

The desire to submit immediately to Your Excellency what has been related to me compels me to omit the details of the events that have occurred. I will furnish them without loss of time. Your Excellency will please communicate to His Excellency the President of the Republic what has been set forth [herein], and at the same time all the considerations of my subordination and respect.

God and Liberty.

JOSE CASTRO
September 7, 1846

Captain Eugenio Montenegro*	Ensign Manuel R[udecindo?] Castro*
Lieutenant Manuel Márquez **	Sergeant Eugenio Martínez
Lieutenant Juan N. Padilla	Sergeant Anastasio Chavoya
Ensign Ignacio Servín	Sergeant Manuel Cantúa
Ensign Francisco Arce*	Corporal Joaquín Pollorena
Ensign Guadalupe Soberanes	Corporal Domingo Mesa
Ensign José María Soberanes*	Private Manuel Rosas
Ensign Solomón Pico	Private Marcos Arias[?]

* Listed in *The Guide to Manuscritps Concerning Baja California in the Bancroft Library*, indicating that they remained for some time in Baja California under either Manuel de Jesús Castro or José Castro.
** Shot and killed his former commander, Vice-Governor José Castro, on April 5, 1860 at Mission Vieja, Baja California.

American and Mexican Editorial Commentaries
on the Conquest of California

Castro's letter to the Mexican Minister of War was framed by two editorial statements, the first expressing the triumphant views of Washington's Daily Union, *the second reproducing the* Diario del Gobierno's *exhortations to the embattled citizens of Mexico. They convey the tenor with which Castro's notice of the loss of the Californias was received by the warring nations. The contrast between the fulminations of the press in both countries and Castro's more level discourse registers in his favor.*

Daily Union, Washington DC
December 4, 1846

We are indebted to the Navy Department for the following translations from Mexican papers recently received. They furnish new evidence of the empty gasconading character of the Mexican race. We are not surprised at the coarse and vituperative language that General Castro and the *Diario* editor employ towards our country. It is consistent with the character of this rude, braggart, semi-barbarous race.

[Here] we have a glorious picture indeed of the "firmness" of this General Castro...[who] fled from Colonel Frémont at the first moment. When Frémont afterwards pursued him with a few dragoons and seamen, the Mexican took to his heels and scampered out of California, and his four hundred troops were scattered over the face of the earth... How little have [the Mexicans] to depend upon for recovering a territory that they have shamefully abandoned, and for wreaking upon us the revenge which they so idly threaten.

...In fact, California has for some time past been connected by no ties worth speaking of to the Mexican government. And now, if we please, the opening declaration of the *Diario* will be made good – "the loss of the Californias would be consummated" and it would be idle for the Mexicans to attempt its recovery by force of arms.

General [Stephen] Kearny is expected to arrive there by the end of November, and what with the troops that he carries with him, the reinforcements which will join him, the regiment of Stevenson, the force which Colonel Frémont and Commodore Stockton [command], the... distance of California from the capital, and the difficulty of sending [Mexican] troops, the fate of [the Californias] is consummated: it will depend on our own will and pleasure.

If Mexico has lost it, we have gained it. We now hold it by their own confession, and it is thus formally announced to all the representatives of other nations that California is in our possession, and the Mexican scepter has, for the present at least, in fact and form departed. [California] is therefore *de facto* in our possession, and it is hoped that all foreign agents will conform themselves to the revolution.

Diario del Gobierno, Mexico City
September 16, 1846

The loss of California is consummated. The documents that we insert here, received yesterday by the Supreme Government, will apprise the public of the new lamentable misfortune and will doubtless increase the patriotic enthusiasm of all Mexicans to free themselves from the domination of an invader so perfidious and unjust.

These losses will be repaired within a very brief time, with interest, if the national spirit takes the flight that is everywhere indicated by the sacrifices of every kind that the citizens are hastening to make. Guanajuato, Jalisco, Zacatecas, and all the states of the interior, with the noblest emulation, are preparing for the contest, and entire numerous battalions are proceeding to join our army to combat usurpation.

This vivid enthusiasm will no doubt be heightened on beholding the example of firmness and patriotism on the part of the Commander General of the Californias, Lieutenant Colonel Don José Castro, and the officers and troops accompanying him who – having no means of resisting the enemy's forces, and being tempted by seductions in every shape to hoist, themselves, the American flag in the Californias – have preferred to depart in search of the means of warring against the enemy, exposing themselves to every kind of suffering, and exhorting the inhabitants there to preserve their affections and ties to Mexico. This conduct is worthy of good Mexicans, and will require the Republic to use the most energetic efforts to cast out of that fertile and coveted territory the flag of the stars.

…In spite of the culpable neglect with which preceding administrations of the Republic have treated the Californias, and of the continual instigations of the Americans, California has fallen without renouncing the Mexican name. Let us deplore that loss and swear to avenge it. The blackest perfidy casts infamy and dishonor upon the enemy in the midst of his triumphs. His power and might, and even victory itself, will never efface, in the eyes of the civilized world, the stain and injustice of this war of ambition and crimes.

And if Mexico, exhausted by her continual discords, impoverished and feeble, should succeed at last in bringing to the ground that American Colossus, what glory will redound to her name! Are we not the same men who wrested from the hands of the Spaniards, thanks to our struggles, their conquest of three hundred years standing? Shall we not, to preserve the national independence, use the same efforts that the astonished world beheld us make to achieve it?

The few troops of the line of the United States, almost destroyed at Monterey, and their volunteers – can they ever equal in number the defenders of Mexico? They may be able to assemble twenty or thirty thousand men, but what are twenty or a hundred thousand men for the conquest of a nation of eight million inhabitants, resolved to defend their hearths and their honor?

Let us be united, and we shall triumph. The repetition of this idea may perhaps be now tiresome, but it is necessary that we should have it ever present. The most powerful weapon of the enemy consists not in his rifles or cannon but in our internecine discords… This is the great battle that we must struggle to gain… We will not grow weary of repeating it: united, we shall reconquer the usurped Mexican territory. Discord is the most splendid triumph to which the enemy aspires, and the most shameful for us.

Genealogy of José Castro

Compiled by Los Californianos Genealogist
Judith M. Rodriguez

Abbreviations: b.=born ch.=baptised conf'd=confirmed m.=married d. =died bur.=buried
Principal relatives appear in UPPER CASE.
Preferred name, if known, is underscored.
"Mission San Carlos" always refers to Carmel Mission.
"Villa de Branciforte" eventually became known as Santa Cruz.

Josef Antonio María de Jesús Castro, known as José Castro, descended from some of the earliest Alta California families, carried on the family tradition of military and civic service. His grandfather, soldier Macario Castro, came to Alta California about 1783 from Sinaloa on the mainland coast of the Gulf of California. Macario devoted his life to military duties, including the protection of the missions and the exploration of the vast territory that Spain was eager to settle at long last, in order to deter Russian incursions from the north as well as possible maritime threats from the British and French. Eminent historian of California Hubert Howe Bancroft described Macario as "the most prominent among the Castro founders."

MACARIO CASTRO
    b. About 1753/1754 at Villa de Sinaloa
    bur. 25 July 1809 at Mission San Carlos
    m. MARÍA POTENCIANA RAMÍREZ Y VALDENEGRA in Sinaloa
        b. About 1755 at Villa de Sinaloa
        d. 30 Dec 1811
        bur. 31 Dec 1811 at Mission Santa Clara

Macario Castro and Potenciana Ramírez had 12 offspring:
1. María Manuela Castro
    b. About 1773 at Villa Sinaloa
    chr. At Guasave in Sonora
    conf'd 2 Nov 1783 at Mission San Gabriel
    m. Luis Gonzaga Pérez, son of Ygnacio Pérez and María Catarina Paredes, on 25 May 1787 at Mission San Juan Capistrano
        b. About 1764 at Cócorit [Yaqui River], Sonora

2. JOSÉ TIBURCIO CASTRO
    b. About 1776 at Pueblo de Guasave (Huasave), Sonora
    chr. At Guasave
    conf'd 2 Nov 1783 at Mission San Gabriel
    bur. 6 July 1841 at Mission San Juan Bautista

    m. MARÍA RUFINA ALVAREZ, daughter of Juan Alvarez and María Bernarda Silva, on 12 Dec 1802 at Mission San Carlos
        b. 10 July 1790 at Pueblo de Los Angeles
        chr. 12 July 1790 at Mission San Gabriel
        bur. 13 Jan 1840 at Mission San Juan Bautista

3. Agapito José Castro
    b. About 1778.

conf'd. 2 Nov 1783 by Fray Junípero Serra at Mission San Gabriel, with brothers Tiburcio and Dionisio and sister Maria Manuela

Agapito came to Alta California with the family in 1783 and is listed on the 1790 census. He is possibly the same Agapito who won local fame as a silversmith.

4. José Ramón <u>Dionisio</u> Castro
    b. at Villa de Sinaloa
    conf'd 2 Nov 1783 at Mission San Gabriel
    bur. 13 Nov 1783 at Mission San Gabriel

5. José Juan Nepomuceno (<u>Simeón</u>) Castro
    b. 24 Feb 1784 at Santa Barbara Presidio
    chr. 7 Mar 1784 at Santa Barbara Presidio Chapel
    bur. 16 June 1842 at Mission San Carlos
    m. María Antonia Pico, daughter of José Dolores Pico and María Isabel Asención Cota, on 18 Aug 1819 at Mission San Carlos
        b. About 1803 at Villa de Branciforte
        bur. 14 Dec 1883 at Mission San Carlos

6. María Felipa de Jesús Castro
    b. 23 Aug 1785
    chr. 26 Aug 1785 at Mission San Diego
    m. Pedro de la Mora on 30 Sept 1804 at Mission Santa Clara

7. María de los Dolores Castro
    b. 10 Jan 1787 at Pueblo de San José
    chr. 12 Jan 1787 at Mission San Juan Capistrano
    d. after 1841
    m. José Dionisio Bernal, son of Juan Francisco Bernal and Ana María Josefa Soto, on 7 July 1806 at Mission Santa Clara
        b. 1765 in Sinaloa
        d. 21 July 1828
        bur. 22 July 1828 at Mission Santa Clara

8. Mariano de la Trinidad Castro
    b. 8 Nov 1788 at Presidio de Monterey
    chr. 9 Nov 1788 at Mission San Carlos
    bur. 12 Mar 1849 at Mission San Carlos
    m(1). María Francisca Escamilla, daughter of Tomás Escamilla and María Ygnacia Gloria Alba, on 12 Dec 1813 at Mission San Carlos
        b. 10 Oct 1800 at San Francisco Presidio
        chr. 12 Oct 1800 at Mission Dolores
        d. 1 Oct 1815 in childbirth
        bur. 2 Oct 1815 at Mission San Carlos
    m(2). María Rufina Galindo, daughter of Juan Venancio Galindo and María Ramona Lorenzo Sánchez, on 26 May 1817 at Mission Santa Clara
        b. 6 Sept 1800
        chr. 17 Sept 1800 at Mission Dolores

9. <u>Juan Antonio</u> (José Antonio) Castro
    b. 17 Jan 1791 at Real Presidio (Monterey)

chr. conditionally and privately on 17 Jan 1791 with supplemental ceremonies on 18 Jan 1791 at Mission Santa Clara using the name Juan Antonio

bur. 21 Oct 1791 at the Monterey Presidio Chapel and recorded at Mission San Carlos using the name José Antonio

10. María del Carmen Josefa Castro
    b. Apr 1792
    chr. 27 Apr 1792 at Mission San Carlos
    bur. 20 Feb 1864 at Mission San Luis Obispo
    m(1). Buenaventura (Ventura) Amezquita, son of Manuel Francisco Amezquita and María Bárbara Graciana Hernández, on 4 Dec 1814 at Mission Santa Clara
        b. 13 July 1784
        chr. 16 July 1784 at Mission Santa Clara
        d. 1 Nov 1819 at Pueblo de San José
        bur. 2 Nov 1819 at Mission San Juan Bautista
    m(2). José de Guadalupe Cantúa, son of Ignacio Cantúa and María Gertrudis Castillo, on 9 Nov 1822 at the Capilla Real, Presidio of Monterey
        b. 10 Dec 1786 at Monterey Presidio
        chr. 12 Dec 1786 at Mission San Carlos

11. Angel María Dolores Castro
    b. 11 Apr 1794 at Pueblo de San José
    chr. 12 Apr 1794 at Mission Santa Clara
    m. María Isabel Butrón, daughter of Manuel Butrón and María Ignacia Rita Higuera, on 12 Dec 1812 at Mission San Carlos, with a nuptial blessing given on 17 Feb 1813 at the Capilla Real, Monterey Presidio
        b. 20 Nov 1796 at Pueblo de San José
        chr. 22 Nov 1796 at Mission Santa Clara
        bur. 1 Feb 1848 at Mission San Juan Bautista

12. María Josefa <u>Lugarda</u> Castro
    b. At Pueblo de San José
    chr. 21 Mar 1796 at Mission Santa Clara
    bur. 19 June 1848 at Mission Santa Clara
    m. Salvador María Espinosa, son of José Cayetano Espinosa and María Rosa Tapia, on 4 Dec 1814 at Mission Santa Clara
    chr. In a supplemental ceremony while in danger of death on 28 Mar 1796, recorded at Mission Soledad

The eldest son of Macario Castro and Potenciana Ramírez was JOSÉ TIBURCIO CASTRO, who came to Alta California as a child with his parents. A soldier like his father, he later became a landowner and a man of political influence. Bancroft notes his "excellent character." José Tiburcio and his wife RUFINA ALVAREZ had 5 offspring:

    1. JOSEF (<u>JOSÉ</u>) ANTONIO MARÍA DE JESÚS CASTRO, who became Comandante General of Alta California and attained the rank of Colonel
        b. 1807 at Presidio de Monterey
        chr. 7 Aug 1808 at Mission Soledad
        d. April 5, 1860 in Baja California (buried 20 miles north of Ensenada)
        m. MARÍA JOSEFA VICTORIANA MODESTA CASTRO, daughter of José Antonio Castro and María Merced del Socorro Ortega, on 12 Aug 1831 at Mission San Carlos
            b. 15 Jun 1816

chr. 19 June 1816 at Mission San Carlos
d. 1899 at Alameda
bur. July 5, 1899 in the Catholic Cemetery, Monterey

2. María Cruz <u>Francisca</u> Dolores Ramona Castro
b. 12 Sept 1809
chr. 14 Sept 1809 at Mission San Carlos
d. 14 Nov 1890 at the home of her daughter near Salinas
m. José Santiago Moreno, son of Francisco Moreno of Cartagena, Spain, and Manuela Valle of Guayaquil, Ecuador, on 12 Oct 1826 at Mission San Carlos
b. At Guayaquil, Ecuador
d. June 1881
bur. At San Carlos cemetery

3. María Antonia Eusebia Ramona Gracia Castro
b. 5 Mar 1811
chr. 6 Mar 1811 at Mission San Carlos (Carmel)
bur. 12 Mar 1812 at the cemetery at the Capilla Real, Monterey Presidio and recorded at Mission San Carlos

4. José del Rosario Castro
b. 2 Dec 1815
chr. 3 Dec 1815 at Mission San Juan Bautista
bur. 19 Dec 1815 at Mission San Juan Bautista

5. María Castro
m. Ignacio Soto, widower

JOSÉ CASTRO, eldest child of Tiburcio Castro and Rufina Álvarez, led a life committed to the causes he championed, like his father and grandfather before him. He was barely twenty when named Secretary of the Monterey Ayuntamiento (town council) in 1828, a precocious beginning to many years as military and political leader. JOSÉ and his wife MODESTA CASTRO DE CASTRO had at least 14 offspring:

1. María Isabela de la Visitación (Visitación) Castro
b. 2 July 1832
chr. 4 July 1832 at Mission San Carlos (Carmel)
bur. 25 Sept 1836 at Mission San Juan Bautista

2. José Gabriel <u>Esteban</u> Castro
chr. 4 Aug 1834 at Mission San Juan Bautista
d. After 6 Dec 1904
Esteban served in the California State Senate in 1856-57, perhaps longer. The 1880 federal census shows him living in San Luis Obispo with Adelaida Limas and her two children; the census enumerator reported that Esteban was single and Adelaida a young widow. Whether or not they ever married, they maintained a long-term relationship. On 6 Dec 1904, "for love and affection," Esteban deeded to Adelaida his interest in Casa Castro on the Monterey Mesa, previously deeded to him by his mother, Modesta Castro de Castro, who had acquired it from her grandmother, María Victoria Beltrán de Castro, widow of its orginal builder, soldier [Josef?] Antonio María Castro via attorney Miguel Avila.

3. María de los Dolores Castro
b. 25 Mar 1836
chr. 2 Apr 1836 at Mission San Juan Bautista

bur. 1 Jan 1837 at Mission San Juan Bautista

4. Maria Visitación <u>Francisca</u> Castro
    b. 10 Oct 1837
    chr. 14 Oct 1837 at Mission San Juan Bautista
    bur. 8 Aug 1840 at San Juan Bautista

5. <u>Rufina</u> (Rufinita) Felicidád Castro
    chr. 3 Mar 1840 at the Capilla Real, Monterey Presidio

6. María Modesta (<u>Modestita</u>) Castro
    b. 23 July 1842 at Mission San Juan Bautista
    chr. 23 Feb 1843 at at the Capilla Real, Monterey Presidio
    m. William Charles Dana, May 26, 1861, cousin of author Richard Henry Dana
    d. 1893 at Monterey
Modesta gave birth to 14 children, one of whom was Francisca Dana, who married Rafael Diaz and upon her second marriage became Mrs. Francisca Diaz-Tucker, last family owner of Casa Castro on the Monterey Mesa.

7. María Candelaria Griselda Castro
    b. 2 Feb 1844
    chr. 26 Mar 1844 at the Capilla Real, Monterey Presidio

8. José Tiburcio Castro
    b. 18 Dec 1845
    chr. 2 Jan 1846 at Mission San Carlos (Carmel)

9. <u>José</u> María (Joseíto) Castro, Jr.
    b. 1846/1847
    m. Flora Graciola between 1870 and 1880
José worked as a painter for many years and later became a liquor merchant. His mother was living with him and his family in Alameda at the time of her death. It may have been this couple's daughter who, as Mrs. Modesta Castro Smith, gifted her grandfather's letters to the Society of California Pioneers.

10. José <u>Job</u> Castro
    b. 20 Nov 1848
    chr. 22 Nov 1848 at Mission San Carlos with his father present
    d. After 11 June 1900
It appears that Job never married. He was living in the household of his mother at the time of the 1860 and 1870 census at Monterey and San Luis Obispo, respectively. He was noted to be an invalid in 1870 and again in 1880, when he was living with his brother José. By 1900, he had moved with José's family to Alameda, California; no trade or occupation was listed for him in that census.

11. Cesario Castro
    b. 25 Feb 1851
    chr. 2 Mar 1851 at Mission San Carlos (Carmel)
    d. After 11 June 1880
Cesario was living with the family of his brother José in San Luis Obispo at the time of the 1880 census; he was about 29 years old, single, and working as a laborer.

12. Eleanora Elizabeta Castro
  b. 14 Apr 1854
  chr. 24 Apr 1854 at Mission San Carlos (Carmel)

13. Moisés Castro
  b. 1853/1854
  d. After 11 June 1880

14. Miriam Romanum (<u>María Romana</u>) Castro
  b. 29 Feb 1856
  chr. 1 May 1856 at Mission San Carlos
Esteban informed his father in Letter 3 (April 10, 1856) that this baby died within two weeks of her birth.

Oriana Day's depiction of Carmel Mission, based on Mariano Guadalupe Vallejo's recollection of how it looked in its heyday; courtesy of the Fine Arts Museums of San Francisco.

Ownership History of Casa Castro/La Mirada on the Monterey Mesa

Casa Castro's chain of ownership began with soldier [José or Josef?] Antonio María Castro, for whom the house was constructed on the choicest Mesa site of "noble" stone rather than "humble" adobe. It subsequently passed through his widow Victoria Beltrán de Castro to their granddaughter Modesta Castro de Castro, wife of Colonel José Castro, having skipped her father José Antonio Castro and his wife María Merced del Socorro Ortega de Castro, and only temporarily involving attorney Miguel Avila.

Modesta deeded the property to her eldest son Esteban Castro. From Esteban it proceeded through his companion, the non-relative Adelaida Limas to whom he deeded it "for love and affection" in 1904, back to fifth-generation Castro descendant Francisca Dana de Díaz (de) Tucker, whose ancestors comprise two Alta California Castro lines–her grandmother Modesta's that began in Alta California with soldier [José] Antonio María Castro, and her grandfather José's inaugurated in Alta California by the Sinaloa-born soldier Macario Castro. Both of her grandfathers (and likely a great-grandfather) bore the name José María Antonio Castro, but whether the two family lines intersected prior to the marriage of José Castro and Modesta Castro is yet to be determined.

Francisca Dana Castro was the daughter of Modesta (Modestita) Castro Castro de Dana, Esteban's sister. Modestita married William Charles Dana of Nipomo (second cousin of Richard Henry Dana, author of the early California classic, *Two Years Before the Mast)* on May 26, 1861, some fourteen months after her father's assassination. Their daughter was given the primary baptismal name of her paternal aunt, José Castro's sister María Cruz Francisca Castro de Moreno. (Wife of José Santiago Moreno, an Ecuadorian of Spanish father and Ecuadorian mother, the elder Francisca died in 1890 at the home of her daughter near Salinas).

Francisca Dana Castro presumably married twice, first to Rafael Díaz, a band conductor known as "Maestro," and later to Mr. Tucker. Casa Castro's Victorian embellishments preseumably date from her ownership. After securing a quit-claim deed from real estate baron David Jacks, who claimed the entire Rancho Aguajito tract that had once belonged to her grandfather José Castro, Francisca Díaz-Tucker (sometimes incorrectly rendered Francesca Dona Diaz) sold Casa Castro and its surrounding three acres to Gouverneur and Ruth Morris by 1921, inaugurating the property's post-Castro era.

In the 1880s Casa Castro fell into disrepair while tenanted under the supervision of Miguel Boronda Allen, at right.

West elevation of Casa Castro in 1902, courtesy of the Monterey Public Library California Room.

Contractor James Clarence (J.C.) Anthony remodeled Casa Castro extensively for the Morrises in 1922. It was the first of three colonial-era homes he revived on the Monterrey Mesa, expanding them into estate-style residences that featured Spanish styles, methods, and materials. In 1929, Anthony's colleague S.H. Hooke undertook another major remodel for the Morrises, who lost the property to foreclosure during the Great Depression. Local builder, banker and real estate investor Thomas A. Work and his wife Maude Porter Work subsequently acquired Casa Castro in the name of their daughter, Betty Work Kirby, who transferred ownership to her brother, Frank Work, after World War II.

In the mid-1980s, Kay Dietterle helped negotiate a transfer of the 3-acre property to the Monterey Museum of Art and then spearheaded the recruiting and training of docents. Jane and Justin Dart spearheaded a fund-raising campaign on behalf on a major addition that would provide needed gallery and preparation space for the renamed La Mirada. Designed by nationally renowned architect Charles Moore, the new wing was dedicated in 1994.

Historian and La Mirada docent Virginia Woodward Stone was the first to research the history of Casa Castro in connection with her illustrated brochure *The Story of La Mirada* (1990). The author of the present volume began research into builder James Clarence (J.C.) Anthony in 1999 as a Monterey Museum of Art docent trainee. That research led to the discovery of the signal importance of the Monterey Mesa neighborhood as the only original Novohispano settlement area in the United States to be revived and perpetuated into the present through the incorporation of surviving colonial buildings, materials and methods. The resulting book–T*he Monterey Mesa: Oldest Neighborhood in California* (Burton-Carvajal. ed., City of Monterey, 2002)–includes a chapter by the late State Historian Edna Kimbro. The different appearance of Casa Castro in its various pre-revival phases (tile roof and exposed stone, stone with shingle roof, and stucco exterior coating with shingle and later tile roof, as shown below) gave rise to the long-lived misnomer "Castro Adobe." Kimbro's essay untangled the visual record by establishing conclusively which unidentified or improperly identified early photographs and paintings depict Casa Castro. The editor's essay reconstructed the history of the building and the neighborhood since 1920. In late 2007, Monterey Museum of Art docent John Greenwald uncovered the long-missing "first piece" of the Casa Castro puzzle–the name of its original owner-builder, soldier [José?] Antonio María Castro, a founding figure who awaits further research.

West-facing portico added by Mrs. Francisca Diaz-Tucker; 1917 photo courtesy of Monterey Public Library.

Eastern elevation of Casa Castro after 1929; unfinished oil painting by Mary Evelyn McCormick.

Biographical Sketches

Names of the following individual appear in **bold** in Parts I-IV;
José Castro's name is also bolded below.

Henry-Jacques-Antoine ALRIC was born in Aveyron, France on November 28, 1805. He was a member of the priesthood in the diocese of Rodez and that of Verdun before departing in 1850 as chaplain on a ship bound for San Francisco. **Monsignor Joseph Sadoc Alemany** assigned him to the gold fields at Sonora, named after the Mexican mining region, where he spent five trying years trying to stem the widespread mistreatment of Mexican and other Spanish-speaking miners. Monsignor Alemany then sent him to the northern district of Baja California to replace the recalled **Padre Suárez del Real** as chaplain of the military colony at Santo Tomás. Under special dispensation from the archibishop, Father Alric was granted three plots of land by **José Castro** which he irrigated and farmed with great success as an example to his neighbors. Father Alric spent the first eight months of 1858 as military chaplain at Fort Yuma, on the California-Arizona border, returning afterwards to La Frontera. By 1860 escalating violence in that region drove him to Mexico City, where he attended to the spiritual needs of the large French community. Before the French imperial army departed Mexico for good, Alric was named Chevalier of the Legion of Honor. He died in France in 1883, having published three versions of his new world memoir between 1865 and 1869. Because his years in Baja California coincided with **José Castro's**, his memoir is an essential historical source.

Juan Bautista Valentín ALVARADO y Vallejo was born in the capital of Monterey in 1809 to José Francisco Alvarado and María Josefa Vallejo. His father died immediately; three years later his mother remarried José Raimundo Estrada and left her young son in care of relatives in the large Vallejo household. Along with his uncle and contemporary **Mariano Guadalupe Vallejo** and their close friend **José Castro**, he was mentored in his education by Governor Solá and the English-born polymath William E.P. Hartnell. Alvarado became Secretary of the *Diputación* (Assembly) from 1828-1834 and continued as a member of that body until 1837 while working at the Custom House. In 1836 he led the revolt against Governor Gutiérrez. From that date until 1842 he served as the first full-term California-born governor. He has many accomplishments to his credit, but his weakness for drink and taste for the high life constrained his potential. As attested by Letter 5, Alvarado entered into business with his *compadre* **José Castro** in the unproductive salt quarries at Cabo San Quintín and the more successful guano-exporting operation from Cedros Island, both in Baja California. After **José Castro** accepted a Mexican government post in Baja California in the mid-1850s, Alvarado kept up a regular correspondence, looking after young Esteban Castro and the rest of the family from his relocated home base at Rancho San Pablo and often San Francisco. In 1859 he transferred a quarter of his Ocampo property in Baja California to **Manuel de Jesús Castro**. In early January 1860 he petitioned for eleven square leagues (about five square miles) of Cañada de San Andrés in Baja California, granted and certified to him by **José Castro**. Like so much of the Baja California property allocated under **Castro's** vice-governorship, this title was transferred to Antonio Milatovich, frequent partner of **Jacques Moerenhout** (Baron Mörner). Alvarado died in 1882 at Rancho San Pablo, inherited by his wife. See biography by Robert Ryal Miller.

Juan Lorenzo Bruno BANDINI was born in Lima, Peru on October 4, 1800. He accompanied his father, a merchant trader, to Alta California in the 1820s and had become a prominent citizen of San Diego by 1827, serving in the *Diputación* (Assembly) that year, then as a Customs officer until 1832. An active member of the opposition to Governor Victoria in 1831, he represented Alta California in the Mexican congress of 1833, later becoming involved in colonization efforts and a trading concern called the Cosmopolitan Company. Having opposed Governor Juan Bautista Alvarado in 1837-38, he nonetheless acquired an appointment as administrator of Mission San Gabriel during the secularization period. In the 1840s he was *síndico* at Los Angeles and secretary to Governor Pío Pico. Neither resisting nor supporting the American takeover of 1846, he accommodated himself to it once it was a *fait accompli*. Rancho Santa Gertrudis at Santo Tomás was one his landholdings, along with ranchos at Guadalupe and San Antonio in La Frontera, the former a mission property that was granted to him in 1846. Surviving correspondence shows that Bandini supported and mentored Castro when he assumed the vice-governorship of La Frontera. Along with San Diegueño **Santiago Argüello**, owner of Rancho Tía Juana, Bandini was accused by **José Matías Moreno** of planning to annex Baja California to the United States. A supporter of **Feliciano Ruiz de Esparza** over **Juan Mendosa** in the civil conflict that devastated La Frontera from 1859 to 1861, Bandini reportedly "applauded with his feet" when Esparza recounted his wartime misdeeds to Judge Benjamin Hayes (Shipek 63). Bandini died at Los Angeles on November 4, 1859.

General José María BLANCARTE refused to turn over the governorship of the Baja California territory to **José Castro** in 1855. Named to that post the preceding year by General Santa Anna, he deviously arranged for the execution of Antonio María Meléndrez, hero of the resistance to American filibuster William Walker and, at the time of his execution by Blancarte, Vice-Governor of La Frontera.

María Amparo Ruiz de BURTON was born in southern Baja California on July 3, 1831 and raised in La Paz. She and her mother were among some 350 supporters of the American military takeover who, in August 1848, were shipped out and given asylum at Monterey when the Treaty of Guadalupe-Hidalgo, under which Mexico unexpectedly retained Baja Calfornia, put all US-sympathizers there at risk. Less that a year later (July 9, 1849) she married Captain (later Colonel) Henry Stanton Burton of the US Army and leader of the first expeditionary forces to occupy her homeland. The couple's time in Monterey (1848-52) coincided with **José Castro**'s return from Sonora, so it is possible that they were acquainted, although Mrs. Burton's marriage to (and by) a Protestant made Roman Catholic Montereyans loathe to associate with her. By the time she was widowed twenty years later, she had two nearly grown children, spoke and wrote polished English, and had enjoyed a cosmopolitan lifestyle in power circles at Washington DC, New York City and other points east. Foremost among the influential men with whom she corresponded was Alta Californian **Mariano Guadalupe Vallejo**. Her exchange of letters with fellow Baja Californian **José Matías Moreno** continued from 1857 until his death 22 years later. During her widowhood she became the first writer of Mexican extraction to publish novels in the United States: *Who Would Have Thought It?* (1872) and *The Squatter and the Don* (1885). She died in 1895 at the age of 64, waging until the end a relentless and often unscrupulous campaign (her own mother brought suit against her for fraud) on behalf of family property claims in the San Diego area (including Rancho Jamul that had belonged to Governor Pío Pico) and others in La Frontera. See her novels and correspondence edited and annotated by Rosaura Sanchez and Beatriz Pita.

Manuel de Jesús CASTRO was born in Monterey in 1821 to José Juan Nepomuceno (Simeón) Castro and María Antonia Pico de Castro. He served as secretary to the prefect from 1842 to 1844 and was one of the instigators of the revolt against Governor Micheltorena that spilled over into 1845, the year that he became Prefect of Monterey. During the last phase of resistance to the American takeover of Alta California, he replaced his cousin, Commander General **José Castro,** leading Californio forces alongside José Maria Flores, a Mexican who had come to Alta California in 1842 with Governor Micheltorena. According to Neal Harlow, the pair departed for Mexico in August of 1846, whereas Robert R. Miller maintains that Manuel disbanded his troops at San Luis Obispo before "taking refuge in the mountains." As officially designated captain of a troop of soldiers in Baja California from mid-1849, Manuel Castro led a long march north from La Paz to Santo Tomás, becoming the founding captain of the military colony established permanently at Santo Tomás in October 1850 with Sargeant José Antonio Chaves. Manuel Castro returned to Upper California in 1852 to testify before the US Land Commission on behalf of family holdings, among them Punta Año Nuevo north of Santa Cruz. In Baja California, he was co-investor with **Juan Bautista Alvarado**, **Jacques Moerenhout** and his elder cousin **José Castro** in the salt flats at Cabo San Quintín. He continued to hold some interests in land and mining enterprises in Baja California at least through the 1860s and still considered himself a military man when photographed in his declining years (page 169).

Feliciano Ruiz de ESPARZA, originally from San Luis Obispo, worked as a silversmith at San Diego in 1854 and later as a *vaquero* (cowboy). In the late 1850s he served as **José Castro**'s secretary and designated surrogate when the Vice-Governor had to attend to pressing obligations in American California. Esparza's refusal to turn over the military command to **Juan Mendosa,**

José Matías Moreno's designated candidate, and later to Castro himself, unleashed tumultuous violence in the region, claiming the latter among its casualties. Disparaged by Moreno as a "border chieftain," by **María Amparo Ruiz de Burton** as a "*macaco*" (monkey), and by others as a "*cholo*" (ruffian of mixed blood), Esparza struck San Diego **Judge Benjamin Hayes** as "lucid, frank and plain" and even thoughtful and repentant of his misdeeds (Shipek 64). Pursued by a batallion of some 200 men led by Eustaquio Cota and **José Matías Moreno**, Esparza retreated with his family in March of 1861 to the island of Guadalupe off Cabo San Quintín, formerly granted to him by **José Castro**, where he died some time later under suspicious circumstances. Rescued as castaways by a passing whaler, his wife and children relocated to San Diego. Esparza's papers reside at the Huntington Library.

Ambrosio GOMEZ was in living Monterey in 1857, when he served **Modesta Castro de Castro** as scribe for Letter 7 He added his own postscript inquiring about conditions in Baja California, whence he fled within the year, driven out of Alta California by accusations made against him. In the Biliographical Guide to Bancroft's Baja California holdings (Beebe and Senkewicz), he appears as a Baja California property owner (packet #4785), granted eleven square leagues by **José Castro** on November 29, 1858. The legal rights to his property were transferred to **Manuel de Jesús Castro** on June 20, 1863, and then on June 25 of the same year to **Antonio Milatovich.**

Jose Yves LIMANTOUR, a Frenchman who had lived in Mexico, was infamous for making fraudulent land claims in San Francisco and San Diego. His jailing is mentioned in Letter 5 from **Juan Bautista Alvarado** to **José Castro**. One of his claims in Baja California comprised three ranches north of San Quintín as well as Mission Santo Domingo with its 400 square miles (roughly 200 leagues). One square league of the latter section was granted by **José Castro** (See Shipek 68-69).

Juan (Bautista) MENDOSA (Mendoza): origin unknown. In 1853 and early 1854, he and La Frontera rancher Antonio Maria Meléndrez led the forces that expelled American filibuster William Walker. The Bibliographical Guide to Bancroft Library sources contains five listings: two in 1852 having to do with the death of "foreigner Issac Banes," one from Santo Tomás on March 3, 1852 identifying Juan Bautista Mendosa as interim commandant of the national guard, another from February of that year reporting on men, munitions and horses. The earliest (January 21, 1851) links him to **Manuel de Jesús Castro** through a loan of sixteen pesos. In 1859, Moreno engineered his appointment from the territorial governor to replace **Feliciano Esparza**, then acting Vice-Governor amd military commander as **José Castro**'s delegated second. Mendosa was to replace José Sáenz, an elderly landowner who, also on the recommendation of **José Matías Moreno,** had been the Governor's first choice to permanently replace **José Castro**. Sáenz sent Mendosa to attack Esparza, who resisted and had himself elected provisional governor. Esparza exiled Mendosa, who reportedly worked as a foreman on **Juan Bandini**'s Rancho Guadalupe, to the San Diego side of the border. Their subsequent confrontation in La Frontera escalated into a frenzy of death and destruction lasting into 1861. Faced with the threat of a contingent from San Diego led by Major Lewis Armistead, Mendosa escaped to Sonora after his efforts to recruit members of the Yuma tribe to his cause failed (Moyano Pahissa in Alric, 26). Back in San Diego, he was shot in the back by **Cave Couts**, a son-in-law of Juan Bandini, who was exonerated of the murder (See Sanchez and Pita in Ruiz de Burton 128, 176 n.85).

José Matías (Brown) MORENO was born in San Antonio, Baja California, in 1819. His father and namesake, Joseph Matthew Brown, an English whaler, died when his offspring was two years old. Moreno, educated by an unconventional Dominican priest, later became a fiercely anti-clerical liberal. Departing for San Diego in 1843 with his remarried mother, Moreno was appointed secretary to Alta California Governor Pío Pico in 1845, traveling with him on government business to Monterey, where he probably met Pico's rival **José Castro** for the first time. In Monterey in 1846, he barely escaped capture by American forces. Back in Baja California soon afterward, he took part in the resistance to the American takeover as commander-in-chief of the Guadalupana Guerrilla of Comandú, gaining heroic stature among his countrymen. He spent another dozen years in San Diego after the US-Mexican war ended in 1848, marrying **Prudenciana López**, an unrecognized natural daughter of **Mariano Guadalupe Vallejo**, in 1851. That same year, with **Guillermo (William) Norrlin**, he formed a company called La Margarita to extracting silver from San Isidro Ajojolojol in La Frontera. Appointed by President Benito Juárez, who sent troops to install him,

Moreno held the post of Vice-Governor of that region from March 1861 to March 1862, succeeding his enemy **José Castro** for only one year. In 1863, having been indicted and tried in San Diego for interference in the affairs of another sovereign country (Mexico), he resettled his wife and five children on **Juan Bandini**'s former property, Rancho Guadalupe in the northern section of La Frontera, which he purchased that same year. Moreno died there of a stroke on December 1, 1869 at age 51. His extensive report on La Frontera, published serially in the *San Diego Union* the year after his death, gave him the last word on that beleaguered region's most contentious period. Among his long-time correspondents was **María Amparo Ruiz de Burton**. His papers reside at the Huntington Library.

Jacques Antoine MOERENHOUT (Morenhout), better known in La Frontera as **Baron Juan J. Mörner**, was French (vice) consul at San Francisco, Monterey, and Los Angeles, where he served from October 1859 until his death in January 1879. He was one of **José Castro**'s associates (and delegated report-writer/bookkeeper) in the salt extraction enterprise at Cabo San Quintín, Baja California. He received La Frontera land grants from Castro including Las Juntas, which consisted of seven leagues (about 14 square miles) at Jacumé. In October 1858 he was imprisoned at Grulla, B.C. by **Juan Mendosa**'s forces on the pretext that he might be a spy for Castro; **Father Alric** secured his release.

Francisco (Pancho) RICO was canoneer under Comandante General **José Castro** in the siege of Frémont's forces at Pico Gavilán in 1846. He and **José Castro** held property jointly in Alta California. On March 2, 1860, he was granted eleven square leagues of property in La Frontera by **José Castro** and duly paid for them (Bancroft bibliography #4821). On August 3, 1863 he gave power of attorney for this property to **Manuel de Jesús Castro**, and on February 24, 1864 he transferred property rights to Antonio Milatovich. He is mentioned in Letter 4 (from Esteban to his father) as godfather to the last child born into the Castro family, who survived barely a week. Delegated by Hubert Howe Bancroft, Thomas Savage took 54 pages of dictation from Rico at his Rancho Zenobio near Gonzales in the late 1870s.

José María del Refugio SUAREZ DEL REAL was born in New Spain (Mexico) about 1804. Ordained in 1831, he was a member of the first group of Mexican (Zacatecan) Franciscans to enter Alta California with Governor Figueroa two years later. Serving at Carmel Mission from 1833, he purchased a house in Monterey in 1837, when secularization left the mission decaying and exposed. In 1844 he relocated to Mission Santa Clara and in 1851 returned to Mexico where he left the Franciscan order. In April 1852, about to depart for upper California, **Captain Manuel de Jesús Castro** named him chaplain of the military colony at Santo Tomás. Soon afterwards Father Real, recalled by the head of his order, El Colegio de Guadalupe in Zacatecas, was stripped of his spiritual jurisdiction and later briefly imprisoned. He decided to remain in Baja California regardless, and by May 1853 was serving as parish priest at San José del Cabo.

Mariano Guadalupe VALLEJO was born at Monterey in 1807, the same year as **José Castro**, with whom he was educated along with his own nephew **Juan Bautista Alvarado**, two years their junior. Having entered military service in 1824, he was promoted to *alférez* (ensign) in 1827 and involved in a number of expeditions against the indigenous peoples of the Central Valley. He married Francisca Benicia Carrillo in 1832. Serving in the *Diputación* (Assembly) in the early 1830s, he was also commander of San Francisco from 1831-1834. After founding Sonoma in 1835, he remained primarily in that area, which he developed extensively with astute management and the cooperation of various indigenous groups. Appointed by his nephew Governor **Juan Bautista Alvarado** as Military Commander of Alta California in 1836, he held the position until the arrival of Governor Micheltorena in 1842. Despite his arrest by the rag-tag perpetrators of the American-led Bear Flag rebellion in June of 1846, he continued to be a sympathetic to the official American takeover of California that immediately followed. A delegate to the state constitutional convention of 1849, he was elected to the state senate the following year. This patriarcal elder statesman encouraged his former compatriots to collaborate in the history being compiled by Hubert Howe Bancroft and his assistants, maintained an extended correspondence with **María Amparo Ruiz de Burton**, and compiled his own history of California (twice, since the first was destroyed in a fire along with pertinent documents). He died at his Sonoma residence in 1890 at the age of 83, having lived three decades beyond his exact contemporary **José Castro**. See biography by Alan Rosenus.

Index of Individual Names

Includes full names and, when available, ranks and titles of individuals mentioned in the Dedication, Introduction, and Parts I-V, except for the letters reproduced in facsimile in Part II and the genealogy provided in Part V. Also excluded are the names of the subject of this volume and its author-compiler. Illustrations appear in bold type; "f" designates footnote. Several Castros share identical names, a redundancy that defies the practical limitations of this Index. – *JBC*

T

V

W

Y

Z

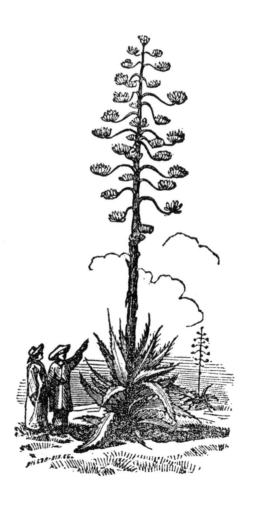

*Hand-colored photograph of Modesta Castro de Dana, daughter of Colonel
Castro and his wife Modesta; courtesy of the Monterey Public Library*